Victims
and
Victimhood

Victims and Victimhood

TRUDY GOVIER

broadview press

Library and Archives Canada Cataloguing in Publication

Govier, Trudy, author
    Victims and victimhood / Trudy Govier.

Includes bibliographical references and index.
ISBN 978-1-55481-099-4 (pbk.)

    1. Victims of crimes—Philosophy. 2. Victims of crimes—Moral and ethical aspects. I. Title.

HV6250.25.G69 2014   362.8801   C2014-906706-2

Broadview Press is an independent, international publishing house, incorporated in 1985.

We welcome comments and suggestions regarding any aspect of our publications—please feel free to contact us at the addresses below or at broadview@broadviewpress.com.

North America
PO Box 1243
Peterborough, Ontario
K9J 7H5, Canada
555 Riverwalk Parkway
Tonawanda, NY 14150
USA
Tel: (705) 743-8990
Fax: (705) 743-8353
email: customerservice@broadviewpress.com

UK, Europe, Central Asia,
Middle East, Africa, India,
and Southeast Asia
Eurospan Group
3 Henrietta St.
London WC2E 8LU
United Kingdom
Tel: 44 (0) 1767 604972
Fax: 44 (0) 1767 601640
email: eurospan@turpin-distribution.com

Australia and New Zealand
Footprint Books
1/6a Prosperity Parade
Warriewood, NSW 2102
Australia
Tel: 1300 260 090
Fax: (02) 997 3185
email: info@footprint.com.au

www.broadviewpress.com

Edited by Betsy Struthers
Book design by Michel Vrana
Typeset in Adobe Caslon Pro

Broadview Press acknowledges the financial support of the Government of Canada through the Canada Book Fund for our publishing activities.

PRINTED IN CANADA

In memory of
Doris Eda Govier
October 3, 1918–April 19, 2014

CONTENTS

ACKNOWLEDGEMENTS

I first wish to acknowledge Wilhelm Verwoerd and Alastair Little, whose stories of work with people affected by the Troubles in Northern Ireland did much to stimulate my interest in victims' issues.

For their generous support, I would like to acknowledge Anton Colijn, Beverley Tollefson Delong, Janet Keeping, Janet Sisson, and my colleagues in the Department of Philosophy at the University of Lethbridge. For probing questions and helpful suggestions, I am indebted to audiences at the Western Canadian Philosophical Association (2011), the Ontario Society for Studies in Argumentation (2013), the Ethics Research Group at the University of Calgary (2014), a Calgary philosophy Meet-Up group (2014), and students in my University of Lethbridge course "Victims and Perpetrators" (2012). During the summer of 2012, Colin Koerselman's interest and energy, especially with regard to questions of testimony, provided considerable stimulation. David Boutland assisted with enthusiastic questions and editing. I am grateful for the timely medical intervention of Dr. Rick Morris in June 2014: it was his assistance that made possible my own final editing. And, of course, this work owes much to Stephen Latta and staff of Broadview Press.

INTRODUCTION

A look at any newspaper will show much attention to victims and their rights and needs. Great variety is likely to appear: people are victims not only of wrongs such as fraud, burglary, rape, and murder but of disaster and disease. Although there are significant differences between these contexts, there exist sufficient similarities to apply the term "victim" in all of them: victims are persons harmed and harmed by forces they do not control. There is damage to one who is a victim and the cause of that damage is something outside that person's agency.

Over the past decade or so, challenging comments about victims have come to my attention. A respected anti-terrorism expert who was attached to the idea of innocent victims objected with outrage to the claim that someone who was a victim of a wrongful act could, in another context, be responsible for wrongdoing. An experienced conference participant stated that the concept of a victim needed to be "problematized." A barrister reported what she regarded as the exaggerated influence of victim impact statements. A legal analyst argued that it would be unfair if the murderer of a man with a forgiving family received a lesser sentence than the murderer of another with a vindictive family. An experienced mediator reported that ongoing moral indignation and righteousness in victims' groups made them so recalcitrant and difficult as to constitute an obstacle to peace. I heard rumblings about governments being afraid of political backlash from victims whose claims were denied, and found written complaints that some victim groups were exploiting their status to avoid criticism and—in some political contexts—literally get away with murder. As persons meriting consideration and attention, is there a sense in which victims enjoy a privileged social position?

So far as the perpetrators of wrongdoing are concerned, the topics of guilt, blame, responsibility, and punishment have long been central in philosophy, with a lineage of discussion going back to ancient times. The same cannot be said of the victims, even in these times when media exhibit a fascination with their suffering and struggles to overcome it. Although news and popular culture indicate considerable interest in victims and their mistreatment, needs, and rights, these topics have received little or no attention in the fields of philosophy and applied ethics. The topic of forgiveness might seem to be one exception. Not only has it been prominent in popular discussions, over the past several decades it has received considerable attention within philosophy, due in part to enormous fascination with the forgiveness of Nelson Mandela and the work of the South African Truth and Reconciliation Commission. Forgiveness, after all, is primarily an issue for victims. But even discussions of forgiveness easily slide away from the concerns of victims to its impact on perpetrators and society at large.

What are the temptations of the victim role? How do these temptations affect capability and agency? What is competition among and between victims, and where do we see evidence of it? In what sense and to what extent must a person be innocent of wrongdoing to qualify as a victim? Victims seem to have a certain kind of authority over their own stories. But what sort of authority is that? What is its foundation and what are its limits? If we feel an obligation to show respect for victims, what should that respect amount to? Should it extend so far as deference to their testimony? To their expressed wishes with regard to sentencing, memorialization, and other aspects of public policy? Given that some victims may, deliberately or unintentionally, offer false testimony as to what they have gone through, may we rightly criticize their stories, even to the point of rejection, without indicating disrespect for their suffering? Can victims be perpetrators? Can perpetrators be victims? Can a person be both a victim and a perpetrator with regard to the same act in the same context? I argue that these questions should be answered in the affirmative. The case of child soldiers provides a convincing, and highly disturbing, example.

These many questions interested me, and it was that interest that led me to write this book. To be sure, victims' issues relating to court proceedings have been explored by legal scholars. And many such issues have been raised within the specifically designated subject of victimology and in the closely related fields of sociology and social psychology. But for the most part, these questions have not been philosophically explored. I thought, and continue to think, that it would be worthwhile to explore victims' issues from a more philosophical perspective than is usual. Questions about victims relate importantly to philosophical topics that have received significant attention. These include authority, testimony, forgiveness, punishment, and agency. I sensed that there would be much to be gained from relating victims' issues to mainstream discussions of these themes. I was convinced, and remain convinced, that reflections on these topics would be improved by such philosophical practices as testing definitions, exploring assumptions, closely examining arguments, and bringing abstract theory to bear on specific cases. Many of the cases I discuss are real ones; others are invented, but realistic.

Such is the background of this book. Given the scarcity of attention to victims' issues within philosophy and applied ethics, this work is something of a pioneering effort. As such, it has been difficult to write, and I am aware that much further work could be done on the topics discussed. I only hope that *Victims and Victimhood* can serve to stimulate further thought and action.

CHAPTER 1

FOUR ATTITUDES TO VICTIMS

There are four common perspectives on victims, and their popularity varies with time and with culture. Those details will not be addressed here; the point is to explore and illustrate these perspectives and consider their merits. They are:

> *Silence:* Victims should be quiet; if they speak out about their
> suffering, they will be alarming and depressing to others.
> *Blame:* To a considerable extent, victims are to blame for their
> own situation.
> *Deference:* Victims should be honoured and respected.
> *Agency:* Victims are agents and as such share responsibility for
> the responses to wrongdoing, ill fortune, and disease.

SILENCE

It is hard to believe, but there was a time when the crimes of the Holocaust were not only figuratively, but literally unspeakable. Survivors from eastern Europe were not supposed to tell of their experiences. People knew the death camps existed. They knew that there were persons alive who had lived through horrors, but they did not wish to hear their reports and stories. Persons returning to Europe from Japanese camps in the Pacific were similarly regarded; in Holland, for instance, the government was concerned to provide special rations for them but was unwilling to hear about what they had gone through. Victims and survivors of the camps were not ignored, but they were not heard; there was no notion that their suffering should be displayed and brought to public attention or that they deserved special consideration for the brutality and agony they had gone through. A plausible explanation for this attitude in the early postwar period was the desire to rebuild and recover from the war; the enormous physical tasks required consumed available resources and attention. People wanted to establish and lead a normal life; they did not wish to dwell on the horrors any longer. They knew that victims were among them and had sympathy for those victims, but they did not want to hear from them—they did not want even to attend to the past, much less dwell on it.

What was the message to victims and survivors?

> Keep quiet about what you have gone through. Do not tell us about your suffering; keep it to yourself. We know something happened to you, and it was no doubt terrible … but we need know no more. The details of your suffering, of what you went through, must be awful. We will accept in general terms that you were seriously harmed, but we are not willing to hear about it. It cannot do you much good, and it will certainly be unpleasant for us. The sorrow and suffering are yours; for as long as you continue to feel them, you must bear them alone. We will not help by sharing, and if we could, it would not be our responsibility to do that. If you insist on telling us what you went through and how you feel about it, you will disturb or even destroy our lives, which is clearly something you should not do. You went through these things and we did not and we do not wish to. The suffering was yours and should remain with you. You can get over it; you should get over it; you will get over it. Keep silent; do not belabour the point. The world is all right, and we are all right within it, and we do not want to consider evidence to the contrary. Keep quiet for our sake and your own.

On this view, a victim should cope and support the functioning social world by keeping his sorrows to himself; he should remain silent and preferably cheerful so as not to disturb the normal life so treasured by his fellow citizens. The attitude of silence and emotional stability, prominent in the early aftermath of the horrendous political wrongs of World War II, has been described by a number of survivors and commentators.

A representative account is that of Petra G.H. Aarts, who describes Dutch attitudes to returning citizens who had survived concentration camps in Indonesia. These people, of whom there were several hundred thousand, had been interned, starved, and humiliated by the Japanese, only to face an anti-colonial war in Indonesia after their release. Many returned to the Netherlands in the late 1940s, only to face new problems adjusting to life in an unfamiliar, small, cold country. Aarts says the Dutch were largely indifferent to the situation of these migrants, though they did give them some material support.[1] The war in Indonesia had been far away, and the involvement of the Dutch military in a subsequent war to defend its colonial empire was something that people did not want to think about. This response of silence was not helpful therapeutically for the victims.

The notion that victims should be silent and not claim attention to their suffering is less common today, though it persists for certain sorts of harm and suffering. A recent example is the case of Susan Brison, who survived a brutal rape and attempted murder.[2] In their aftermath, she sought to describe what it was like to be a victim of the crimes. She was walking in the French countryside in broad daylight when she was grabbed from behind, pulled into the bushes, beaten, and raped. Her assailant made three attempts to strangle her and eventually knocked her on the head with a rock. Though the brutality of the attack was obvious from her injuries, and Brison received decent treatment from police and medical personnel, she admits to at first not wanting to tell people about it. One reason lay in her feeling of shame; another stemmed from what she came to regard as curiously inconsistent attitudes toward sexual violence against women. It was her sense that many people tend to take such violence for granted as a natural and nearly inevitable feature of social life while at the same time being quite convinced that they themselves would never be its victims.

Brison experienced what she describes as an almost universal response to rape: people sought so much to protect themselves from bad news about social reality that they found it hard to identify with her as the victim of such an unanticipated and apparently random attack. To do that would be to accept that such viciousness can occur randomly to anyone at any time in any place. Most could not hear her story. Even family members reacted as though the crimes had not happened. Without empathizing with her as victim, some posited God and His purposes in their attempts to render the crimes intelligible. An aunt commented that it was good that God saved her without asking why God would have allowed such a violation to happen in the first place; she then stated that God must have made her stronger by having her live through the brutal assault.[3]

Nowadays, many people get cancer and are referred to as its *victims*. Many die of the disease; many recover from it and go on to enjoy years of decent health after effective treatment. In Western societies at least, cancer can be openly discussed: most people who have it tell their friends and relatives, who listen to the diagnosis and consult about the merits of various treatment plans. It was not always thus. Several decades back, cancer was an unspeakable disease. If one mentioned it at all, it was alluded to cautiously and euphemistically as "the big C." If someone appeared pale and in a turban at a social event, no one would ask whether they were undergoing chemotherapy treatments that had necessitated the head covering. Even 30 years ago, cancer seemed too terrible to be alluded to directly, and many felt that it should not be acknowledged except, perhaps, to a close friend or relative. People able to discuss cancer with its victims felt themselves progressive and some-how superior; though they did not suffer themselves, they were at least capable of acknowledging that the disease caused its victims considerable pain and anxiety before their premature deaths. Other diseases were not unspeakable to the same degree but—as with criminal and political wrongs—the assumption generally was that one should keep one's pain and suffering to oneself. The normal cheer of social life should not be disturbed by the ill and disabled. They should keep quiet about what they were going through, manage with a minimal amount of health, and let other people get on with their lives.

What can be said of the "silence" approach to victims and victimization? It is now relatively uncommon, at least in Western countries. In its favour, some points merit consideration. In some cases, for people to describe the terrible things that happened to them will be in a sense to go through them again and suffer again. Whereas the standard contemporary assumption is that talking about sorrows will relieve them, there are people for whom the telling of such stories will amount to reliving them, multiplying painful experiences. In such cases, silence on the part of non-victims may indicate respect for a victim and have positive value for that reason. Some victims of some harms may not want their suffering noted or commented on. For example, an older man with a strong ideology of masculine strength and power may find it embarrassing to have his infirmities noted. To fail to ask about his limp, memory failures, or skin lesions may be a display of respect toward him, a support for his desired self-presentation, and protective of his dignity. To recount an occasion on which such a man was a victim of telephone fraud could amount to emphasizing his vulnerability as an older adult; he might ask his adult children "don't mention this again" to protect his sense of his own competence.[4] Similarly, in some cultures, sexual wrongs are so widely assumed to impugn the honour of the victim that they had better go unmentioned.

There are further arguments for silence. In contexts where present needs are urgent, one could argue that taking notice of injuries and suffering robs atten-tion and resources from recovery and rebuilding—that focusing on repairing the wounds of the past will result in lost opportunities to build the future. As applied to the immediate aftermath of World War II, such arguments had some force.

While, ideally, one would both attend to the suffering and needs of victims and rebuild infrastructure and institutions, time and resources seemed insufficient to do both. Some argued that when a more physically secure and economically wealthy society had developed, there would be more resources for victims and other vulnerable people. Moreover, children might be affected not only physically but psychologically if they grew up in an atmosphere in which grievous wartime wrongs and suffering were continually emphasized.

Thus, an argument for silence is that acknowledgement can be overdone and go too far. Much-acknowledged victims might come to see themselves as privileged and deserving of prolonged support. Obviously, the counter-argument is that silence itself can be overdone and go too far. The interesting question is where the line is to be drawn: the answer depends importantly on context.

As a general rule, silence about suffering and wrongdoing is not to be recommended. It is likely to be therapeutically harmful to victims and their families, who will find no opportunities to express feelings and to understand what has happened in their lives. Victims' suffering, which may have been fundamental to their development, sense of self, and ability to function in work and relationships, will remain unshared and unacknowledged. A considerable burden is placed on victims who feel an obligation to support the desired social pretense that everything is "all right." Deception and self-deception will be required to keep the damage hidden. Damage due to the imposition of a burden of silence has been called "the second wound of silence."[5] The expression indicates that victims are hurt again by the failure of others to acknowledge what they have gone through. Something likely to be of enormous import for their lives and well-being cannot be shared with others if there is no acknowledgment and accordingly no basis for solidarity and social support. These others, who avoid the knowledge that bad things do happen at the cost of failing to empathize and sympathize with the sufferers, gain their comfort at the cost of a false picture of the world. Their overly cheerful picture of life will result in a failure to recognize realities that they might amend if they understood them.

BLAME

Pressure to keep quiet will not always achieve its goal. Though victims of catastrophe, disease, and wrongdoing may be discouraged from talking about what they endured, evidence will remain in photos of starving children, pictures of survivors of concentration camps, and newspaper accounts of criminal trials. Accidents happen and some will be publicized. People will die of disease. Even for those unwilling to acknowledge the existence of these troubles, the evidence will be there and will cry out to make the degree of denial required for cheerful silence impossible.

And yet the desire for a friendly universe remains. Many of us want to believe that the world is a tolerably benign place where not too many seriously bad things will happen to seriously good people. And, most importantly, we want to be at ease in the belief that nothing really terrible will happen to *us*. This is a comforting belief, and we like comfort. If we no longer believe in a provident God, we will have to get that comfort elsewhere, and we often seek it in the conviction that somehow we can exert forms of control over what will happen to us. If we wish to protect ourselves from earthquakes, we can stay out of certain parts of the world such as Japan or southern California. If we do not want to be attacked by sharks, we can refrain from swimming in tropical waters, avoiding, for instance, the Great Barrier Reef. And as for disease, we can eat properly, exercise regularly, avoid stress, get enough sleep, and have regular medical check-ups. To avoid theft, we can install alarm systems on our houses or refrain from purchasing expensive art and furniture. We can protect ourselves from sexual assault by not walking on dark streets or wearing revealing clothes. We seek to protect ourselves; we believe, and want to believe, that we live in a world that is orderly enough for us to be able to do that.

In short, we want to believe that a world without God makes enough sense for us to be safe within it. An element of this belief is that we can understand and anticipate certain sorts of harms that might befall us, and we can act so as to prevent ourselves from suffering from them. Bad things happen to good people and to bad people; we have evidence of that. But we have nevertheless a powerful inclination to believe that bad things will not happen to us. Why not? We presume that the world is sufficiently intelligible for us to know how to protect ourselves from these things. We resolve to do that for ourselves. The notion is something like this: "Bad things happen. *Others* are victims. I am not *others* and I will not be a victim, because I will be able to protect myself."

Such an attitude may sound impressively and heroically stoical, but it has a most unfortunate corollary for those persons who are victims. If I can protect myself, they could have protected themselves. And if they could have protected themselves, could have exercised some control over their fate, and did not, then they have failed in some way. Accordingly, they have been agents whose acts and failures to act shaped their own fate. We may think initially of victims as innocents on whom harm has been inflicted, but if we reflect on the predictable nature of our world, we can see significant acts and omissions and consider ways in which these victims may bear some responsibility for what happened to them. We may be inclined to conclude that what happened did not *just happen*: these people helped to bring their fate upon themselves. After all, the earthquake victim did continue to live near a fault line. The man attacked by a shark was swimming in waters known to be dangerous. The cancer victim worked in a restaurant where smoking was permitted. The woman with diabetes spent too much time watching television and not enough on a treadmill. And the victim of sexual assault should not have been walking alone, not after dark to be sure. If we find out that she was attacked in daylight, as in Brison's case, we may adapt our hypothesis and insist that she should have known not to walk alone in the countryside, even on a sunny morning. There will always be some available hypothesis that can be adopted to allow the safe ones to blame the victim.

The "blame the victim" attitude has been exposed to much of the criticism it richly deserves. But that does not mean it has ceased to exist. The problem is, victimization challenges beliefs that are basic for many people: the world is benevolent; it is meaningful; and the self is worthy. Within social psychology this view has been much discussed and goes under the name Just World Theory.[6] According to this theory, we have a need to believe in a world where people generally get what they deserve. To put it in simple terms, we want to suppose that good things happen to good people and bad things happen to bad people; in the end, everyone winds up with the condition he or she deserves. We have a need to believe somehow in a kind of cosmic justice. Because there is considerable evidence that such justice does not exist, we invent hypotheses to protect our comforting illusion.

Evidence that some good person, apparently similar to me, has met an unpleasant fate due to catastrophe, disease, or crime threatens my belief in a Just World where I can protect myself. Thus, such evidence is unwelcome. An hypothesis that can protect my view of the world is that the suffering victim is accountable for her own suffering. She has failed in some way in which I myself would not fail. She is suffering. She is damaged, harmed. *Why?* How could this happen? How could it happen to her? Why do these things happen? Many of us will be aware that this is somehow a flawed question, that it is the wrong question to ask—but that awareness is easily overcome by our powerful desire to think of ourselves as having control in a safe and predictable world.

If we see ourselves in a secular framework or in a theological framework that does not permit us to blame ill fortune on God, then someone must be "to blame." Who? We think of the victim and think, "She must have done something to bring this on." The corollary thought is: "We can figure out what this thing was and make sure we never do it." What did she do that she could have avoided doing and that we can avoid doing? We speculate, taking care to posit an action or event that would not apply in our own case. Because of our need to see ourselves as invulnerable, we differentiate ourselves from the victim, attributing her vulnerability to some action or characteristic that we would not share. How do we do that? *We blame the victim.* She did something we would never do; it was her fault since she could have avoided doing it. The greater the need to differentiate ourselves from her, the more we will be inclined to blame her. We may go so far as to conclude that in a world without God, people deserve what they get and get what they deserve.

What emerges from the Just World Theory if one is oneself a victim? The Just World hypothesis blames the victim—but in this case the victim is oneself. Therefore, blame oneself. If I fell on a slippery sidewalk, I should have looked more carefully when walking; if I had a miscarriage, I should not have become pregnant so soon after my last child was born; if I was victim of a home invasion, I should have done a better job repairing those basement windows or moved out of my home when I learned that such a crime had happened only half a kilometre from my house. Self-blame in this way is rarely well-supported by evidence. Though dysfunctional in the way it undermines self-trust and self-esteem, a Just World interpretation can serve to buttress favoured beliefs about one's ability to predict and control the world so as to protect oneself within it.[7]

This being said, we can nonetheless appreciate important considerations supporting victim blame in some contexts. The notion of agency is important, as are notions of precaution and care. Victimhood implies passivity, and this may encourage us to neglect the agency of victims. Most adult victims are, after all, capable of deliberation, reasoning, and acting on the basis of their own decisions. It is true that in some cases people who have been harmed by disaster, disease, or wrong-doing have acted unwisely. One example, from the summer of 2012, involves four people who were floating down the Bow River in Calgary in an inflatable raft at a time when the river was unusually high. Though warned by river safety personnel that the waters were dangerous, they chose to continue. Their raft capsized. Three persons survived and one drowned. They did not deliberately harm themselves (it was not their intent to have the raft capsize, after all), but they did make an unwise choice and suffered harm as a result. Their choice contributed to their being in circumstances where there was a significant risk of serious harm.[8]

Speaking of such cases we often use the terminology of victimhood and speak of people meeting their fate; however, it is clear that these people heard the warning and chose to ignore it. They were in rough waters, knew themselves to be there, were warned away, and yet kept going. Is the drowning victim responsible, or blameworthy, for his own drowning? He did not choose to drown and presumably would not have so chosen; however, he did choose to engage in the risky behaviour that led to his drowning. Is he an "innocent victim"? Not quite. To blame such a person to some degree for the harm that led to his own death is reasonable, and the same may be said for his companions. They are likely suffering sorrow and guilt in the aftermath of this accident, and an accident it truly was. But it was an accident that was not entirely accidental. Human actions and decisions had much to do with it, and some of those were the unreasonable actions and decisions of the victim himself. These aspects of failing to take reasonable preventive measures, or willfully exposing oneself to harm, are taken into account in judgements of legal responsibility and liability.

It goes without saying that there are many similar cases: skiers, ski-doers, and climbers who proceed against warnings into avalanche zones; climbers of Mt. Everest who insist on trying for the top when they are already suffering altitude sickness; Olympic contestants who persist in competition despite injuries; people who dive into shallow lakes or pools; those who travel to be mercenaries or join in *jihad*; and many others. After such people are killed or seriously injured, we may think of them as victims. And yet there are significant aspects of agency in the context of their victimhood. The drowned rafter was an *agent* in the events that led to his death. He was unwise, even reckless. It is interesting to note in this example that the man who drowned was not only imprudent and then a victim in a drowning for which he bore some responsibility, he was also a hero. He could swim and was an experienced rafter, and he drowned trying to save one of his companions. The case illustrates the point that what human beings do and suffer can be described in many ways: this man made an irresponsible choice; he was imprudent. He was in the end the victim of a drowning. And at the same time he was a hero for saving his friend.

Thus, time, context, and agency need to be considered in judgements about victims and victimhood. Although there are cases in which victims bear some responsibility for their fate, we should not generalize from them. Blaming the victim is faulty as a general response. It often (though not in the Calgary river case) requires the adoption of implausible *ad hoc* hypotheses and is for that reason cognitively objectionable.

As with the illusions imposed by silence, there are deceptions and self-deceptions used to support the Just World Theory and blaming the victim. We may want to believe that we can protect ourselves against disease and catastrophe, but that comforting belief is not true in general. Things do just happen to people; our fate is not wholly the result of our choices. To indulge our desire to live in a Just World will be to construct for ourselves an inaccurate picture of the world in which we do live. And if we do not understand the world, we cannot work to improve it.

Blaming the victim often involves making unwarranted attributions of actions and intentions to persons already suffering from the effects of disaster, disease, or wrongdoing, thus raising ethical objections as well as cognitive ones. In short, blaming the victim imposes more suffering on those who are already suffering. It is likely to be both cruel and unfair to victims, many of whom will be blamed even when they had little or no control over their situation. Even in cases where there is sound evidence that victims have contributed to their fate, we too easily exaggerate their causal role due to our desire to see the world as benign enough to be controlled by human agents.

DEFERENCE

The obviously flawed assumptions underlying *silence* on the one hand and *blaming* on the other have led to increased sensitivity to the position and role of victims. This concern has led to expanded respect for victims and widespread interest in the confessional discourse in which they tell of their suffering and their efforts to overcome it. Accompanying this concern is the conviction that victims should not be silenced, blamed, or ignored; they deserve consideration and respect because of their suffering and innocence. Respect extends into many areas.[9] Victims should be acknowledged and not silenced, understood and not blamed. Individually and as a society we should stand in solidarity with victims and put their interests first, rather than seeking to isolate ourselves so as to buttress comforting illusions about the world.

On a common current understanding, victims are innocent people to whom bad things have happened. As *innocent* sufferers of *harm*, they are presumed to be virtuous people who should be beyond criticism. Victims have been harmed and have suffered from harms that have come upon them due to events in the natural world, actions of others who have wronged them, or a combination of both. Harmed, they have suffered and continue to suffer through no fault of their own. Far from seeking to silence victims, contemporary Western culture shows fascination with their struggles, extending respect and acknowledgement very far indeed. To understand and sympathize with victims, we need to attend closely to their stories. However appalling the details, we should be ready to empathize and offer whatever support we can. Too often victims have been marginalized in court proceedings, official historical narratives, or philosophical theories focusing on the punishment of perpetrators. Victims are innocent persons damaged by things done to them, sufferers and not blameworthy agents, human beings in need of attention and resources directed to their repair. These convictions underlie the common contemporary attitude of deference toward victims.

Such concern for victims manifests itself in many contexts and deference has gone too far in some. In court cases, we find appeals to the notion of closure extended to imply that even legal proceedings and results should contribute to healing. Victim impact statements are deemed to have a role in the sentencing of convicted persons. Treatments of transitional justice feature discussions of apology and redress and frequent appeals to the prerogative of victims as the only persons with the moral authority to forgive perpetrators. Truth commission proceedings and less formal workshops on peacemaking place great emphasis on victims telling their stories, the implication being that these stories have a power and authority all their own and should not be critically questioned. In their sense of righteousness, and in their demand and need for social resources, victims may acquire a powerful sense of entitlement and even become obstacles to peace processes.

In historical debates and conversations about acknowledgement, we find competition for status as victim, referred to sometimes as Victim Olympics. Who deserves the most memorial attention? Whose group was the worst and most grievously wronged? Who suffered the most? If the Holocaust is memorialized, African Americans may question why slavery has not received similar attention; the Chinese may wish to commemorate the Nanking massacre, while the Japanese would ignore it and emphasize their suffering at Hiroshima. Political victims include the Palestinians, the Armenians, and many others. In a culture convinced that we should not silence victims and should not blame them either, we have come to a kind of valorization of victims. We have come to respect their suffering to the point of granting to them a sort of epistemic privilege. We deem them innocents over a range of contexts; we think of them not only lacking in culpability for their own suffering but lacking it in a broad array of other contexts. Argue the possibility that a victim of terrorism was guilty of something else and you are likely to be vociferously attacked by highly offended others. Could a man killed on September 11, 2011 at the World Trade Center have been guilty of deceiving his wife about an extramarital affair? Lying about his income on a tax return? Neglecting the needs of the Third World poor while supporting policies of the World Bank? One might defend such possibilities on the basis of sheer good sense.[10] But given the common, though fallacious, assumption that a person who was passive in a victim role did no harm in others, one can anticipate a hostile response to an implication of fault in this context.

Attitudes of deference to victims are prominent in contemporary Western cultures, and there are powerful impulses to support them. Many victims are members of marginalized groups that have been too long denigrated or ignored. To pretend that nothing bad was ever done to them, to insist that they are fine, to deny resources for compensation or rehabilitation, to remain oblivious to the harms done to them—all this is in effect to injure them again, imposing a "second wound of silence."[11] What is "second wounding"? The point of this expression is that silence about a person's wounds is itself a wound, because wounded people need acknowledgement and attention. If their wounds are unseen and their stories unheard, their needs will be unmet. To be met, they must be acknowledged. In virtue of their suffering experience, victims merit deference and respect. In the immediate context of their victimhood, they are not responsible for what has been done to them.[12] They have been passive in their own harm, not responsible for their misfortunes, innocent—but suffering. To the extent that they are victims, they are suffering from the harm they have experienced. Our cultural deference to victims is based on these aspects: innocence and suffering. We rightly sense that moral repair and deference arise from them. We need to consider the nature and extent of the respect we owe to victims.

The problem with deference is that we may come to a point where victims are virtually beyond criticism, placed on a pedestal erected on their perceived epistemic privilege and moral innocence. When it comes down to it, few would disagree that victims should be *respected* in some sense. There is such a thing as the unique experience of victims; the point is to identity what that is and to recognize the limits of its authority. There is such a thing as the innocence of victims; the point is to explore its limits and implications for agency. To be a victim, one need not be a perfect human being. The compassion we feel for victims and the justice that we feel is due to them are not compatible with marginalizing them, insulting them, or colluding in their humiliation. We need to attend to victims; we need to treat them fairly; certainly, we do need to respect them. It is a harder question, and one that will receive considerable attention in the chapters to come, just what *respect* for victims should amount to and how it is best expressed.

AGENCY AND RESTORATIVE JUSTICE

A fourth set of attitudes to victims may be identified in the restorative justice movement, which is based on a conception of justice in which the central emphasis is on the healing of victims, perpetrators, and the communities in which wrongs have been committed. Here, victims are understood as agents with capacities and powers to be used in the aftermath of crime. The focus is on wrongs committed by some persons against others, and on the resolution of the conflicts and problems surrounding those wrongs. In a restorative justice process, all the parties with a stake in a particular offence come together to resolve issues arising from it. Restorative conceptions of victims, offenders, healing, and justice were developed first in the context of individual crimes in which the offenders were juveniles guilty of vandalism and other petty crimes.[13] They have now been extended to adult wrongdoing and even to the aftermath of political conflict, most famously in South Africa. Advocates of restorative justice do not concern themselves with victims of disease, accident, or natural disaster.

In an influential early article, the Norwegian criminologist Nils Christie described crime as a conflict between offenders and those against whom they offended, and conflict as the property of the persons in conflict.[14] He took the view that laws are passed and enforced by dominant groups in a society with the view to limiting acts against their interests. On his view it is these laws alone that establish offenders as members of a minority group, the group of criminals. Persons are defined as criminal or as committing a crime because of other people's attitudes to them; when a behaviour is defined as criminal, then action is taken against it and against the committing agent. On this account, there is no sound justification for punishment as legally instituted in Western societies: it should be abolished.[15]

Christie understood crime as implying a conflict between victims and offenders. He argued that the persons directly involved in the crime, victims and offenders, "own" the conflict, which is something potentially of value to them and can be conceived as property. Conflict is valuable property, on his view, because its resolution can yield useful insights and outcomes. Christie claimed that modern states have "stolen" this property (crimes) from those directly involved in a conflict. His concern was that victims, in particular, lose power when the state defines itself as the one harmed and takes over the management of crime's aftermath in a system of formal legal justice. In that system, victims become, at most, witnesses in a criminal procedure within which they exercise little or no control. Wrongs were done against them, harms imposed on them, but in the aftermath, they lack power to seek a solution.

Criticizing the "state as victim" presumption of standard legal proceedings, Christie emphasized the power and responsibility of victims. He understood victims as *agents* in a conflict and not as purely passive objects of the actions of others. In his view, victims should be regarded as persons with capacities and responsibilities. They deserve to be heard, not silenced; respected, not deferred to; they are active agents, not passive recipients. Victims share responsibility for restoring their relationships and their own well-being in the aftermath of crime. These views have been tremendously influential in the restorative justice movement.

To think of someone as a victim is to think of that person as passive with regard to a specific harming act. But that does not mean that she is passive and lacking in responsibility with regard to the context of the act or what is done in its aftermath. Christie and later advocates of restorative justice emphasize that victims are often *agents* in structuring the situations in which harm falls them. They want to make this point about *agency* without going so far as to *blame* the victims.

In restorative justice, a fundamental notion is that decent relationships matter. What is to be *restored* in restorative justice is persons and their relationships. A wrong committed by one person against another means that there is damage to the relationship between the person harmed and the perpetrator who inflicts that harm. In wrongdoing as understood in restorative justice, both the victim and the perpetrator are harmed as individuals; additionally, family and community members are also affected since they are likely to suffer some insecurity, fear, and distrust in the knowledge that the wrongful acts have been committed in their midst.[16] In the aftermath, the victim in particular is likely to feel anger, resentment, and distrust—and possibly also a desire for revenge. The perpetrator, if he or she was not already, will be in a state of some alienation from the victim and from community members.

Restorative justice aims to restore victims and perpetrators and to rebuild or build decent relationships in the wake of wrongdoing and harm. Ideally, in the wake of a significant wrong, proceedings would serve the interests of victim, perpetrator, and community so that everyone concerned benefits. Typically, restorative justice proceedings involve communication between victims and perpetrators in the form of individual meetings or community meetings attended by family and friends of both perpetrator and victim. At these meetings, feelings are expressed; the perpetrator will explain his or her circumstances surrounding the crime, how he or she came to commit the crime, how the victim was selected, and the perpetrator's feelings about the crime—hopefully remorseful, though sometimes otherwise. The victim will describe the crime and its aftermath as they feel to him or her and seek relevant information from the perpetrator. In the ideal case, the perpetrator would come to appreciate further the significance of the crime committed and express to the victim remorse or apology, together with some form of restitution. The victim would accept the apology and forgive the perpetrator. A facilitator or, in the case of a community circle, community representative will make some note of the restitution offered to make sure that the agreement is properly implemented.

In theory, restorative justice processes are quite distinct from official court proceedings and do not include legally imposed punishment. The resolution of a case through restorative justice proceedings does not require a jail sentence or other form of punishment for perpetrators. In practice, however, restorative justice proceedings may occur in conjunction with the more standard judicial practices. Restorative justice and more traditional court justice can and do coexist and are related in a number of different ways. Restorative justice proceedings may occur as a substitute for court proceedings or as an optional supplement to them.

Proponents of restorative justice argue that the responsibility for wrongdoing should be borne by the community in which the wrongful act has been committed. Victims are agents and are members of that community; accordingly, they share responsibility for resolution of conflict in the aftermath of wrongdoing. They are not to be regarded as merely passive or "helpless" sufferers in the context of responding to crime and wrongdoing. They are community members who have been harmed, who may have had a role in constructing the context in which a crime was committed, and who (unless dead or gravely disabled) may be expecting to contribute to restorative proceedings.[17] Victims benefit from their encounters with the perpetrator and others insofar as they gain information and understanding that will often serve to reduce their fear of being harmed by similar crimes. For example, if a victim fears that there was some specific reason that he and his house were singled out for a home invasion, he may be reassured upon learning that the choice of his home by the attackers was basically random and that, being high on drugs, they did not understand the severity of the assaults they committed.

Meetings with the perpetrator should also provide for the protection of the victim, through facilitation and the role of family and friends, and the benefits of apology and restitution. The victim is an agent with a role to play. As someone harmed by the offending act, the victim is owed something in the way of restitution and compensation. He or she may benefit from information, support, and an opportunity to express his or her feelings. The healing and recovery of individuals and relationships may be enhanced if the victim forgives the offender. However, victims should not be pressed to forgive.[18] Forgiving is something they may freely offer, particularly in response to expressions of remorse and apology from the offender. Thus, restitution and apology are more likely results of restorative justice proceedings than of standard court procedures in which the victim and offender may never meet or may meet only in a formalized context providing little room for exchange of feelings and information.[19]

Restorative justice advocates insist that the needs of victims and perpetrators do not establish a zero-sum game in which gains for victims (assumed often to be retributive satisfaction) require losses for perpetrators (stiffer sentences and harder treatment). Rather, meetings providing for good communication can serve the needs of both, providing for the honest information and empathetic understanding that will enhance healing and address fears. They provide meaningful participation for victims, in the aftermath of wrongs, and give them an opportunity to be treated respectfully and fairly and pose the questions most important to them. It is expected that victims who have some moral power to shape the future benefit from the sense that they are not helplessly passive. If it is assumed, as is common, that what victims want is some kind of retribution, then the theory of restorative justice is open to criticism on the grounds that it will deprive victims of the satisfactions to be gained from the knowledge that the agent who harmed them is suffering in his turn. (The assumption that victims want retribution has been questioned on empirical grounds.[20])

In restorative justice theory, the victim is regarded as needing healing and repair, both in himself or herself, and with regard to relationships with the perpetrator and the community. He or she is seen as owed some expression of remorse, often in the form of an apology, and some form of restitution or compensation. Restitution need not be monetary; it could take other forms, such as practical assistance. Any participation by the victim should be optional and freely chosen, and any forgiveness or token of reconciliation should be freely offered. Facilitators should be trained to meet the needs of victims, and proceedings should provide occasions for them to honestly and safely express their thoughts and feelings.

Many victims do not want more judicially imposed punishment for offenders; instead, they want a fairer process showing them more respect and giving them some legitimate role. They also want information about the status of their case and emotional restoration, preferably through apology. Fairness, information, and respect are more important to victims than longer jail sentences for offenders. Since the 1970s, a victims' movement has supported some of the ideas underlying restorative justice, such as Christie's assertion that the state has stolen conflict from the victims. Complaints that victims play little or no role in court proceedings, appearing only as witnesses open to questioning (often hostile in nature), have led to changes within the traditional justice system in many Western countries: better facilities for victims in courts, improved access to counselling, modest compensation for some crimes, provision for victim impact statements, and some innovations in court procedures. In response to the victims' movement, legislation now provides for victim impact statements in almost all US states and in Canada and Australia. There are, however, problems about the uses of such statements, outstanding among them being the far greater impact of statements from articulate victims than from others.

The aims of restorative justice regarding victims are to give them a larger role, meet their need for information, allow them to be heard, and assist them in getting back the independence and power that the crime may have taken away from them. In restorative justice proceedings, there appear to be real benefits for victims. Participants report general satisfaction, reduced fear and anger, and an increased likelihood that perpetrators make reparations.[21] Problems are that victims may feel pressed to engage, may be reduced by facilitators to subordinate or intermediary roles, and may find or feel that the needs of the perpetrator are dominating proceedings. In theory, all victims are to be treated in a similar way, but in practice, there are relevant differences. For instance, for victims of intimate violence, meetings with perpetrators may not be appropriate.

A criticism of restorative justice from the point of view of victims is that they may be incorrectly regarded as having a responsibility to assist perpetrators and even to forgive in contexts where such actions do not suit their own needs. Supposedly, victims are central in the concept of restorative justice. Assessments of its success should attend importantly to their views on the effects of its procedures so far as the repairing or enhancing of social ties is concerned. Yet here, just as in traditional court proceedings, attention too easily shifts from victims to perpetrators. Issues of perpetrator rehabilitation, possible punishment and appropriate amends, and future reintegration into the community are pressing. In contrast, victims do not seem to threaten anyone. It is perpetrators who seem threatening and to whom something may be "done." It is perpetrators who require reform. All too readily, the interests of victims may come to be dominated by the needs and situation of perpetrators and the fears of the community. Victims may feel manipulated, even coerced and exploited, when they are urged to participate in restorative justice proceedings. A victim might think, "It is bad enough to have suffered this break-in; now, they expect me to use up a lot of time attending emotional meetings, just to help out this character whose actions have already caused me to suffer." They may be anxious about such proceedings, worrying that they will be disturbing, depressing, and time-consuming. In some cases, such as spousal abuse, the power situation between the offender and the victim may have been such that it is unreasonable to think a victim could contribute honestly and freely to proceedings; she may be fearful and intimidated.

The benefits of restorative justice have been many and its emphasis on victims' agency is valuable. The assumptions underlying restorative justice differ greatly from the assumptions of retributive justice: contrasting the two exposes central questions about responsibility and responses to wrongdoing.[22] Though relatively neglected in applied ethics, a key topic here is that of victims. In the discussion of victims, a central major introductory topic is both ethical and conceptual. Who is a victim?

NOTES

1   Petra Aarts, "Intergenerational Effects in Families of WWII Survivors from the Dutch East Indies," *International Handbook of Multigenerational Legacies of Trauma*, ed. Yael Danieli (New York: Springer, 1998) 175–87.

2   Susan Brison, *Aftermath: Violence and the Remaking of a Self* (Princeton, NJ: Princeton UP 2003).

3   A brief discussion about God's alleged responsibility for victimhood is offered in the appendix.

4   Based on personal experience.

5   See, for instance, Randi Gunther, "The Second Wound: Blaming the Innocent Victims of Sexual Abuse," *Psychology Today* 26 Oct. 2012 <http://www.huffingtonpost.com/randi-gunther/sexual-abuse2_2013443.html>, last accessed 20 Sept. 2013.

6   Just World Theory has been much discussed. See, for a thorough account, Melvin Lerner, *The Belief in a Just World: A Fundamental Delusion* (New York: Plenum, 1980).

7   Doris Brothers, *Falling Backwards: An Exploration of Trust and Self-Experience* (New York: W.W. Norton, 1995).

8   This sort of case will be discussed further.

9   More can be said and will be said about problematic aspects of these shifts toward deference.

10   I experienced this reaction when writing about the 9/11 bombings. Though it is a commonsense point of view and it should be quite obvious that someone could be a victim of a terrorist attack without being a morally pure and innocent person in all aspects of his life, stating this truism evoked a reaction of rage, even from one person well-recognized as an expert on counter-terrorism. The myth of the pure victim is a powerful one and does not always receive the scrutiny it deserves.

11   See, for instance, Gunther.

12   Ways in which innocence factors into concepts of victimhood are considered in Chapters 2 and 3 of this book.

13   See R. Braithwaite, "Restorative Justice: Assessing Optimistic and Pessimistic Accounts," *Crime and Justice* 25 (1999): 1–127.

14   Nils Christie, "Conflicts as Property," *British Journal of Criminology* 17.1 (1977): 1–15. See also Nils Christie, *A Suitable Amount of Crime* (London: Routledge, 2004).

15   In discussions of punishment, this view is called the Abolition View.

16   Complicating accounts of restoring relationships is the fact that in many contexts a decent relationship between the victim and the perpetrator did not exist even before the crime was committed: there may have been a flawed relationship or none at all. (For example, typically, a pedestrian hit by a car has no prior relationship with the driver of that car.) To handle this problem, advocates of restorative justice must extend their account to *building* decent relationships, rather than literally *restoring* them. A pivotal

assumption in restorative justice is that for relationships to be built or restored, some kind of repair is required for both victims and perpetrators.

17   A cautionary note must be struck here: there are aspects of wrongdoing for which victims truly are passive and do not share responsibility.

18   Forgiveness is discussed in Chapter 9.

19   Heather Strang, "Victim Evaluations of Face-to-Face Restorative Justice Conferences: A Quasi-Experimental Analysis," *Journal of Social Issues* 62.3 (2006): 281–306.

20   Heather Strang, *Repair or Revenge: Victims and Restorative Justice* (Oxford: Oxford UP, 2002).

21   Strang, *Repair or Revenge.*

22   See Chapter 8 of this book.

CHAPTER 2

WHO IS A VICTIM?

Look at almost any newspaper: the word "victim" is commonly used. We might reasonably suppose that this word is well understood. Here is a simple definition: a victim is an innocent person harmed, through no fault of his own, by an external force or the wrongful act of another. Two elements: innocence and harm. Both raise unexpected complications.

People are said to be victims of disease or natural disaster and also of wrongful acts. So far as wrongful acts are concerned, the paradigm is that of a guilty perpetrator and an innocent victim. There are the agents who bring harm and those damaged by their actions, those who act and those who are acted upon, the perpetrators and their victims. A murderer is a wrongdoer, offender, or perpetrator; the person he kills is the victim, object, not agent, in the attack. Similarly a thief is a perpetrator; the person whose property she takes is the victim. As agent, a con man deceives another; as passive recipient, his victim is the one deceived.

In these apparently straightforward examples we have two parties—the actor and the acted upon. The perpetrator is distinct from the victim; the perpetrator does something and his passive victim is harmed by it. We can clearly distinguish the killer from the one killed, the thief from the one robbed, the deceiver from the one deceived, and so on. From these apparently clear physical contrasts we readily infer moral distinctions. The perpetrator has done something harmful and wrong to another human being; as an active agent and subject, he may be presumed responsible for his actions and guilty of wrongdoing. The victim has done nothing wrong; as a victim, a person is the passive and innocent object of a harmful action. The oft-used expression "innocent victims" serves to emphasize victims' lack of responsibility for what they have suffered. To be a victim is to be innocent, harmed by the act of another.

A PERPLEXING CASE

In May 2011, Nafissatou Diallo accused Dominique Strauss-Kahn of attempted rape, committing a criminal sex act, and sexual abuse in a New York hotel room.[1] At the time, Diallo was a chambermaid and Strauss-Kahn was the high-profile head of the International Monetary Fund. A hard-working single mother, Diallo seemed at first to the Department of the New York Attorney-General to be an ideal victim, deserving but vulnerable to a powerful assailant. Following up on her accusations, Strauss-Kahn was arrested, jailed, and led into court handcuffed, in a somewhat dishevelled state. But the department found that Diallo had lied to gain entrance to the United States, was wavering in her testimony, and had some morally questionable associates. In short, she could not be an ideal victim in court: she would not seem to have strong moral credentials as a person whose testimony would be deemed reliable. Concluding that she would not be a credible witness in a case that would depend crucially on her testimony, the attorney-general dropped the criminal charges against Strauss-Kahn. Diallo filed a civil suit, claiming monetary damages. Eventually that civil case was settled by negotiation. Details were not made public, but it was reported that Diallo received a payout of some $6 million. Strauss-Kahn admitted sexual contact—for which there was forensic evidence—and moral wrongdoing but denied committing any illegal act. Diallo's case might have been helped by the fact that there had been other charges and allegations regarding assault and rape against Strauss-Kahn. Whereas a criminal case against him would have required demonstration beyond any reasonable doubt, the civil case required only a preponderance of evidence.

There were concerns about the withdrawal of the case, expressed especially by feminists who expressed a fear that women vulnerable due to immigration issues or other aspects of their past would not be willing to appear as victims of rape or sexual assault because of credibility problems. Rich and powerful men who could afford skilled attorneys would be able to act with impunity against poor and vulnerable women. Women might fear being "dragged through the mud" or ostracized by their communities. The Department of the New York Attorney-General may well have been correct in its estimation that Diallo's testimony, essential to its case, would not stand up in court so as to prove beyond a reasonable doubt the allegations against Strauss-Kahn. For the success of the civil suit, the evidence of his prior behaviour was enough to allow her to negotiate from a position of strength.

Morally, Diallo could clearly have been a victim of sexual assault and attempted rape even though, legally, Strauss-Kahn was never convicted. The settlement she received makes it likely (not certain) that he did assault her. To be sure, she would not have been a credible witness in court, due to the fact that she had demonstrably lied in other contexts. But that legal situation does not imply a factual or moral conclusion about what went on. This case vividly illustrates the point that people who have committed some wrongs can be victims of other wrongs. People who lie can, after all, be victims of sexual assault.

In short, not all victims have characteristics that can elicit maximum public sympathy. In 1986, Nils Christie wrote about the ideal victim. (He was satirizing the notion, criticizing the norms presumed.) The ideal victim according to Christie is a person who would be likely to elicit the most public sympathy after an attack.[2] She would be vulnerable (a little old lady), having done something virtuous (visited an ill relative), and attacked by someone more powerful (a large man) who used his power to wrong her (bang her on the head) so as to pursue his own evil purposes (getting her money so that he could buy illegal drugs). This supposedly ideal victim should be weak, relatively powerless, and above all respectable. Clearly Diallo was not an ideal victim in this sense, and indeed, many victims are not. Still, there remains a tie between notions of victimhood and ideas of innocence or blamelessness.

REFLECTIONS ON INNOCENCE

Are victims innocent *by definition*? Innocent in what sense? And of what? By what standards? Moral, in the sense that they did no wrong? Legal, in the sense that they broke no law? Causal, in that they did not cause bad things to happen? And innocent of what—of causing the harming act alone? Or of causing any act or acts that served to provide the context of the harming act? Is the implication of victim innocence so strong that it is contradictory to think of a guilty victim? Confounding cases are readily found. Can a person be a victim of his own acts or of his own character traits?[3] Is it contradictory to speak of a victim as sharing responsibility for what happened to her? Are those who blame the victim guilty not only of moral and causal mistakes but also of logical ones?

In the paradigm, there are two parties, two clearly defined and differentiated roles, and a clear line regarding innocence and guilt. The innocent and passive party is the victim; the guilty and active party the perpetrator. This fundamental and intuitive "good guy" and "bad guy" situation merits scrutiny. It is just too simple. There are many cases that do not fit the victim/perpetrator paradigm in which a passive and entirely innocent victim is harmed by the wrongful act of an active and guilty perpetrator. The term "victim" implies moral as well as causal judgements, and these sorts of judgements interact in complex ways. When we consider contexts and circumstances, we can readily construct realistic cases in which harmed parties are in significant respects guilty and harming parties in significant respects innocent.

Consider, for example, the case of persons who were brought into a country by their parents, who were illegal immigrants. This is a situation tragically common in the United States. Young people have been brought up as Americans, attended US schools, and have the language, culture, and friendships typically of US citizens. Yet, when they graduate from high school, hoping to attend university, they inquire about their papers only to find they are ineligible for many admissions and scholarships. These young people are in many ways beneficiaries of the actions of their parents, but with regard to their awkward legal status in the United States, they are also victims of those actions. In this aspect, their status as victims is not in doubt, because as children without knowledge and decision-making power, they bear no degree of responsibility for their parents' decision to enter the United States illegally and build a life there. The children of illegal immigrants did nothing to place themselves in the situation they are in. A parent who entered illegally made some choice—albeit a choice in difficult circumstances. If a man entered the country illegally and was, as a result, unable to obtain a driver's licence, it would be inaccurate to see him as a victim of the law on this matter, because he would bear responsibility for his circumstances. He, after all, took a decision to enter a context in which defensible legal restrictions, harmful to him and his family, were predictable aspects of his situation. The situation of the child brought at a young age and the parent choosing to come are different. Children brought to a country illegally by their parents are, indeed, innocent of responsibility for the situation in which they find themselves.

Considerations of innocence are more complex in other cases. Many examples can be found in which people undertake what would be illegal activities and encounter crime along their path. Consider, for example, a man, Adrian, who has flirtatious contacts with a young woman over the Internet. She tells him she is 14 and he believes it. They arrange to meet for sex and Adrian goes to their rendezvous. When he gets there, he is met by a group of young men who beat him viciously to the point of unconsciousness, leaving him for dead. In this scenario, is Adrian a victim?[4] Obviously, he would not qualify as an ideal victim in this situation. Yet, he is surely a victim of the vicious beating; in that act, he is a passive recipient rather than agent. And he was harmed. So far as the beating is concerned, Adrian is the person harmed rather than the person(s) harming and was passively affected by external force imposed wrongfully by others. He is innocent of responsibility so far as the physical attack itself is concerned, so of that act we may say that he is a victim. In the broad sense, Adrian is in a culpable position, given the sexual exploitation that is his plan; however, he is certainly not a perpetrator of this beating. Of that act, he is a victim. For it, he lacks responsibility. To be a victim of a certain action is not to be innocent of intent with regard to some related actions.

In this sort of case, a person is innocent with regard to an attack although not innocent with regard to its context. Adrian was of guilty intent regarding sexual activity with a minor. His going to the rendezvous was an expression of that intent to commit an act of which he would have been a guilty perpetrator. Adrian acted illegally, unwisely, and immorally in leading the girl on; he had criminal intent when intending to participate with her in sexual activities. If they had had a sexual encounter, due to the girl's age, he would have been morally and legally judged the responsible party and as such a guilty perpetrator. And yet, with regard to the beating, there is a clear sense in which Adrian was a victim; he was harmed by actions for which he was not responsible.

The example of Adrian is that of a person intending to violate moral and legal norms and, along the way, falling prey to the harmful actions of others. We can complicate the example to pose further questions about innocence and victimhood, illustrating the point that the concept "victim" strongly suggests a lack of responsibility with regard to the harming act and wrongdoing on the part of the harming agent (assuming it is a human being, not a force such as a tidal wave or earthquake). Suppose the person coming to the intended rendezvous was not a teenager but an undercover cop? In that case, Adrian would still have been harmed, due to an encounter with an unanticipated external force. He would likely have been arrested and charged with a serious offence. He would have been harmed in the undercover scenario, but not harmed by *wrongful* actions of any person. In such a case, we would not speak of Adrian as a *victim* of arrest, because we would presume that he deserved to be arrested. (In other words, we would presume that the arrest was not a wrongful one.) Although arrest will typically be harmful to the arrested person, we do not presume that it is a wrongful act.[5] In an arrest where there is an undercover cop but nothing amiss so as to constitute wrongful arrest, we find no perpetrator. That is because there is no personal agent harming *by doing wrong* even though there is a personal agent harming (on the presumption that a person is harmed by being arrested). There is no victim on the presumption that the person harmed deserved to be harmed and was thus not wronged when he was harmed.

Examples of this type are easily constructed and they indicate that being harmed is not sufficient to establish one's victimhood. There is a kind of innocence that is needed: one must not deserve the harm imposed by the damaging act itself, even though one might have acted so as to create the context in which that act occurred. Standards for judging that innocence are contested in some cases, a fact that emerges prominently in discussions of political conflict.[6]

Qualifications are needed when we seek to incorporate notions of innocence and guilt into the story of victimhood. It would be too simple to say that a person is a victim of a wrong only if he or she did nothing at all to contribute to the commission of that wrong, because there are too many ways in which people act to set the context of their lives. After all, a necessary condition of being beaten on a downtown street is being on that street. Adrian was a victim of a beating, though he was an agent—and not a morally upright agent—in the situation that provided its context. His status as a victim is relative to that act and not to his intended sexual activity. We cannot endorse the view that to qualify as a victim, a person must bear no responsibility for his presence in the situation of harm. We need to examine the distinction between the harming act and its context. For "innocent victimhood" what is required is that the victim not be responsible for the harming act itself.

Suppose that Adrian simply walks alone on a dark street in a neighbourhood widely believed to be dangerous and is set upon and beaten by a gang along the way. He decided to walk at this time in this place and arguably that decision was unwise. But to say that is not to say that Adrian was an agent in the wrongful attack on himself; it is not to blame the victim for the attack. Clearly, he lacked responsibility for the beating itself, was passive in the context of that act, and was a victim. In this case, Adrian was harmed by a wrongful act; he was innocent with regard to that act, and he is a victim of it. It is crucial here to note that seeing this man as a victim presumes judgements based on a sense of normality and fault. These judgements are both causal and moral. When we deem Adrian a victim, we at the same time judge that *he should not have been beaten*, that *his beating was wrong*, and those who beat him were *perpetrators of a wrong*.

These norms of responsibility are implied by the feminist organizers of "Slutwalk" protests. In such protests, women appear dressed in ways conventionally deemed to be overly exposed or "slutty." Their message is: "We can dress in this way if we so choose. We are entitled to choose how we dress, and our dressing in this way does not mean that we ourselves bear responsibility for any sexual assaults that might be launched against us. If any person does attack us, it is that person who is responsible for the attack." Norms of taste and prudence can indeed be debated, and people may deem their dress tasteless or imprudent. But whatever the conclusions of such debates are, it will remain the case that any persons who molest or rape these women will themselves be the agents of those acts. Women who dress in a "slutty" manner do not assault themselves.

ANTICIPATING VICTIM PASSIVITY

One might argue, as some commentators have, that among those killed and injured in the 9/11 attacks were some persons involved in international financial management and, directly or indirectly, complicit in poor governance and extreme poverty in various countries around the world. One could argue that such persons causally contributed to the context of the terrorist attacks, when that context is defined in terms of global economic inequality. Some of the persons killed or injured did, after all, share responsibility for the us direction and management of global financial power and thus for the context. To point out this contextual role is not to say that such persons themselves planned or implemented the attacks or intentionally brought about their own victimhood in those attacks.[7] Their situation is like that of an individual who is vulnerable in a context that he has established and for which he bears some responsibility. If that individual is attacked by external agents, they who commit the attack bear responsibility for it.

A different issue of agency, and one of tragic interest, arises in the context of the 9/11 attacks. This issue concerns persons who chose to jump from the Twin Towers. There is no exact count, but it is estimated that there were about 200 persons who did so. Their actions have received relatively little attention, and the likely reasons for this illustrate some of our concerns here.[8] Save for conspiracy theorists, most people would regard those who died as a result of the 9/11 attacks as innocent persons, victims of those attacks who bore no responsibility either for the attacks or for their own deaths resulting from those attacks. Persons who jumped would seem not to fit the victim paradigm: they presumably decided (in a very bad situation) to jump, and in that decision they would have exhibited some degree of control over what happened to them. We do not know exactly who they were, and it is likely that they came from various walks of life. What is fascinating about their situation is not any contribution to the context in which the attacks occurred, but rather something else: their agency within the attack situation.

Insofar as these persons made a decision to jump from the towers and did so, they were not purely passive victims. For those who accept that these people "voluntarily" jumped and committed suicide, they would appear to be agents of their own death. The attacks on the Towers left them in burning buildings; in a situation of desperation, they made this choice and as a result ended their own lives by jumping. From some religious viewpoints, such persons *chose* to end their own lives and acted wrongfully in doing so, since their acts would count as suicide and thus as wrong. Their choice would amount to an individualized resistance to the fate that God had intended. For persons sharing these ideas, the revelation that a family member had chosen to jump from the towers would be most unwelcome; on their view, the jumper, as a "suicide," would be innocent no more and would not in the full sense count as a victim of the 9/11 attacks. Rather, he or she would be seen as an agent who had chosen death, albeit in highly extraordinary circumstances. On this view, there can never be a *victim* of suicide: religious faith dictates that a suicidal agent, active (not passive) and guilty (not innocent), must have been wrong to deliberately bring about his or her own death. Accordingly, no person who jumped from the towers would qualify as a *victim* of the terrorist attacks. Since persons killed in the attacks should have been victims of them, the jumpers constituted an anomaly most conveniently forgotten. The anomaly of a "choice to die" was so unwelcome that the phenomenon of jumping persons has been mostly ignored or, at the very least, downplayed. There may be a small display at the Ground Zero Museum in New York, dedicated to those who jumped; however, this display will be tucked in an alcove so as not to be conspicuous.

The anomaly points to presumptions about the passivity that is expected of victims and that is linked to notions of their vulnerability and innocence. Innocence here is both causal and moral. Victims should not be the cause of the damage done to them, nor should they be the agents responsible for its wrongful aspects.[9] As a victim, a person is expected to be innocent, not guilty, and passive, not active.

HARM AND SUFFERING

That victims suffer from the harms inflicted upon them is a truism. Some aspects of damage are readily seen and apparently understood by onlookers. To be a victim one must be harmed, which is to say that one's interests must be in some way adversely affected. Typically, harm can be most clearly seen and understood when it is physical. After he is beaten, Adrian's bruised body, broken jaw, missing teeth, and so on will be clearly evident and show the damage done to him as a victim. Those who jumped from the Twin Towers died, and elements of their smashed bodies remained.

Although we can never feel the pain of another person, we can often imagine its intensity, especially when there is physical injury. We can to some extent grasp the pain of a broken limb or blackened eye, or the anxiety and nuisance brought by a stolen passport. If Adrian is robbed, damage may not bring physical pain but can be clearly specified in terms of lost funds, documents, and so on. Both physically and economically, the damage will bring costs in terms of comfort and efforts to recover. The beating is wrong; Adrian is damaged, he is harmed. To recover from this harm will take energy, effort, and time. Long-term effects of a primarily psychological nature—as in cases of PTSD (post-traumatic stress disorder)—are more difficult to understand. Victims of childhood sexual abuse often suffer for years after the abuse itself has ended. Notwithstanding their frequent efforts to describe what they have gone through, their suffering is difficult for non-victims to comprehend.

A person who is a victim of wrongdoing typically suffers from the harm brought by that wrong. He or she may continue to suffer long after the harming acts are committed. Suffering is primarily a conscious matter; when a person suffers physical pain, he or she is aware of it. The same may be said of most psychic pain. One suffers when one is aware of pain and unease; one suffers from physical pain or from psychic discomfort, anxiety, and unhappiness; or from all of these at once. It is more difficult to make sense of the notion of unconscious suffering, though one could posit it in some cases, as when a person with an estranged child might be said to suffer unconsciously from the alienation. Suffering can be distinguished from harm. A person is harmed when his or her well-being (physical and psychological) or interests (financial, concerning personal prospects) are adversely affected. He or she is likely to suffer when the harm is imposed but may not do so after a period of time. While no longer suffering, a person may continue to be harmed in the sense that these interests have been adversely affected.

Short-term harms may even become benefits over a longer term. For example, consider the case of a man who loses his job as a result of a betraying and deceptive colleague and is in the short term harmed by economic losses, dislocation, and damage to his self-esteem. As a result of these events, this man—let's call him Ralph—moves across the country and finds alternate employment, which in the end turns out to be highly advantageous to his career and relationships. Ralph was and remains a victim of his colleague's actions; in the short term he was harmed by them, although in the long term he has benefitted. In all likelihood he suffered when he lost the job but is no longer suffering at the end. Was Ralph harmed? In the short term, yes. In the longer term, no. Was he a victim? Yes, he was a victim of the colleague's acts, and it remains true to say that he was and regard him as a victim. Did he suffer? Almost certainly. But can we say that over the longer term Ralph was harmed? Fundamentally, he was not, though he might continue to remember with bitterness his colleague's betrayal.

To be harmed by, and a victim of, a particular wrongful act done at a specific time and in a specific context does not entail either that one is harmed in the long term or that one is suffering from that act over the longer term. In many contexts, it would be tactless to dwell on the point and one would make oneself quite unpopular by mentioning it. Nevertheless, it is obviously possible to have cases such as that of Ralph. Even a very serious harm might turn out to be beneficial over the longer term. Someone widowed as a result of the 9/11 attacks might remarry a person more kind and generous than her first husband, to her benefit and that of her children. Only in the shorter term would she be harmed as a result of the death of an abusive husband; that could be liberating, though it would be inappropriate in many contexts to make this point.

The central and necessary (though not sufficient) element of victimhood is that of harm. Suffering is different from harm, typically involving awareness of pain or ill-ease. How enduring suffering is, how intensive it is, how it feels, what it is like all vary with different persons and different wrongs. It is possible that people may be wronged without suffering, and it is certainly possible for them to suffer without being wronged. (Clearly, victims of disease or natural disaster may be harmed and suffer without being wronged by any agent, unless one defines God as the agent in such cases.[10]) To be a victim, one must as a matter of logical necessity be harmed. One need not suffer. We can envisage, for instance, a victim of financial fraud who loses his money and whose interests are adversely affected, but who does not suffer because he did not really care about that money in the first place. Victims are harmed, and they are harmed through no responsibility of their own. But the harms of victimhood need not last a lifetime.

HARMS OVER GENERATIONS

There has been much discussion in Canada concerning the appalling wrongs committed at residential schools for Aboriginal children, which were run by governments and churches. Poor food and education, poor facilities, physical abuse, cultural abuse, and in a horrifying number of cases sexual abuse were characteristic of these facilities for 150 years. With the growing public awareness and discussion of the alarming details, some have disputed claims of victimhood by claiming that there were some benefits of the system. Many children learned to speak, read, and write in English, and some gained a love of reading and other skills they were able to use in their adult lives. Such gains would not mean that children were not victims of physical and sexual abuse. Beating, sexual interference, and rape are brutal and painful acts damaging to those on whom they are imposed, and they remain so, even in cases where there were some benefits from the primarily abusive context. These children were victims of the abuse they experienced; they were innocent of responsibility, harmed by others. Many suffered over long periods of time. Arguments to the effect that there were some benefits to their education or that they could not possibly have continued to suffer decades after their schooling do not rebut those fundamental facts of victimhood.

There undoubtedly remains much to be discovered about the workings of the residential school system. The Canadian Truth and Reconciliation Commission has struggled with only partial success to get access to relevant archival documents.[11] Library and Archives Canada maintains that it would cost some $40 million dollars and take 10 years to locate and digitize all the relevant records. Recent disturbing reports, based on academic research by food historian Ian Mosby, indicated that in the late 1940s, nutritional experiments were performed on Aboriginal children in northern Manitoba. When children were found to be seriously malnourished, scientists gave them vitamins and supplements, instead of more food, to test the effects of those elements. In effect, Aboriginal children forced into residential schools were used as guinea pigs in experiments about nutritional supplements.[12]

The tragic case of residential schools provides a powerful illustration of the extent of victimhood over persons and over time. A child mistreated in a residential school is a victim of that mistreatment. As a person malnourished, humiliated, and (in many cases) abused, that child is a primary victim of wrongdoing. He has been harmed, he has suffered, and in all likelihood he will have continued to suffer over a long time. But this is not to say that the child is the only victim. His parents and other family members are secondary victims of what is done (the removal of the child from his home and his alienation from his home culture), and if he has descendants, there is a tragic likelihood that their lives will be damaged by the damage originally done to him. The notion of secondary victims is based on the fact that wrongful harm to one person typically brings harm to other persons closely connected to him or her.[13] Often, harm goes further still—a point again convincingly illustrated by such phenomena as the residential schools. When children are taken from their communities and families are damaged, parenting skills are lost and problems of damaged individuals persist, often at tremendous cost to communities. In such cases, it makes sense to identify a third level of victimhood: the entire community is affected as a tertiary victim. The case of Canadian residential schools is one in which primary, secondary, and tertiary victims are all likely to suffer long after the original wrongful acts were committed. Even persons who ceased to suffer and in some ways benefitted from training or education in the schools remain victims of the mistreatment they experienced.

VICTIMS AND SURVIVORS

The idea of a victim is typically that of a vulnerable person, damaged by the wrongful acts of others, passively the recipient of harm, unable to protect herself from the original damage or rescue herself in its aftermath. What does it mean to be in the role of a victim? To accept that role? To take it even as an aspect of one's identity? One problem about the "victim role" is that expectations of passivity are extended into the aftermath of wrongs, to contexts beyond that of the original harming act. On this view, victims are expected to do little for themselves. Injured persons can be limited by such expectations and the sense of powerlessness they may create. Clearly, there are negative aspects attached to the victim role.

Though victims' entitlements are embraced by some, the notion of being a victim is firmly rejected by others who resist notions of vulnerability and passivity in the aftermath of wrongdoing. We tend to regard victims as needy and helpless, meekly anticipating sympathy and assistance, expecting the compassion of others while doing little to assert themselves and help themselves. These expectations have led to rejections of the victim label and role in some circles. At the hearings of the South African Truth and Reconciliation Commission, more women than men testified at Victim Hearings. Most often, these women were wives, widows, daughters, and sisters of men who had fought in the struggles against apartheid. Men involved in that struggle tended to reject the victim role, leading them to stay away from Victim Hearings. If they had been injured, even tortured, even if they continued to suffer physical and psychic damage, they did not want to be regarded as victims in need of sympathy and assistance. They tended instead to regard themselves as fighters, warriors, and heroes in a liberation struggle.

A preferred term, in this context as in many others, is "survivor." Unlike "victim," "survivor" does not connote passivity, vulnerability, and need. Instead, it connotes activity and strength—sometimes even heroism. For understandable reasons, victims may wish to be deemed survivors. There are many references to "victims and survivors," as an Internet search will quickly reveal. To many, "survivor" has seemed a better term than "victim," and due to its connotations of endurance and effort, it is preferred by many.[14]

Erin Greene is a Canadian woman who survived an attack by a polar bear in the minimal sense that she lived through it and lived after it. The bear thrashed her, with the result that her scalp was torn, a piece of her left ear was removed, and three arteries were severed. Greene was air-lifted to Winnipeg from the northern city of Churchill, Manitoba, and successfully treated in hospital. According to a news account, she recovered but will face a hefty bill for the airlift.[15] Greene was the victim in an attack; she was helpless against the force of the bear, lacking in responsibility for its actions. She was harmed; she was treated; she survived. The *victim* became a *survivor* in a clear and literal sense in this case.

What is implied by being a survivor? First and most obviously, the implication is that one has survived; one has endured, has lived on after going through something difficult that involved harm and suffering. But more is implied. To say that a person survived is to imply that he or she came relatively unscathed through significant challenges. To be a *survivor* is to have exhibited some energy and even heroism in facing up to difficulties and living through them and not merely to have been a passive *victim*.

One clear objection to replacing the term "victim" with the term "survivor" is that not all victims survive. Many victims survive; many others are killed. These persons are obviously not survivors, however heroically they might have struggled. For this reason, the term "survivor" simply cannot replace the term "victim." And there are further reasons that any systematic substitution of "survivor" for "victim" would only be confusing. For all the implicit norms and resulting complications accompanying the word "victim," we do still need the term. It makes sense to speak of those who have lived through sexual abuse or torture as survivors of those wrongs in more than the minimal sense that they continue to live. The richer sense—that they have struggled against tough challenges and come to function well in their aftermath—is often warranted. But when a wrong is more slight, as in a case of burglary or mis-administration, the term "survivor" has overly heroic connotations. For some crimes such as fraud or burglary, there are clearly victims, and yet "survivor" seems too extreme. Associations with brave struggle and heroic effort would be misplaced in such contexts. To be sure, these people are victims, but it would be misleading to refer to them as *survivors* unless the hardships undergone were considerable. If we were to generally replace the term "victim" with the term "survivor," the likelihood is that our notions of effort and the conquest of challenges would shift so as to incorporate more notions of vulnerability and innocence in survival itself. The term "survivor" would lose aspects of its meaning and little would be gained, at significant cost to clarity.

When the story of Erin Greene as a survivor is recounted, the obvious implication is that she lived through the bear attack and her recovery from it. Serious challenges are presumed when we speak of surviving. The attack was fearsome and painful; the recovery as a result of medical treatment was likely painful too. To think of a bear attack as something one could survive is quite appropriate. For minor hardships, the notion of survival is inappropriate. To say that one *survived* a line in a supermarket would be either misleading or ironic unless there was something unusually challenging about being in that line (high temperatures or a wait of a number of hours with no bathroom facilities, for instance). Similarly, it could be inappropriate to speak non-ironically of surviving a relatively modest wrong, such as the loss of a few dollars or a delay in traffic.

These considerations expose a crucial ambiguity in the term "survivor." As we have seen, in one established sense of the term, referring to someone as a survivor is appropriate only when she has overcome significant challenges. But in another sense, "survivor" is used to refer to persons who have simply lived on in the sense of remaining alive when family or associates have been killed. The family members who are secondary victims are survivors of the person killed simply in the sense that they have lived after his death. They may or may not be survivors in the deeper sense that they have overcome serious challenges in an aftermath situation.[16]

Suppose that Erin Greene had not lived through the bear attack. We would speak then of her survivors: her parents, siblings, husband, and children, for instance. These people were never attacked by a polar bear as she was, but there is a sense in which they were victims of the attack. They were secondary victims harmed by the loss of a family member.[17] Whether these secondary victims are survivors in the stronger and more honorific sense of having overcome challenges in the aftermath is an open question.

To sum up, there are three clear reasons for not recommending that the term "survivor" replace the term "victim." Speaking here of primary victims, we can see the points most clearly. First and most importantly, some primary victims do not survive. Second, the terms "victim" and "survivor" have very different emotional and moral connotations as to passivity, struggle, and the overcoming of obstacles. Third, there are potentially confusing ambiguities in the term "survivor" as between simply living on and living on so as to overcome fundamental challenges.

A SCENARIO AND ITS PITFALLS: VICTIMS AND PERPETRATORS

In the classic victim scenario involving moral agents, a guilty perpetrator acts to wrongfully harm a passive and innocent victim. Yet there are pitfalls when we consider some cases through the lens of this scenario. There are aspects in which a victim may be less than passive and less than innocent regarding the act that harmed him or her. We have also seen that the damage from wrongful acts can extend to persons other than the primary victim and can last over a considerable period of time, extending in some tragic cases even to communities and subsequent generations. These aspects of victimhood have implications for perpetrators as well. Persons who are secondary or tertiary victims of some wrongs may be perpetrators of others. To say the least, any firm dichotomy of victim and perpetrator should be resisted.[18] What should be firmly rejected is extending the victim/perpetrator role in one act or context to others. Especially distorting is the ossification of such roles so that they become a basis for identity.

Individuals and groups can exploit the victim role and attitudes of deference to victims. The notion of innocence implied by victim status may serve to buttress an enduring sense of grievance and self-righteousness that may perpetuate individual or group conflict. Highly significant in this context is the fact that as a "victim" a person or group will be regarded as lacking in responsibility for its damaged situation, deserving of sympathy, and having an entitlement to resources required for recovery. Sympathy for the victims may lead to overly deferential attitudes and even to a kind of "victim's licence," based on the sense that a person or group that has suffered severe wrongs is entitled to protect itself and stands beyond criticism because of the damage done to it. This sort of deference can be seen in political cases in which a horrendously damaged group is deemed entitled to go to any length to protect itself.[19] The resolve is "never again"—seen so clearly in the cases of Israel and Rwanda. Having been grossly damaged by horrendous wrongdoing, a group will understandably go far to protect itself, motivated by fear of similar damage in the future. In its understandable sense of vulnerability, it may feel entitled to oppress others deemed to be enemies who could, as in the past, set out to ensure its destruction. Stress will be on the fact that this group was once a victim of terrible wrongs, and this emphasis will inhibit recognition that in a subsequent situation, the group has become a perpetrator, sometimes of grievously serious wrongs against others.

Contrary to the simplistic presumptions of some popular cultures, the world is not divided into two sorts of people: good guys and bad guys, victims and perpetrators. Most individuals, and most groups, have a mixture of characteristics and act in varying ways in various contexts. It is even possible for a person to be a victim and a perpetrator with regard to the same act in the same context. A perpetrator of wrongs may himself or herself be the victim of threats or perceived threats, as in cases of conscripts or torturers under the direction of brutal regimes. A torturer may have been trained and forced to torture persons whom he knows to be innocent. Engaged in torture, such a person may commit cruel and brutal acts as a perpetrator while being at the same time a victim of coercion in difficult circumstances.

Especially tragic cases of pressing humanitarian concern are those of child soldiers, both victims and perpetrators in brutal contemporary wars.

CHILD SOLDIERS AS VICTIM-PERPETRATORS AND PERPETRATOR-VICTIMS

Children as young as eight and 10 fight in wars. Most familiar, perhaps, are examples of children in rebel armies in Africa. The 20-year civil war in Sierra Leone was of appalling brutality. So too have been wars in Mozambique, Angola, the Democratic Republic of Congo, and northern Uganda. Although such conflicts have been widely publicized, Africa is not the only place where children are engaged in intense political violence. The phenomenon also exists in South America, Asia, and the Middle East. There are disputes about the chronological age range for *childhood*, and we will return to these, but these disputes mainly concern the teenage years, say over 15. It is well-known that children far younger are fighting and performing many other roles in armed forces, including cooking, cleaning, and carrying goods as well as direct combat, and they are also involved in coerced sexual activity and entertainment. Memoirs and works by academics and activists amply document the phenomenon. Due to the variety of tasks children may perform in affiliation with fighting forces, an exact definition of "soldier" in this context is hard to come by, and chaotic circumstances make counting difficult. Though exact numbers are not known, it is estimated that some 200,000 to 300,000 children are affiliated with and active with fighting forces around the world.[20]

Many of these children are both perpetrators and victims. They are perpetrators because they are agents of cruel and brutal acts including killings, amputations, threats, torture, and arson. They are victims because they are not in the full sense morally responsible for what they do. They are immature, and they are in coercive and extraordinarily difficult circumstances; even of the acts they perpetrate, they are not responsible agents. In debates about the moral accountability of child soldiers, one central issue is that of how a child becomes affiliated with, or a member of, a fighting group. Often a child affiliated with a military group has been abducted from his or her school or village and compelled to remain with the group after being forced to participate in brutality that may include killing a family member or close friend. After a cruel training period and being subjected to many threats, he or she may be engaged in active combat and gross misdeeds such as torture, rape, and pillage. Prior to participation in such actions, the child will have been brainwashed, subject to threats, and given drugs or alcohol. Some groups force families to give up one child to guerrilla or military operations, and children are handed over so that other family members may be relatively safe. In such circumstances, which are tragically not uncommon, a child is clearly not responsible for his or her brutalized situation.

But there are also cases of voluntary enlistment by children. Those who have studied child soldiers point out that it is by no means the case that all of them have been abducted and forced into combat and associated roles. Children may voluntarily join armed groups. Indeed, in circumstances of war or seriously imperilled peace, there are many reasons that children might volunteer, including identification with the causes for which such groups are fighting or claim to be fighting.[21] A child may be orphaned and have no means of sustaining himself or herself in chaotic circumstances where armed groups seem to be the only source of protection and means of survival. Affiliation with an armed group may seem, and may really be, the only available source of food, shelter, and protection. Alternately, a child may flee desperate family circumstances. She may be persuaded to fight for a cause seeming to support justice and equality. After grave losses, she may seek to fight for revenge. She may see an active role in rebel groups as preferable to a highly restrictive role due to the gender practices of a very conservative society. There are, then, many reasons a child might voluntarily affiliate himself or herself with an armed group. Common though it is, abduction is certainly not the only path to becoming a child soldier.

Whether as victims or as rival combatants, persons who survive the acts of child soldiers may remember children in the role of brutal and apparently enthusiastic perpetrators. While these recollections of horrors must be respected, the view that such child perpetrators are accountable moral agents must be firmly rejected. Circumstances of joining up may vary, but the facts of immaturity and extremely difficult circumstances remain. Typically, a decision to join an armed group will be taken by a child in difficult circumstances where there are few clear paths to survival. But, most importantly, that decision is taken by a *child* whose choice is, due to immaturity, not voluntary even when it may seem to be so. As a child, a person does not have the capacity to make profoundly serious moral choices such as the choice to affiliate with an armed group in circumstances of violence and chaos. The child will typically lack information about life within that group, its circumstances, the sorts of actions performed by its members, and the reasons for those actions and their consequences. With such gaps, he or she could not make an informed decision even with the maturity to do so. And such maturity will be lacking by definition; we are, after all, talking about children.

With regard to the situation in which he finds himself, a child soldier is a victim, one who is harmed through no fault of his own. The boy or girl soldier is a victim sometimes of abduction or dire threats, sometimes of a "choice" made in harsh circumstances. Without power, information, or maturity, the boy or girl living within an armed group is not morally responsible for being in that situation.

Most accounts of child soldiers stress their victimhood. Romeo Dallaire, who encountered child soldiers in Rwanda and later wrote movingly about them, describes them as compelled and indoctrinated, used as tools by adults who wage war. Dallaire states firmly:

> Whether commanders abduct children or recruit them
> voluntarily, using children as combat troops is always a crime

on the part of the leaders. The child in either case should
be viewed and treated as a victim of this crime and not be
held responsible for decisions made under extreme duress.[22]

Dallaire goes on to describe the treatment of children in armed groups and how children in combat appear threatening, brutal, and full of hatred and evil. A person does not have to be morally accountable for his situation or his actions to appear as a fearsome being to others who are threatened by him or her. Horrifyingly, this person remains a child even when committing cruel and brutal acts of maiming, torture, and killing.

There are, of course, some choices and degrees of agency among boys and girls within military groups. For example, a girl might seek a powerful male as her "bush husband" and thereby gain better food and protection from rape. Another child soldier might manage, within an action, to put himself in a position where he burned huts rather than amputating limbs. Memoirs and other accounts of child soldiers establish the point that even in their situations of extreme brutality, some children succeed in making choices to avoid the very worst actions. Even so, children in these circumstances are vulnerable, subject to extreme duress and control, and immature as decision-makers. The fact that some child soldiers can make and implement some protective choices does not show that all or most of them are responsible for the actions they take after brutalizing treatment in the chaotic circumstances of war.

What is especially perplexing about child soldiers is that when they engage in acts of murder, torture, mutilation, and killing, they appear to be perpetrators as well as victims. The child combatant is clearly active and an agent of wrongdoing, even though not morally responsible for his or her situation or individual actions within that situation. This point is at one level clear and obvious, but at another level it is likely to be confusing both for theory and for practice. It is theoretically confusing because the innocent (child) seems guilty and the passive (victim) is highly active. It is practically confusing with regard to issues of military ethics, rehabilitation, and reintegration.[23]

In her recent book *The Violence of Victimhood*, Diane Enns vividly explains the confusion felt when we realize that child soldiers are victims and perpetrators simultaneously.[24] Enns is concerned that the victim aspect of this situation has been exaggerated. She warns of the danger of forgetting that even though they are in many respects victims, these children are like many other killers when they insist that they killed for "right" or "excusable" reasons. She stresses the risks to morality and accurate thinking when human agents understand and represent their situation as one in which they had *no choice*. And to be sure, though they find themselves in appalling circumstances, many child soldiers do have some choices to make. By insisting there is *no choice*, people can deceive themselves, sometimes to excuse or justify horrors. Enns is concerned that if we define child soldiers primarily as *victims*, we will diminish our sense that they are in some sense agents and *perpetrators*; an emphasis on the victimhood of child soldiers will result in a loss of attention and concern for those persons who have been, and are, *their* victims. This concern is understandable and grounded on her awareness of the more general problem that too much deference for victims results in a kind of victim's licence where the victims of some wrongs go on to commit other wrongs and enjoy a sort of reputational impunity.

But there is a problem at this point. Despite her sensitivity to the phenomena of victim/perpetrators and perpetrator/victims, Enns seems here to fall back into the supposition that the child agent of brutality must be *either* a victim or a perpetrator. Her thinking seems itself founded on a false dichotomy between victims and perpetrators. That supposition underlies her claim that if the child is himself deemed a victim of coercive acts, he cannot be a perpetrator (agent of wrongdoing) as regards some other acts. Presupposed is the claim that as a victim, he cannot himself have victims; in other words, because he is a victim, there are no other persons who are his victims. Reasoning in this way, there would be no sympathy or support for those persons who are his victims.[25] That is why Enns wishes to stress the perpetrator status of child soldiers. But the presupposed claim should be rejected. Enns' stance on the perpetrator status of child soldiers is not required in order to justify concern for *all* victims. Victims merit sympathy and care because of the harm that has come to them. If a woman loses a limb due to the action in a civil war of a child soldier who has been abducted, threatened, and drugged, that woman will be vulnerable and in need of assistance, regardless of what is said about the responsibility of the child victim/perpetrator.

Enns questions the classic victim/perpetrator paradigm and is generally sensitive to the fact that victims may exercise some agency and are not in every case wholly passive. Her concern is that those who think primarily within the classic paradigm incorporating victim/perpetrator dichotomy will be led by their identification with child soldier victims to neglect the victimhood of those harmed by child soldier perpetrators. To be sure, many do think in terms of that dichotomous paradigm, and many do ossify the victim role so as to construct "victim" as an enduring identity of innocence. Enns correctly emphasizes that child soldiers may be agents and that many later acknowledge some choice in highly difficult situations.[26] They do make some choices in the sense that they may choose to kill one person rather than another or to avoid participating in some action by pretending to be ill. Against all odds, some even manage to escape. The fact that adults often engage in spurious rationalizations such as "I had no choice" does not show that victimized children in coercive circumstances are properly blamed when they offer such explanations. Enns defends a kind of responsibility in the sense that one has to deal with the consequences of one's actions, and that is of course a worthy norm. However, it is somewhat unclear just what its practical implications would be in the context of child soldiers struggling in brutal and coercive circumstances. More fundamentally, if a person is not morally responsible in the sense of having the capacity to make and implement a choice, it is not clear why, in the aftermath, he or she would be morally required to respond to the consequences of his or her wrongful actions.

To reflect further on these profoundly difficult issues, we need to consider a basic distinction between responsibility when committing an act and responsibility after that act. It is one thing to be morally responsible for one's action in the sense that one has made a deliberate, uncoerced, and informed decision about what to do and has been able to act on that decision. In this sense, child soldiers are not morally responsible either for the situations in which they find themselves or for the actions they take within those situations. It is another thing to accept some responsibility, *after the fact*, for the consequences of one's actions. Enns says of child soldiers after the fact that "they own their actions" and must take responsibility for them and their consequences.[27] This is another matter and something child soldiers can do if they emerge to become adult citizens functioning in a civil society. Astoundingly, some do that, becoming artists and activists for peace, refugees, and other humanitarian causes.[28] The phenomenon is admirable and inspiring. Yet it would be too much to say that recovering child soldiers have obligations to act in these ways. When they do that, it is commendable and amazing, but not obligatory. Given the vulnerability and limited capabilities of former child soldiers, it would not make sense to impose norms of obligation on them in situations of aftermath. Attempts to require them to engage in activism or to offer positive help for their victims would likely be counter-productive.

WHO *IS* A VICTIM?

A victim is a person or agent harmed by an act of external element that is not deserved and not a matter of his or her will but is instead imposed by an external force or agent. It is not a simple matter of fact that a person is a victim; as we have seen, the notion of victim is a deeply moral one, including at its core moral presumptions about responsibility, innocence and virtue, harm, suffering, vulnerability, and passivity. Victimhood is considered to result from wrongdoing in contexts where there are victims and perpetrating agents. A focus on victims and perpetrators is understandable, given legal and moral problems about punishment and process for known and suspected perpetrators. Yet, as the notion of victimhood is employed, we are not always the victims of other agents who are perpetrators. We may be victims of forces and entities other than personal agents; disease, accidents, natural catastrophes, and animal attacks are obvious examples.

When we think of victims, we are apt to think first of individuals. Yet groups can be victims, a fact amply illustrated both in politics and in natural disasters. Truth commissions in many countries have found evidence of harms to damaged communities and marginalized groups. In 2001, the United States was the victim of a terrorist attack. As a society and state, Haiti was the victim of an earthquake in 2010, as was Japan in 2011. In 1998 and again in 2013, Quebec and Ontario were victims of intense ice storms, inflicting serious inconvenience and cost. Enormous damage was imposed on individuals, society, and state in the Philippines typhoon in 2013. Climate change will negatively affect individuals and groups around the globe: they may be said to be its victims. Some will experience more harm than others; many will share responsibilities for the factors causing climate change. The more responsible will tend to be in the industrialized North, the more affected in the less developed South. Wars have destroyed infrastructure, bringing inconvenience, disease, and death. Even corporations can be victims, though the large and powerful ones would not stand out as obvious examples and would certainly not qualify as ideal victims. In the aftermath of a damaging event such as a flood, an insurance company could not only be harmed by the many claims resulting from its customers but could be the victim of fraudulent claims. Individuals could seek to perpetrate wrong against a corporation typically more powerful than they, and they could potentially succeed. In all these contexts, there has been undeserved harm imposed by an external agent, inflicted on social structures and institutions and damaging to many.

Given that there are many sorts of harms, victims may be harmed in many ways. Harm may be physical or mental or both. It may be conscious or (more rarely) unconscious, short-lived or persisting even through generations. Though victims are harmed by externally imposed acts, it is possible even for them to benefit ultimately from those very acts. That fact does not rebut the original victimhood.

Although we expect victims to be passive, in the context in which they are victims, their agency is not always fully suppressed. Those persons who jumped to their deaths in the 9/11 attacks provide an illustration of that possibility. What seems to some to be guilty suicide will seem to others a brave choice and assertion of will in a context of desperation. The context is no less desperate, and no less imposed because the fact of choice remains within it. The same may be said of child soldiers, who exhibit some agency in horrendous conditions of war. They are no less victims, and no more guilty, for the fact that they can deliberate and choose with regard to some aspects of their circumstances.

With regard to victims and victimhood, moral complexities are considerable. Relative to a harming act or entity, the victim is vulnerable, passive, and open to damage, even if he or she was active in some regard. The label "victim" will apply to someone in the context of an act or set of acts and should not be generalized over all contexts. As the case of Nafissatou Diallo powerfully illustrates, a person may be guilty of some wrongs (lying) while a victim of others (coercion, sexual assault). Obviously, not all victims are "ideal." A person is not *simply a victim* or for that matter *simply a perpetrator*. Being a victim should not be taken as a defining element of one's identity. A victim in some contexts—even (as so poignantly illustrated in the case of child soldiers) a victim in many respects and many contexts—may also be a perpetrator and bear responsibility as a perpetrator. Status as a victim is relative to a context and an act. Attending to this point helps to avoid simplistic categorizations and stereotypes.

Victims are persons harmed in ways they do not deserve through no fault of their own. Because there are many perspectives from which fault may be judged, persons deemed to be victims from some perspectives may not be so regarded from others. Differences of this kind are especially apparent in contexts of political conflict.

NOTES

1   Jennifer Poltz, "Dominique Strauss-Kahn Settlement: Former IMF Chief, N. Diallo Settle Sexual Assault Lawsuit," *Huffington Post* 10 Dec. 2012.

2   Nils Christie, "The Ideal Victim," *From Crime Policy to Victim Policy*, ed. E. Fattah (Basingstoke, UK: Macmillan, 1986) 17–30.

3   This interesting question is not considered in detail here. My short answer to it is yes. To say that a person is a victim of his own desires or character or habits is to say that he is harmed by their effect on him; he harms himself insofar as his pursuit of important goals or norms is undermined by not fully controlled aspects of his character and desires. These are indeed his but may be seen as external insofar as he is unable to control their effect on him. There is an implication in the notion of victimhood here that the more rational or "higher" self is undermined by the impact of a lesser self that the higher self cannot control.

4   There is no implication here that these men are beating Adrian *because* he has arranged the rendezvous with the young woman or that they intend to (in some sense) punish him because he has made this arrangement.

5   If we did make that presumption (as in a case of clear police bias), we would then be willing to refer to the arrested person as a victim. He or she would be a victim of a wrongful arrest or false arrest.

6   Examples from Northern Ireland are discussed in some detail in Chapter 3 of this book.

7   Discussed in Trudy Govier, *A Delicate Balance* (Boulder, CO: Westview Press, 2002).

8   "It looked like they were blinded by smoke—they just walked to the edge and fell out." Leonard speculates that people did not want to know whether relatives who died in the attack had jumped, and that their resistance to consider the jumpers was founded in part on religious ideas. Tom Leonard, "The 9/11 Victims America Wants to Forget," *Mail Online* 11 Sept. 2011 <http://www.dailymail.co.uk/news/article-2035720/9-11-jumpers-America-wants-forget-victims-fell-Twin-Towers.html> last accessed 24 June 2014.

9   In a case where a person is a victim of himself, the aspects of which he is a victim are presumed to be aspects over which he lacks control, as explained in note 3 above.

10   This matter is discussed in the Appendix.

11   At time of writing (August 2013), the Canadian TRC continues its work.

12   "Nutritional Experiments Scandal—Rally Organizers Want Documents Released," *Toronto Star*, 26 July 2013 <http://www.thestar.com/news/canada/2013/07/25/ nutritional_experiments_scandal_rally_organizers_want_documents_released. html> last accessed 24 June 2014. The research paper in question is by Ian Mosby, "Administering Colonial Science: Nutrition Research and Human Biomedical Experimentation in Aboriginal Communities and Residential Schools, 1942–1952," *Social History* 46.91 (May 2013): 145–72.

13   The concepts of primary, secondary, and tertiary victimhood are further explained in Trudy Govier, *Taking Wrongs Seriously: Acknowledgment, Reconciliation, and the Politics of Sustainable Peace.* (Amherst, NY: Humanity Books-Prometheus, 2006).

14   For many, "victim" and "survivor" are mutually exclusive in the sense that those wishing to identify as survivors reject the victim label. Strictly speaking, these terms are not exclusive. One might regard oneself as a victim of an act at one time in the sense that one was harmed by the act and was not responsible for it, and then later regard oneself as a survivor of that act in the sense that one deemed oneself to have met its challenges and lived on to become an active agent. One can imagine scenarios— as, for example, with PTSD—in which a survivor, for whatever reasons, encountered further challenges that were too great and fell back into his condition of victimhood. Contextualization as to time and circumstances will help to sort out these puzzles. I owe my sensitivity to these problems to David Boutland.

15   "Woman Recounts Harrowing Attack by Churchill Polar Bear," CBC News, 19 Dec. 2013 <http://www.cbc.ca/player/Embedded-Only/News/Manitoba/ ID/2425494937/> last accessed 24 June 2014.

16   This is not to say that failure to overcome challenges in the aftermath constitutes a fault.

17   The qualifier "secondary" here does not imply either less importance or even less suffering.

18   Govier, *Taking Wrongs Seriously*, Chapter 2.

19   This notion is explained and subjected to criticism by Diane Enns in *The Violence of Victimhood* (University Park, PA: Pennsylvania State UP, 2012).

20   Michael Wessells, *Child Soldiers: From Violence to Protection* (Cambridge, MA: Harvard UP, 2006). I have also gained insights from Romeo Dallaire, *They Fight Like Soldiers, They Die Like Children* (Toronto: Random House, 2010); David M. Rosen, *Armies of the Young: Child Soldiers in War and Terrorism* (New Brunswick, NJ: Rutgers UP, 2005); and Ishmael Beah, *A Long Way Gone: Memoirs of a Boy Soldier* (Toronto: Douglas and McIntyre, 2007).

21   Rosen emphasizes agency and moral accountability more than do other authors with the possible exception of Diane Enns.

22   Dallaire 127.

23   Dallaire; Jeff McMahon, "Child Soldiers: An Ethical Perspective," *Building Knowledge about Children in Armed Conflict*, ed. Scott Gates and Simon Reich (Pittsburgh: U of Pittsburgh P, 2013) 27–36.

24   Enns 118.

25   Pushing the point from a logical point of view, one could even insist that they cannot exist. Enns, of course, does not go that far.

26   Enns 127.

27   Enns 149.

28   Examples of recovered child soldiers who have gone on to become performers and activists are many. They include Emmanuel Jal from Sudan, a hip-hop artist, writer, and activist; Ishmael Beah from Sierra Leone, a writer and activist; Helen Kwac (pseudonym) from northern Uganda, a human rights and anti-corruption activist; and Yordanos Haile Michael from Eritrea, an actor-activist.

CHAPTER 3

SOME CONTROVERSIES ABOUT VICTIMHOOD

In the aftermath of the Troubles in Northern Ireland, disputes about its victims have been prominent. People on one side of the Republican/Unionist conflict object to the victim status of certain persons on the other side, alleging that they do not qualify as victims because they were agents or supporters of wrongdoing and, as such, not innocent parties. They were instead terrorists, paramilitaries, combatants, or in some other way responsible participants in wrongdoing.

HIERARCHIES?

On some views, all victims (all damaged persons) will be equally deserving: one will refuse to consider degrees of innocence or intensity of suffering. These may be referred to as "no hierarchy" views, the underlying idea being that there should be no hierarchy of victims. We may ask here: "equally deserving of what?" What is it that victims deserve, that we might wish to allocate differentially and then decide to allocate equally on the insistence that there should be no hierarchy of victims? Sympathy? Responses from police or medical personnel? Support? Resources for rehabilitation? Compensation? Reparations? Acknowledgement? Attention and space in public memorials, museums, and textbooks? Input into policy decisions? The response to questions of desert will vary according to context. Whatever victims deserve—most obviously, sympathy and care—harmed persons would deserve *equally* if hierarchy and distinctions are fully rejected. Considerations of rights and wrongs, agency and innocence will not be relevant to the case.

In disputes about the entitlements of victims, the notion of hierarchy may play a powerful rhetorical role. Its role is typically negative. The implication is that someone is making a distinction that presupposes a hierarchy, but any hierarchy is misconstrued since, as harmed persons, all who are victims are equally deserving.

Here is an illustrative example. Rob and Unwin are persons who identify with sides opposed during the Troubles. Unwin claims that Sheila, a candidate for treatment and compensation, does not qualify as a victim because though she has suffered harm she did so because she was the relative of a terrorist. In response, Rob accuses Unwin of defending a *hierarchy of victims*, a framework in which some harmed persons are *more deserving* (or more *meriting of status as victims*) than others. Indeed, Unwin's response is dependent on disputed assumptions about the rightness and wrongness of the political struggle over Northern Ireland. Unwin sides with the Loyalists, who support a continued link with the United Kingdom, and it is from that perspective that he makes judgements about the rights and wrongs of political action. During the years of struggle, Unwin opposed the Republicans and in particular the armed fighters in the Irish Republican Army (the IRA), regarding them as terrorist agents working wrongly and violently against the authorities and order of a legitimate nation state—the United Kingdom, inclusive of Northern Ireland. After the settlement worked out in the Good Friday Agreement of 1998, Unwin will allow that persons associated with the IRA were harmed in the struggle. Some were killed, many were injured, others were left in need due to the deaths or injuries of relatives. Unwin will allow that such people can in some sense—a minimal sense—be deemed victims. They have been harmed. But in Unwin's view, they do not fully qualify as victims because they are not innocent of wrongdoing. Rather, they were—and still are—guilty of political wrongs. In his view, they are terrorists and terrorist supporters.

Standing on the other side of the Northern Ireland struggle, Rob does not accept Unwin's standards regarding right and wrong, responsibility and innocence. He makes an argument for the correctness of his own standards, which are based on a Republican perspective. Were they to engage in this dispute, Rob and Unwin would retrace all the major issues of Northern Ireland politics: What is a legitimate state? Did the police and army have a legitimate monopoly on the exercise of violence? What is the time frame of the Troubles? These issues underpin not only the dispute but also questions about who qualifies as a victim. They are sometimes described as problems about the definition of the term "victim." But that description is misleading, for these are disputes about innocence and guilt, and they arise from differing judgements about political rights and wrongs. Who was fighting for a just cause and who was not? What means could agents justly have employed in the struggle? In rejecting the idea that there could be any hierarchy of victims, Rob implies that all persons harmed in the struggle count as victims and that no victim should be ranked higher in entitlement than any other. When he accuses Unwin of relying on a "hierarchy of victims," Rob takes a shortcut in the articulation of this position and in so doing seems to avoid revisiting disputes about the complex substance of Northern Irish politics. There may be some rhetorical appeal to this shortcut, but it is purely superficial and cannot withstand scrutiny.

Claiming a hierarchy or lack of one in disputes over victimhood, a person can avoid committing to any theory of rights and wrongs in a conflict, escaping complex historical and political debates. There are, then, temptations in the view that all hierarchies of victims should be rejected. In rejecting a *hierarchy* of victims one can appear to be in a virtuous and broad-minded position, generous and non-judgemental. It is this impression that may lend effect to Rob's rhetorical question: "Are you saying there is a hierarchy of victims?" Implied is: "You are presuming there is a hierarchy of victims, and there is no such thing, so you are wrong." It is a quick moral shortcut, but the plausibility of such a position is merely apparent. Further reflection reveals that it is ultimately not realistic to refuse to make distinctions between some victims and others.

It would have been more straightforward for Rob to tell Unwin that he objects to Unwin's assumptions about rights and wrongs and for Unwin to reply to Rob that yes, he is presuming a hierarchy of victims and he is prepared to defend that hierarchy on the basis of his Loyalist understanding of the politics of Northern Ireland. Realistically, what Rob and Unwin disagree on is the rights and wrongs of the conflict over Northern Ireland and the accountability of agents acting within it.

The dispute between Unwin and Rob is based on political differences. Unwin has a particular hierarchy; Rob does not like it and endorses a rival hierarchy, while presenting his position as a resistance to any hierarchy at all. The implication that there should be no hierarchy allows Rob to appear the more virtuous of the two: in rejecting any hierarchy of victims, he can appear to be in solidarity, and equal solidarity, with all victims. To be sure, the politics of peace in Northern Ireland would be facilitated if disputes about the entitlements of victims could be avoided. To engage in them is to resurrect the sectarian and political issues that lay at the heart of the Troubles in the first place. To pursue issues of justification, responsibility, and innocence is to open the old wounds.

The presumption that *all hierarchies are objectionable* cannot withstand analysis, if it means that it is always a mistake to make distinctions between victims. Distinctions do need to be made with regard to a number of practical matters, such as acknowledgement, medical aid, and compensation. In all likelihood, both Rob and Unwin will turn out to support distinctions and (based on them) "hierarchies." It is just that they will draw different distinctions, emerging from diverging views of politics. To Rob, the IRA and its supporters were heroic fighters in a liberation struggle against a colonial state. Those who survived were victims deserving sympathy and assistance. To Unwin, agents and supporters of the IRA were guilty terrorists and the people who fought against them loyal employees or citizens of a legitimate state. It is extremely unlikely that Rob would seriously and wholeheartedly reject all distinctions and hierarchies with regard to victims.

A critic of somebody else's "hierarchy" will nearly always himself be prepared to make *some* distinctions between some harmed persons and others. Typically, what we find is that this critic will make distinctions on grounds different from those of the person whose "hierarchy" he disputes. Commentators sometimes call for a definition of "victim" with the implication that if people could only get that straight, they would agree on who is a victim and who is not. But they place the dispute in the wrong place when they do this. Disagreements such as this are not really about the proper definition of "victim." Rather, they are about the rightness or wrongness of political causes and actions within a political struggle—and the responsibilities of individual agents for their actions and affiliations. In short, in conflict situations, the notion "victim" is politicized. Differences about who counts as a victim will involve differences about justice, responsibility, and innocence. They are differences about norms and criteria relevant to them, and not matters of definition.

A REJECTED PROPOSAL

According to the Bradley Eames Report, a sound response to lingering issues about victims of the Troubles would be for the nearest relative of anyone who died as a result of the conflict in and about Northern Ireland since January 1966 to receive a one-off *ex gratia* recognition payment of £12,000. A surviving person would count as a victim and would be entitled to receive a Recognition Payment, given that a family member lost his or her life in the conflict "in and about Northern Ireland" after 1966.[1] This recommendation was roundly rejected by persons of both (shall we say *all*?) sides of the struggle—Loyalist, Republican, and all the variations within. In the sectarian dispute, Republicans saw Loyalist supporters as agents of repressive colonialism. Loyalists saw Republican supporters as supporters and agents of terrorism. If "guilty" agents in the combat were killed, their surviving relatives were tarred with guilt and were not victims because though they were harmed, they were harmed due to a fault of their own. And, accordingly, they did not deserve any form of payment from the government in the name of peace, reconciliation, or other recovery from the bitter past.

DISTINCTIONS AND FRAMEWORKS

Though this sort of rhetoric about (objectionable) hierarchies of victims has been prominent in Northern Ireland since the 1998 agreement, it is by no means restricted to that context. Nor need one be in the early aftermath of a violently waged conflict for such accusations to be made; they can persist in non-political contexts or in political contexts for decades or even centuries after a violent political struggle has ended.[2] Indeed, many commentators have been accused of employing various false hierarchies with regard to victim status, which can be put forward or contested on a wide variety of grounds.

People may object to a hierarchy on the basis of the broad claim that in the context in question, there should be no hierarchy at all. At one stage of the debate about US intervention in Syria, US President Barack Obama argued that intervention was warranted due to the deaths of children killed by *chemical* weapons. An objection to his view was that there should be no distinction between deaths of children due to the use of chemical weapons and those due to the use of *conventional* weapons. To this objection one might respond by pointing to the special status of chemical weapons in international agreements or arguing that dying would be more painful if chemical weapons were used. To consider another example, a columnist might rate victims of murder on the basis of race (whites first), and a critic might object that she is wrong because all such killings are equally serious and equally wrong. Or a Marxist historian might rate victims of discrimination on the basis of social class, putting the least affluent first. An objection would be that he is wrong because people are equally deserving of fair treatment and the affluent and the middle class are less likely to get it than the poor. A psychiatrist rates victims on the basis of how much suffering she attributes to them as a result of wrongful and harmful treatment they have undergone; an objection is that she is wrong because nobody can sensibly evaluate degrees of suffering experienced by others.

In these cases, the objectors seem to resist all distinctions within a certain category. In other cases, people may object to one basis for distinction by advocating some other grounds. An advocate of women's shelters rates victims on the basis of gender (women first). Here, an objection might be made on the grounds that statistics indicate that the phenomenon of gang violence is more serious than domestic violence and far more men than women are victims of gang violence. Or a state agency might rank victims for compensation on the basis of occupational role (police and fire fighting personnel first, sex workers last). An objection will be that the agency has an erroneous policy because compensation should be grounded on the extent of enduring disabilities resulting from one's injury. A doctor might rank victims on the basis of the sort of harm and suffering they experience (first a serious physical injury, then a more modest physical injury, then damage to mental health); a counsellor might object that this ranking is incorrect because mental harms are often more serious and lasting than physical ones.

As these situations suggest, it is easy to multiply examples where distinctions are made and there are plausible-seeming objections to them. And yet, even though a particular *hierarchy of victims* may be objectionable in some contexts, it is not generally objectionable to make *distinctions* between victims and to employ in some contexts hierarchical frameworks constructed around those distinctions. The practice of triage is an especially clear example. Responding to a large number of persons in medical need in the aftermath of some emergency requires distinguishing cases as to the likelihood of benefitting from medical attention. Here, as elsewhere, there will be pressing practical reasons for making distinctions among victims. Such distinctions are often both necessary and reasonable. If one person is a victim of a burglary and another is a victim of sexual torture, it will be reasonable to put the needs and interests of the second before those of the first in contexts of counselling or police investigations.[3]

CASES AND CONTEXTS

The classification of a harming act as wrong or unwanted might be contested by someone who grants that the act did harm someone but argues that it was nevertheless a rightful act for reasons of intention or value, all things considered.[4] The person whose victim status is in question may or may not be identical with the person or persons directly harmed in the initial act. He or she might be a secondary victim adversely affected by harms inflicted on another, as in the case of a child left without a parent. A person may wonder about his or her own status as a victim. Judgements about victims may diverge, given differing perspectives with regard to time, causation, harm, and responsibility. Varying factors give rise to differences about victim status, as is illustrated in the following examples.

Case One: Obesity

An observer is considering the question of whether persons who are obese should be regarded as victims. This question has been argued both ways. In an article entitled "Obesity Patients *Are Not Victims*" (my emphasis), Dr. David Gratzer argues that it is a familiar cop-out to see oneself as a victim. He contends that obese people want to escape responsibility by blaming their failings on others, claiming "It is not my fault, I am a victim." This syndrome, as familiar as fast food, is termed by him "MacVictim." He qualifies his claim slightly to say that for *most* persons, obesity is preventable and results from the consumption of too many calories.[5] On his view, a person who is obese has made her own decisions to eat too much and is *not* a victim either of another person's actions or of a disease over which she has no control. In other words, although the obese person may very well be harmed by her condition and be suffering from it, she is suffering from something for which she bears considerable (or even total) responsibility, given the commonsense causal theory that obesity is the result of consuming too many calories. One chooses, after all, to consume calories, and accordingly, on this theory, an obese person should not be regarded as a victim.

The opposing view, though less common, is also sometimes expressed—and expressed as a matter of fact by members of the medical profession. In an essay entitled "The Obese Are Victims Not Perpetrators," Dr. George S.M. Cowan articulates this position. A professor of surgery, Cowan states that persons who are lean and do not have extra body weight are simply lucky. They have "a gift" and do not deserve any special praise for it. Cowan argues that morbid obesity is like a malignancy; it is a physical ailment and an especially unfortunate one because it is so obvious and cannot easily be hidden (unlike some other personal conditions such as diabetes, high blood pressure, alcoholism, or drug addiction). Cowan maintains that it is not medically understood why the body's biology keeps a person thin or fat. On his account, some persons *suffer* from obesity, which is a biological disorder for which they are not responsible. As suffering persons, they deserve respect and sympathy, not castigation for their supposed "failings."[6] They are not responsible for their suffering or for the harmful biological condition that causes it; hence, they are victims.

In this dispute about obesity, it is especially clear how differences about victim status result from differences about responsibility. In question in this context are both *causal responsibility* and *moral responsibility*. Causal questions concern human biology, food storage, and fat. Differences about causal responsibility lead to different views about the moral responsibility of obese persons for their excess weight. An observer who, like Gratzer, believes that consuming "too many calories" causes one to be obese will accordingly believe that an obese person has done something that she could have refrained from doing. Presuming that she has done that, Gratzer would say that obesity results from actions of her own for which she is responsible. Given that this woman's condition results from her own actions and is in this sense of her own making, she is *not* a victim on this account.

The central issues here are agency and responsibility. The view that obese persons are victims is based on the presumption that they are *not* agents in their own obesity because that obesity results from factors other than their own choices. There are scientific truths about what these factors are, and what is indicated is that *neither causally nor morally are obese persons responsible for their condition.* If obese persons are responsible for their condition they are not victims. If they are not responsible, they are victims. What is contested here is *cause*.

Case Two: Time Frames

Let us shift away from the medical context and consider a different sort of case. Suppose the time is December 2011 and Rajeesh is a middle-class Canadian of South Asian origin who is thinking about another Canadian, Tim, the eight-year-old grandchild of an Aboriginal person who was abused in a residential school. Tim is deemed by some to be a victim of the harm done to his grandfather, with damage transmitted through Tim's abused father to Tim himself. (Perhaps Tim's father became an alcoholic, likely as a result of his own ill-treatment at the hands of the grandfather, whose own capacities and sense of self were damaged in the school.)

Time frame, as it affects causal relationships, is the main underlying issue in this case. One time frame is that of Tim's life (i.e., 2003 to 2011). Another is that of the grandfather's stay in the residential school (i.e., 1960 to 1969); it was during this period that the grandfather was abused and seriously harmed. The perpetrators of that abuse could be narrowly defined as those persons who beat and deprived the grandfather or more broadly defined as those who organized and supported the system of residential schools in general. Those who think of Tim as a victim of the residential school system will think of him as harmed later as a result of the abuse inflicted on his grandfather. (Presumably, intermediate victims would be Tim's parents.) We find in this case three or even four different time periods relevant to the issue of Tim's victim status. These are the time of the acts harming the grandfather when he was in the schools (1960 to 1969), the time during which harm was done to Tim (2003 to 2011), and the time of Rajeesh's judgement as to whether Tim is a victim or not (2011).[7] A likely intermediate phase concerns Tim's parents; we can suppose that this period was between 1975 and 2003.

Rajeesh may dispute the claim that Tim is a (secondary) victim of abuse in the residential school. He might deny wrongdoing in those schools on the grounds that the sort of harsh paternalism characteristic of the schools was not wrong by the standards of their time, presuming that prevailing contemporary standards are the only ones that can reasonably be applied in such cases. Rajeesh might not even grant the fundamental assumption that Tim's grandfather was a victim harmed by *wrongful* acts of abuse. (On this view, issues of individual or shared responsibility for wrongful acts would not arise because there were no wrongful acts.) But this sort of stance seems unlikely for Rajeesh, especially given that he himself comes from a background in which colonialism has been deemed wrong and firmly rejected. Suppose instead that Rajeesh is willing to grant that physically and sexually abusive acts against Aboriginal students in the residential schools were wrong and brought serious, lasting harm to many children in the schools, who were victims. Obviously, none of those persons could have been Tim, who was not alive when the acts were committed. If Rajeesh denies victim status to Tim in this case, it will not be because he alleges any active role or moral responsibility for the abuse on Tim's part. Rather, it will be due to skepticism about harm and suffering and their transmission through the generations—grandfather to father, father to his own son—during the time period between the 1960s and 2011.

While acknowledging that somehow, for some reason, harm has been done to Tim, Rajeesh might dispute causal connections through the generations. To suppose that Tim *as a grandson* has been harmed by what was experienced by his victimized grandfather is to suppose a rather long causal chain and to reject alternate causal sequences. Rajeesh might judge that the time lapse between the 1960s and the 2000s and between the generations makes the causal chain questionable. He might believe that it is empirically implausible that Tim has suffered harm as a result of what happened to his grandfather in the residential schools. Perhaps Tim suffers from a learning disability or has been bullied by some of his schoolmates. Persons disputing Rajeesh's account would seek to defend causal claims about the impact of residential schools on families. They might argue, for instance, that abuse of the grandfather led him to alcoholism and mistreatment of Tim's father and that mistreatment led to drug abuse and dysfunctional parenting on the part of the father, with the ultimate result being the father's mistreatment of Tim and resulting harm and suffering on Tim's part.

The central issue in this case is not whether Tim has been harmed and is a victim of something medical, political, or a combination of factors. It is whether the damage done to Tim can be causally traced to his grandfather's victimization decades before questions about the boy's victimization arise.

Case Three: Moral Judgements

Considering again the context of Northern Ireland, we may reflect on the case of Olivia, a relatively affluent Protestant woman living in Belfast. In 2009, let us say, Olivia comes to consider issues about compensation for victims of the Troubles after reading about the recommendations of the Bradley-Eames Report. Bernadette is a relatively impoverished Catholic woman who has lived in Belfast since 1980. She counts as a victim according to the Bradley-Eames Report because her son, an IRA combatant, was killed by a soldier in the British army during a 1982 action. She broadly supported his activities for the Republican cause, although she did not know the details of what he was doing. At issue is whether, in the time period from 1982 to 2009, Bernadette should be regarded as a *victim* of the Troubles. Olivia objects strongly to the recommendation that Bernadette and persons like her should have status as *victims* (secondary victims) due to the death of relatives and should merit compensation equal to that to be granted to civilians, soldiers, and police on the Loyalist side. Olivia believes that Bernadette's son was not a victim and that she thus does not merit compensation because she does not properly qualify as a secondary victim.[8] Rather, he was a terrorist and she was complicit in his terrorist activities.

To grant that Bernadette is a victim during this time, Olivia would have to grant that Bernadette was harmed by the act in 1982 and that that act was *wrongful*, making her son a victim. Olivia acknowledges that Bernadette's son was killed and she can well imagine that Bernadette still grieves for him and will be adversely affected by the lack of support that her son could have given her. Her denial of victim status will be based on her denial of further presumptions to the effect that the killing of Bernadette's son was a wrongful act, one for which neither Bernadette nor her son bore responsibility. Olivia's understanding of the conflict entails that the shooting of "terrorists" by the police was legitimate, given that these agents were engaging in illicit violence to attack a legitimate state. The son chose to engage; the mother must have known and tacitly approved that engagement. Though the son was killed, he was not a victim. Accordingly, although his mother survived having a family member killed, she does not merit status as a victim, contrary to the recommendations of the Bradley-Eames Report.

Judgements by a person with a different sectarian perspective will almost certainly differ. A Catholic priest living in a working-class area of Belfast would likely grant both that the killing of Bernadette's son was wrong and that Bernadette herself was innocent of any responsibility for that wrong. Accordingly, he would deem Bernadette a victim of the Troubles. From his perspective, she is a mother who is harmed and still suffering from the loss of her son who was *wrongfully killed* while fighting in a legitimate role in a political conflict. On this view, if the Bradley-Eames Report recommends that *all victims* should be compensated in some way, the recommendation properly applies to Bernadette as a victim.

In the winding down of a conflict, there will be problems when people cling to moral presumptions attaching to the term "victim." These problems arise when people continue to hold the moral and political views that structured the conflict itself. The Bradley-Eames Report should be understood as seeking to neutralize the term "victim" and to shift away from the moral presuppositions of the conflict. Intense on both sides of the conflict, the resistance to the Bradley-Eames recommendations points to the difficulty of bringing about such neutralization.

This case illustrates how different moral judgements about actions and attitudes can result in differences about the application of the term "victim." Differences regarding moral judgements here are traceable to differing sectarian views about a lasting political conflict and how people acted within that conflict. After the Good Friday Agreement of 1998, the Troubles were supposed to be "over" and yet sectarian divides and strong differences about politics and political morality were not. Disagreements about victimhood struck some commentators as being about the definition of the term "victim." They did not arise from that, but rather from the sectarian and political differences that characterized the Troubles themselves.

Case Four: Victim or Survivor?

Omar, a man considered by some to be a victim, rejects that label, insisting instead that he be regarded as a *survivor*. He was fighting in a resistance army in Libya, was injured in the fighting, and had one leg amputated. In the aftermath of the war, when the Gadaffi regime was replaced by a more liberal successor, Omar became a competent and successful provincial official. He reflects on his own status. Was he a victim in the struggle for a free Libya? He was harmed when fighting for a just cause and thus defines those who injured him as committing wrong against him; he suffered as a result of events during the violent struggle. There is a sense in which he continued to suffer at later times, even granting the "success" of a prosthetic limb. But is he now, when he is considering the whole affair, a *victim*? As a hospital patient undergoing an amputation, he was a suffering victim of a wartime injury. But some 18 months after the war, he is functioning well in a job that he considers important, and he feels proud to have been part of a successful revolt against a notoriously cruel tyrant.

We have here a case of someone reflecting on his own status as a victim. There is a shift of time frames, however. This man was injured and suffered during the period between April 2011 and December 2011. He comes to consider at a later time, June 2012, whether, overall, he was a victim of the revolution. He concludes that he is not a victim because of his *agency* in surviving the turbulent violence and, in particular, overcoming the serious harm done to him. He sees himself as having triumphed over his harm and suffering to the point where he judges that he is no longer suffering. He was harmed, he did suffer, but at this point he is a functioning agent. He is no longer passive with regard to his injury: he has acted so as to triumph in difficult circumstances. His outcome is not that of a suffering and innocent victim but that of a responsible person who has survived the harm done to him in a rightful struggle to overthrow a (wrongful) tyrannical regime. He was a victim; he was harmed and suffered as a victim. But that was in the past. He is making a judgement now, and he judges that he is not a victim. He is a survivor. Omar's case illustrates how a shift from passivity and vulnerability to activity and competence leads to a rejection of the label "victim."

All four cases reveal that we judge persons to be victims and rely on interpretation and values when we do so. Victimhood is by no means a simple matter of fact. It is often a contested matter relative to contextual factors of agency, moral and political judgements, causation, and time. People are victims at particular times of particular acts that are harmful to them and for which they bear little moral responsibility. They are rarely, with respect to their lives as a whole, simply victims.

VICTIM IDENTITIES

What, then, about victimhood as a basis for identity? At first blush, the response to this question may appear simple: one's status as a victim is likely to be a flawed basis for identity. Being harmed is something that happens during one time frame of a person's life and damage done then affects some aspects of a person's life and not others. Furthermore, moral and political responsibilities vary from one context to another. It would be a reductionist mistake for a person to construct his or her identity on *victimhood*. The point seems especially obvious in contexts of minor harms and minor wrongs. Suppose, for example, that a person had her wallet stolen as a teenager and was a victim of theft. To define herself as a *victim* of that crime many years later, would be to overemphasize the impact of that crime, downgrading the significance of many other things she would have done and experienced in subsequent years.

There are for most of us many aspects of identity. A person may at the same time find himself a father, a millworker, a choral singer, a US citizen of Lebanese origin, and a Muslim. All these aspects of himself may be important to him, and which is of greatest importance is likely to vary with changing life circumstances. If, for instance, this man enjoys an important role and good salary with his job, he may find much of his identity in that role. If he loses his job, his recreational activities may gain importance to him and he may prefer to find his identity as a leader singer in the bass section of a choir or as a community volunteer. If his country is attacked and he sees its security as threatened, his personal security may also be jeopardized, and his US citizenship stands out as his most salient identity. If the resources or status of his religious group come to be threatened, he may come to emphasize most of all his identity as a Muslim. Social identity should be understood as plural and as shifting. To emphasize some strands of identity over and above all others is reductionist and likely to be counterproductive even if that aspect of identity is a positive one (top scholar or Olympic athlete, for instance).

An identity based on victimhood seems especially unpromising, given the presumptions of harm, passivity, and entitlement that typically accompany that identity.[9] Yet, the significance of victimhood for social identity may seem compelling when we consider very serious wrongs. Suppose that, instead of being a victim of a minor theft, a woman was as a teenager a victim of a traumatic rape as a result of which she has continuing nightmares and experiences considerable difficulty regarding trust issues in relationships. If, in those circumstances, she continues to define herself as a victim of rape several decades after its occurrence, that is understandable, given the seriousness of the wrong and her vulnerable age when it was committed. This grave and painful wrong had much to do with her development and current situation and continues to be prominent in her consciousness and her relationships. Even so, there are likely to be negative effects if she incorporates themes of victimhood into her identity and sense of self. Concerning even a traumatic rape, one can make the point that it was committed at one time, not others, and damaged the victim in some respects, not others. One can make the point that the raped woman has many aspects and capabilities that have little or nothing to do with the rape and that there are choices as to how she allows that rape to define her and affect her life. Suppose that given the scope and significance of that damage and given the serious challenges in her life related to it, a rape victim seems not to have recovered from the attack, perhaps not even to be capable of recovering from it. She may seem to have incorporated into her identity her status as a *victim of rape*.

It seems presumptuous and insensitive to insist that at some point even a victim of a serious wrong has had time to recover from what was done to him or her—to state that now is time to "get over it" and "move forward." A friend or counsellor who urges a rape victim to move on, to refuse to give the rape such existential significance, is likely to appear to be lacking in understanding of the seriousness of the offence and its impact. It may seem harsh and offensive to maintain that after a certain period of time the rape victim should move on and resist identifying herself as such. After all, persons are significantly harmed by rape, which is an instance of a serious crime. The victim might insist that no one who has not been a victim of a serious wrong knows what it is like to suffer from one and argue that no one should presume to dictate what the healing path should be in someone else's case.[10] It is, by no means harsh, however, to insist that even a person who is a victim of a serious wrong is not *only* a victim. Except in pathological cases, few would contend that the identity of a victim of rape can be understood by focussing only on the wrongfulness of the attack and the suffering it has caused. The person who is a victim will at the same time be a son or daughter, perhaps also a worker, an activist, a community volunteer, a citizen, a member of an ethnically identified group, a parent, a teacher. Our question here concerns not the facts of victimhood but the role of those facts in a person's identity. Let us simply stipulate that there is no dispute that the rape occurred, that it was wrong, that this person was damaged physically and mentally by what happened, that she was not responsible for it, and that she continues to suffer and be challenged in life as a result. Granting all these points, we go on to ask about the extent to which the facts of victimhood should define the person's identity. The case is a stand-in for more general questions about identity and victimhood.

Should a person find his or her identity in victimhood? The question is one of norm, not of fact. What will be the benefits and costs of understanding one's life in terms of victimizing acts and their effects? As a victim, a person is likely to have a sense of desert, of entitlement to sympathy and resources for rehabilitation and repair. In societies inclined to allocate respect and deference on the basis of suffering, victimhood will confer privileges: a victim is likely to enjoy enhanced attention and resources. And yet the costs of living with a victim identity are many: thinking of oneself as a victim, a person will be recalling and dwelling on painful acts in the past and may regard himself or herself as vulnerable and helpless, suggesting a disempowered self. Thinking of the self as relatively powerless, a self-identified victim risks giving little attention to developing positive capacities that could assist in improving his or her life and the lives of others. As a victim, a person is innocent and not responsible for the action that is the focus of attention. By continuing to define herself in terms of victimhood, she is likely to strengthen her sense of righteousness, removing herself from any implication of guilt or responsibility.

Despite potential advantages of deference and support, the victim role is not generally a creative or constructive one. To be sure, there may be potential for good works based on a person's victim role. A victim may become a kind of survivor-victim—an activist, writer, or speaker whose efforts gain attention to serious social evils—or a museum guide explaining memorials about tragedy and genocide. In such cases, a person's victimhood becomes a plank on which the rest of his life is built, so that his victimhood becomes the basis for his livelihood and success in life.

VICTIMS OF POLITICS, VICTIMS OF DISEASE

Near Cape Town, South Africa lies Robben Island, which for several centuries was a place of banishment or prison. The island is now a World Heritage site and museum, marking the place where Nelson Mandela and other anti-apartheid activists were held for many years. Mandela spent 18 years there, a fact that has done much to mark the significance of the island. Ferryboats go from the mainland to the island, and schoolchildren and tourists take tours to the destination. Trips show geography and sea life and may even have a festive aspect at the outset. But their main point is to show where Mandela and other activists worked and were incarcerated and to convey a sense of the hardships and sacrifices of those who struggled against apartheid. Most guides are former political prisoners who tell their stories to visitors, offering anecdotes and insights into what it was like to live there. Internet reviews of these tours, provided by tourists, are generally positive and praise these guides highly for offering historical and political understanding. And yet, thinking of the phenomenon from the point of view of the ex-prisoners, one can hardly avoid raising questions about the psychological effects of such work. As prisoners, these present-day guides were in many respects victims: they had been victims of apartheid; they were then victims of apartheid law and sentencing, and of cruel treatment and restriction of their freedom. As workers on the island, they remain in the same geographical vicinity, retelling and presumably (in some sense) reliving what they experienced over many years of uncomfortable incarceration while gaining their livelihood from their status and experience as victims.

Robben Island is not the only site where political prisoners earn their livelihood by recounting their victimhood. In Vilnius, Lithuania, there is a museum in the former KGB headquarters whose purpose is to expose abuses under communism. Persons who were previously interned in the building serve as guides. In Berlin, in a museum about abuses in East Germany, tours are given, mostly by former prisoners of the secret police, the Stasi. These guides describe the ways in which they were mistreated in state institutions. The museum once offered free tours to schoolchildren. That policy was so successful that the museum nearly had to close: numbers were too great to be accommodated.[11] As in the South African case, one can only wonder about the effects of occupational victimhood on a person's psychological health and development of capacities and interests. While it is understandable that economically vulnerable people might choose to live in this way on their "commodified" victimhood, it seems unlikely that the effects of continually recalling and reiterating brutalizing experience would be positive.

Regarding victims of disease, a tragic case of commodification and identity is described by anthropologist Nadine Beckmann. Beckmann outlines some unintended and perverse consequences of international programs intended to benefit persons living with HIV-AIDS.[12] For victims, the sick body may become a resource for living because the disease has enabled them to obtain from international donors the economic basis for survival. As persons living with HIV-AIDS, they learn to better tell and exploit their personal stories to gain more support, more respect, and more treatment. They may obtain additional income from offering public testimony, attending workshops and seminars, and gaining positions in action groups. There is a sense in which these people gain their livelihood by marketing their suffering. One might even say that they market their very selves as a means of survival. They are typically suffering and suffering badly, victims of this cruel disease. The costs of livelihood by victimhood are many: dependency on donors; alienation from family, friends, and community as a result of exposing oneself in open (Western-style) testimony; conflicts as to just how sick one should seem; and the resentment of other community members with regard to the direction of resources. Beckmann reports that many living with HIV-AIDS do not seem to others in the community to be *victims.* They are often judged to be non-innocent because they are thought to have brought disease and suffering on themselves by violating basic social norms. Lives are saved, but only very diminished lives are lived as a result. Beckmann draws the conclusion that HIV-positive people in poor and marginalized countries need to use their bodies and stories of suffering as a last resort for survival.

While the pitfalls of victim identity are many, it must also be acknowledged that there are contexts in which the position of victim has provided opportunities for healthy self-development and good works. Opportunities and even advantages may come to persons harmed by wrongful actions and adverse events. The potential is illustrated in the many cases in which victims have become heroic athletes, activists, memoirists, and leaders. Having suffered and overcome substantial challenges, they have accomplished much, using to good effect the interest and appeal of their experiences. A classic case is that of Canadian Terry Fox, a victim of cancer who commenced in 1981 a cross-country run to raise not only awareness of the disease but money for cancer research. Fox had had his right leg amputated due to cancer. He ran determinedly but awkwardly, employing a kind of hopping gait and using a prosthetic device. After running over 5,000 kilometres on his campaign, he had to quit on discovering that cancer had spread to his lungs. His efforts inspired annual runs held ever since not only in his home country but in some 60 other countries around the world. He sought to influence others and to raise funds for research. In that he succeeded. It is estimated that various Terry Fox Runs and Walks have raised at least $500 million for cancer research. Fox did not want himself to be defined by his disability; it would be a mistake to regard him simply as a victim of cancer. He was surely not a disempowered or passive victim, nor was he a person who emphasized limitations and sought privileges on the basis of his disease. We cannot say, however, that Terry Fox was a survivor: he died of his disease.[13]

Gabrielle Giffords provides another inspiring example of heroic struggle. Seriously injured by gunfire in an attack in Tucson, Arizona on January 8, 2011, Giffords was at one point falsely reported to have died. Amazingly, she lived on after being shot in the head. She has struggled mightily to recover from serious injuries to her brain and even had a large skull fragment removed, to be replaced by a prosthetic device.[14] She walks shakily and speaks slowly. She has worked hard to achieve a form of recovery, showing great personal strength in doing so. Her 2013 testimony to the US Senate Judiciary Committee and plea for more background checks prior to gun purchases were deeply moving, as are her slow but ongoing efforts to restore her abilities. With her husband, Mark Kelly, Giffords has founded Americans for Responsible Solutions, a fundraising SuperPac intended to counter the lobbying power of the National Rifle Association. Given her determination, action, and activism, Giffords is a survivor in the rich sense of that term. She was a victim and in some sense remains a victim, and there is a sense in which she has grounded her present activities on that victimhood. But it would be inaccurate to say that she has found her identity in victimhood. Giffords is a survivor—an active and determined survivor who has lived on to fight adversity and use her painful experience for the public good.

The cases of Terry Fox and Gabrielle Giffords are only two among many illustrating the fact that victims may accomplish much despite—and even due to—the fact that they have constructed an identity and social role from the circumstances of victimhood. These are phenomena of heroic victimhood, and the notion of heroic victimhood is not to be interpreted ironically. Victims may be led to awareness, empathy, and concern for others on the basis of what has happened to them. As persons struggling to recover, exerting their capacities as proponents of worthy causes, they are likely to enjoy considerable sympathy and to be found credible representatives and spokespersons. Given that there are so many moving examples of victims who have been highly successful in such roles, it would be inaccurate to judge that the identity of "victim" is always a negative and limiting one.

An important problem about the understandable public fascination with heroic victimhood is its potential to encourage unrealistic expectations about what victims can do. Not all can become athletes, celebrated political figures, or accomplished authors. This much is a matter of necessity, given that cultures have room for only a limited number of such figures at a time, meaning that public attention is a scarce resource. (Not everyone can appear on the Oprah Winfrey show or its like.) From a more psychological and personal perspective, realism about victim resources and recovery is needed. Victims of serious harms may be too traumatized and damaged to have the strength for heroic struggle. They may lack the talent and energy needed to make conspicuous contributions. Clearly, if such people could manage their challenges in the manner of a Terry Fox or Gabrielle Giffords, that would be a wonderful thing and would merit our sympathetic attention. But to expect someone in the victim role to be able to reach such heights of achievement is to expect too much.

COMPETITIVE VICTIMHOOD

Victim groups may compete for resources and attention. A common basis for such competition is suffering. The underlying argument here is that "my group" has suffered more than "your group," and because we have status as the greater sufferers, we are the greater victims and hence are the more deserving of sympathy and consideration.

Competition between groups vying for victim status can amount to a significant obstacle to peace processes. In the quest for peace and political reconciliation, the groups contending for status have typically been engaged in conflict with each other. They are likely to lack empathy for persons on "the other side" and have little interest in listening to stories of the suffering of these others. A concentration on grievances may support and stimulate desires for revenge. The conviction that "our group" qualifies as the more significant victim, perhaps even the only victim, in a conflict will block efforts to build understanding and trust. It will serve to excuse failures of empathy and inhibit initiatives towards cooperation. The idea that "our group" has higher victim status relieves us of the need to make friends or engage in cooperative activities outside group boundaries. Any sense that "our group" might have acted unjustly or cruelly is likely to be overwhelmed by the conviction that we are, above all, victims of wrongdoing at the hands of you *others*. Competitive victimhood is likely to discourage initiatives in the direction of forgiveness or trust-building and, for these reasons, poses a significant obstacle to political reconciliation in the aftermath of conflict.[15]

The phenomenon of competition among victim groups has been pejoratively referred to as Victim Olympics. Widely recognized and tragically persistent, this sort of competition is manifested not only in the immediate aftermath of conflict but even decades or centuries after contested events, when the quest for peace is not an immediate concern. Competition for victim status appears when groups find their identity, or central aspects of their identity, in historical victimhood and seek recognition and resources on that basis. In doing so, they often come into competition with other groups since the resources for acknowledgement and memory are scarce. Public attention is, after all, a scarce resource because people cannot pay attention to all tragedies and calamities. It is also scarce because it may require other resources, money being the most obvious one. Societies cannot publicize and memorialize all political wrongs, and even if they could, people would not have the time and energy to attend to them. Treatment in school texts is an example. It is important for a society to acknowledge and seek to understand past wrongs by having them discussed in the classroom. It is fair to comment that most societies should do more in this area. Realistically, however, attention paid to one tragedy will not be given to another; a better treatment of slavery may necessitate a more cursory treatment of Aboriginal land issues, for instance. Competition in such contexts is one aspect of Victim Olympics.

In terms of group victimhood, the Jews as victims of the Holocaust are probably the most widely acknowledged case in human history. The gross abuse and horrendous killing are well-known and need not be revisited here. Silence in the early years after World War II has been replaced by numerous histories, testimonies, memorials, acts of recognition, and attempts at reconciliation and repair. In some countries, Holocaust denial is illegal, and in the Western world it is almost everywhere regarded as indicative of profound irrationality and prejudice. Scholars have argued for the uniqueness of the Holocaust. Consider, for instance, Emil Fackenheim's widely read book *To Mend the World*,[16] which cites the desire to exterminate all Jews, whatever their age or innocence, on the basis of "blood" alone as proof of the totalistic and unique goals of this particular genocide. The recognition of the Holocaust as an appalling humanly caused calamity has led to knowledge, understanding, criminal trials, and innumerable narratives of suffering and bravery. It has also inspired competition among victims.

A contemporary Canadian example of competition between victim groups affected the development of a human rights museum in Winnipeg. The case is that of the Holocaust and the less known calamity of the Holodomor, a genocide of Ukrainians brought about by cruel policies of Stalin in the early 1930s. In horrifying abuses of power, the Stalinist state turned on its own citizens in the Ukraine, forcibly denying them food with the result that millions starved to death. The Holodomor, called by one author the "harvest of sorrow," has received relatively little attention from historians, activists, and popular culture. As more information emerged after the fall of communism, its status as a genocide began to be discussed. Planning for the Canadian Museum of Human Rights, based in Winnipeg, included two permanent galleries dedicated to memorialization of victims and information about genocide. One was for the Holocaust; the other for First Nations people of North America. The city of Winnipeg has at least 167,000 citizens of Ukrainian descent, and some activists among them argued that concentrating on these two groups denied proper status to the Holodomor. To be sure, a permanent gallery or "zone" was to be dedicated to the victims of the Holodomor, but that gallery would include material regarding other genocides and atrocities as well. The Holodomor would apparently not receive a status equivalent to that of the Holocaust, which would have a permanent gallery all to itself. One might not think that recognition is a scarce resource—but space and public attention are scarce, and the debate about the Holocaust and the Holodomor became intense.[17]

In this context, some commentators wisely advised that memorialization and attention should not be understood as a zero-sum game. Even though resources may be scarce, paying attention to one calamity does not mean dismissing or ignoring another. The case of the Holocaust and the Holodomor was not even an example of a group insisting on its victim status in relation to a perpetrator. Groups competing for victim status struggled against each other, not against perpetrator groups. It was the Germans who perpetrated against the Jews the crimes of the Holocaust, and it was Stalin and his government in Russia who cruelly deprived the Ukrainians of food.[18] But the opposition in the museum dispute was not between Canadian Jews and German Nazis, it was between Canadian Jews and Canadian Ukrainians. The intense competition concerned claims to recognition.

Which group suffered more than which other group? In what ways did group members suffer? Over how long a historical period? With what degree of guilt or innocence? How, and how cruelly? How many were killed? How do the numbers compare? Which horror was worse? It is generally agreed that some 6 million Jews were killed by the Nazis. The numbers in the Holodomor are disputed: 3.5 million? 5 million? 7 million? 10 or 11 million? In terms of historical accuracy, the numbers matter, but in what other ways do they matter? When one person who is a descendent of Holocaust survivors debates another who is a descendant of Holodomor survivors, their discussion descends to arguing about whether "my group suffered more than yours because more of *us* were killed than of *you*." This is not a productive dispute.

The US philosopher Laurence Thomas is both Black and Jewish. He has discussed strained relations between Blacks and Jews in the United States, with its unhealthy dynamic in which people stress the suffering of "my group" while downplaying the suffering of "your group."[19] (Thomas is not in favour of such competitions; he is describing them, not recommending them.) Thomas describes what he calls a Principle of Job, according to which great suffering conveys deep moral knowledge. Presuming the Principle of Job, one might claim that greater suffering conveys deeper moral knowledge and infer that if one group is deemed to have suffered more than another, its judgements should be regarded as more wise. The supposedly greater authority of the more suffering group will lend to it a credibility advantage, which can be used in political competition for recognition and resources. In such competitions, American Jews have generally won compared to Black Americans. But, as Thomas maintains, the Principle of Job is not credible. Such competition is ill-construed and has baneful effects.

When Europeans came to North America and took over the continent, it is estimated that some 80 million Native Americans died as a result. It is not known how many Africans lost their lives due to the slave trade and institution of slavery; estimates range from 12 million to 20 million. As we have seen, some 6 million Jews are estimated to have died in the Holocaust and anywhere from 3.5 to 11 million Ukrainians died of state-induced famine. One might try to establish a hierarchy of victimhood based on numbers of people killed in a given calamitous wrong. But not only are such numbers contested and sometimes unknowable, time frames may be not comparable. In any event, comparisons and hierarchies of this type serve no good purpose. All such wrongful policies—the Holocaust, the slave trade, and the colonization of the Americas—brutalized and killed large numbers of people. Such wrongs should be acknowledged and understood and (obviously) not repeated. It makes little sense to ask which is the greatest wrong.

One might argue that the Holocaust was more evil than slavery since slave-owners did not seek to exterminate Africans, whereas in the Holocaust there was an effort to exterminate Jews. On the other hand, one might argue that slavery was more evil than the Holocaust in its demand for complete subordination on the part of enslaved persons accompanied (perversely) by a demand for their complete loyalty. One might argue that wrongs against Aboriginal people in North America were greater than either of the others on the grounds of their greater duration and the profound cultural assaults that accompanied them. Indeed, such arguments can seem interesting and important. Yet engaging in such disputes should be resisted. One cannot sensibly rank group suffering on a continuum from greatest to least.

Questions of the evil of institutions and the suffering of individual persons within them should not be "measured" by estimates of numbers of deaths. Purely quantitative considerations would omit the intensity and nature of suffering, the period of time during which it occurred, and the intent of individuals and institutions. Obviously, there are aspects of brutality and cruelty that are incommensurate. How, for instance, could we compare the suffering due to anxiety about the fate of a loved one to tortures endured by a victim of kidnapping? We need to reject such questions as which was the greater evil, whose intentions were most evil, which group was the greater victim, and whose suffering merits the most recognition.

Thomas speculates that the ideology of the "American Dream," with its individualistic presumption that success comes only from talent and hard work, has contributed to competition between Jews and Black Americans as victim groups. If Jews have achieved more even in the aftermath of greater suffering, one could argue their greater superiority on those grounds. But Thomas's real point is a more fundamental one: he decries competition between victim groups, regarding it as tasteless and counter-productive. One wrong does not become less because another different wrong, arguable greater in some magnitude, was committed. We should not attempt to rank evil, or human suffering, on a continuum. To do so will only warp our moral sensibilities. Evil, Thomas rightly states, should be understood for what it is in its particular circumstances.

Competition for victim status is disparaged when it is referred to as "Victim Olympics," but the dismissive label has by no means sufficed to end it. In fact, its very existence is an indicator of the deference and entitlement that so often accompany victimhood in contemporary Western culture. Who suffered more? Who suffered the most? There is some compulsion to ask—but there is an equal compulsion to reject the question. We need to ask about the knowledge that suffering is supposed to convey and the respect it is supposed to warrant.

NOTES

1   Report of the Consultative Group on the Past (Bradley-Eames Report), Belfast 2009, Chapter 4: "Victims and Survivors" <http://www.parliament.the-stationery-office.co.uk/pa/cm200910/cmselect/cmniaf/171/171.pdf> last accessed 24 June 2014. Deaths of persons due to the direct or accidental result of paramilitary group action or security force action were to be treated equally. The report did not allocate responsibility or blame; it noted that when the needs and concerns of one group are addressed, another group is likely to be offended and stated that victims and survivors exist because of societal failings. The equalization of "victims" proposed in this report was met by vociferous objections from all sides, as it was seen as falsely neutralizing and immorally equating *combatants* with "innocent" *victims*.

2   A small amount of Internet research will suffice to establish this point.

3   Medical triage may provide a useful analogy here.

4   For example, suppose that someone shot to wound a hostage-taker, but killed him instead or that civilians were seriously injured while defending a military outpost in a just war. An even more straightforward example of an act that is harmful, though not wrong, is a surgery that goes amiss; for example, a man might undergo what was supposed to be a routine eye surgery and wind up losing the vision in one eye; this happened to someone I know.

5   David Gratzer, "Obesity Patients Are Not Victims," KevinMD.com, 13 Dec. 2010, <http://www.kevinmd.com/blog/2010/12/obesity-patients-victims.html> last accessed 24 June 2014.

6   George S.M. Cowan MD, "The Obese Are Victims Not Perpetrators," n.d. <http://www.obesity-online.com/ifso/lecture_CowanG.htm> last accessed 24 June 2014.

7   Note here that to think of Rajeesh as reflecting on Tim's status is not to think of Rajeesh as complicit as a perpetrator, as guilty or complicit with wrongs against Aboriginal people, or as a beneficiary of them. At this point, Rajeesh is an observer reflecting on whether or not it is correct to think of Tim as a victim of the residential school system.

8   A touching story about the secondary victim of a horrific murder and dismemberment is told in Michelle Lalonde, "Luka Magnotta Case: Father of Victim Rushes Out of Courtroom Again," *Montreal Gazette* 15 Mar. 2013 <http://www2.canada.com/story.html?id=8104832> last accessed 24 June 2014.

9   See also Anthony Appiah, *The Ethics of Identity* (Princeton: Princeton UP, 2005) and Amartya Sen, *Identity and Violence: The Illusion of Destiny* (New York: Norton, 2007).

10   This sort of argument is discussed at length in Chapter 4.

11   David Crossland, "A Victim of Its Own Success: Berlin Stasi Museum on Brink of Bankruptcy," *Spiegel Online* 10 Aug. 2009 <http://www.spiegel.de/international/germany/a-victim-of-its-own-success-berlin-stasi-museum-on-brink-of-bankruptcy-a-641534.html> last accessed 24 June 2014.

12   Nadine Beckmann, "The Commodification of Misery: Markets for Healing, Markets for Sickness," paper for the Open University (U.K.); and Nadine Beckmann, "AIDS and the Commodification of Suffering," talk delivered to the Centre for African Studies, University of Leeds, Nov. 2010.

13   There are many accounts of the work of Terry Fox and its continuation after his death. See, for example, Leslie Scrivener, "How Terry Fox Changed Canada," *Toronto Star* 11 April 2010 <http://www.thestar.com/news/canada/2010/04/11/how_terry_fox_changed_canada.htm> last accessed 24 June 2014.

14   Gabrielle Giffords and her husband Mark Kelly are speaking out against gun violence. For a report on her testimony at a US Senate hearing, see Ed O'Keefe and David Fahrenthold, "Gabrielle Giffords Speaks at Senate Hearing on Gun Violence: 'You Must Act. Be Bold,'" 30 Jan. 2013 <http://www.washingtonpost.com/politics/gabrielle-giffords-to-testify-at-senate-hearing-on-gun-violence/2013/01/29/ffba6a30-6a61-11e2-95b3-272d604a10a3_story.html> last accessed 24 June 2014.

15   Luca Andrighetto and Ishani Banerji, "The Victim Wars: How Competitive Victimhood Stymies Reconciliation Between Conflict Groups," *The Inquisitive Mind* 5.15 (2012) <http://www.in-mind.org> last accessed 12 Oct. 2013.

16   Emil Fackenheim, *To Mend the World* (New York: Schocken, 1982).

17   See Dean Pritchard, "Holodomor vs. Holocaust: Controversy Dogs Human Rights Museum," *Winnipeg Sun*, 5 May 2011. <http://www.winnipegsun.com/2011/05/05/holomodor-vs-holocaust> last accessed 24 June 2014.

18   Complications in historical analysis exist. For example, some argued that Jewish political figures in the USSR cooperated with Stalin and that some Ukrainian nationalists participated as perpetrators in Holocaust crimes.

19   Laurence Thomas, "Suffering as a Moral Beacon," *The Americanization of the Holocaust* (Baltimore: Johns Hopkins UP, 1999) 198–210. See also Laurence Thomas, "The Morally Obnoxious Comparisons of Evil," Fritz Bauer Institut Papers, 2002 <http://www.laurencethomas.com/Evils.pdf> last accessed 24 June 2014; and Laurence Thomas, *Vessels of Evil: American Slavery and the Holocaust* (Philadelphia: Temple UP, 1993).

CHAPTER 4

SUFFERING, DEFERENCE, AND RESPECT

There is a widespread sense that we should respect victims, and such respect should involve deference based on what they have gone through and endured. Many of us are strongly inclined to endorse the following line of thought: because only the victim of a wrong or harm knows what it is to experience that wrong or harm, there is an important kind of authority that rests with the victim. As to her suffering, she and she alone is the expert; thus, others must defer to her awareness and understanding. Since deference is due, criticism would be inappropriate. In this way, suffering seems to support respect, including a deference that has the public implication that criticism of victims is inappropriate.

We can spell out the line of thought like this:

1. Only the victim of a harm knows what it is like to suffer from it.
    So,
2. No one other than the victim of a harm knows what it is like
    to suffer from it.
    Accordingly,

3. The victim of a harm is the person in the best position to
    determine what is the appropriate response to it.
    Therefore,
4. No one who is not the victim of a harm is in a position to
    criticize the victim's response to it.

This line of thought begins with considerations about the uniqueness of a victim's experience and proceeds to a conclusion about the respect and deference owing to that person as regards responses to his or her suffering. (Such responses might concern the treatment, medical or psychiatric, of the suffering or public processes such as trials, apologies, and memorials.) Let us call this argument the Deference Argument. It represents an influential and apparently powerful line of thought. Because of our sense that they have suffered in ways that we have not, we believe that in some very fundamental respects victims know best. They merit our respect and stemming from it gain a kind of authority. Reasoning in this way, we become reluctant to criticize individual victims and spokespersons for victim groups, given what they have gone through and the risk of appearing insensitive and presumptuous.

The Deference Argument is an important one about privilege in the victim role. Given the conclusion that their experience establishes a kind of authority, to which we should defer, victims are seen to have a morally and epistemically privileged position. On the basis of that position, they are given a type of social privilege in the sense of being exempt from criticism. Their experience of harm and suffering seems to ground a special status. In virtue of the understanding presumed to emerge from personal experience, their epistemic privilege establishes a basis for moral authority. The Deference Argument serves to support a sense of authority bearing on action and policy. It is based on a premise about the victim's unique access to his or her experience of suffering and proceeds to a conclusion of victim authority extending to other potentially sensitive matters.

To reflect on the relationship between suffering and authority, we need to consider further in what sense a victim and she alone can be deemed to understand her own suffering. We then need to explore the sense in which she has special or privileged knowledge, and how far that privileged knowledge extends. What sort of knowledge of her own experience does a person have? In what sense is that knowledge unique? And what are its implications for moral authority?

A young Afghan woman, Sahar Gul, was married as a child bride into a family that sought to force her into prostitution. When she refused, they starved, beat, and tortured her. She was eventually rescued and hospitalized with severe injuries and possibly permanent hearing loss. Reading accounts of her terrible story, we can only imagine the fears and agonies this young woman must have experienced.[1] Even with this indirect exposure to her story, we are likely to wince and cringe. We may pause to imagine her circumstances and ask how we would feel, young and vulnerable and horribly insecure in a family to whom we had been sold, in a culture with no solid mores against violence against women in general and young brides in particular.[2] Obviously, for most Western women, there are aspects of this young woman's experience that are beyond our grasp. We will recognize that we cannot comprehend her suffering. She has gone through this; we, readers of accounts about it, have not and have only exposure to the story. There is a fundamental sense in which we do not know and cannot know what it would be like to go through these things. Tragically, she can know and does know. She is the victim of these crimes; she felt the pain and fear; she was injured; she has endured agonies—and we, who hear her story have not.

Somehow, Sahar Gul survived. She is being treated, is recovering, and is regaining the capacity to speak for herself. To the extent that she can, again, speak for herself, she may try to communicate to others the nature of her suffering. If she does that, she will deserve attention and every consideration from others and in particular from those with whom she is engaged during her healing and the aftermath of the appalling treatment she received. The suffering was hers; the knowledge of it is, terribly, hers; she knows what it was like to go through these things, and others do not. To even pretend to comprehend the nature of that suffering—the beatings, torture, captivity, and humiliation that this victim has gone through—would be insulting and insensitive. We are likely to feel that, were we to do that, we would be augmenting the wrongs done to her; we would likely hurt her further, harm her further.

SUBJECTIVITY: WHAT IS IT LIKE TO BE ANOTHER?

In his widely read essay "What Is It Like to Be a Bat?," Thomas Nagel argues for the irreducibility of a subjective stance to an objective one.[3] Every subjective experience, he states, is essentially connected with a single point of view from which it cannot be separated. Nagel maintains that having a perspective on the world is fundamentally distinct from having properties as an entity in the world—so distinct that we cannot understand what it would mean to reduce the subjective to the objective or the mental to the physical. Nagel forcibly argues that an organism has conscious states if and only if there is something it is like, for the organism, to be that organism. This "something it is like" is the subjective character of experience, the *pour soi*, what the organism is like for itself, as distinct from the objective character, the *en soi*, or what the organism is like in itself.

There is something it is like to be a bat. No one who is not a bat can know what it is like to be a bat; no human being can know what it is like to be a bat. Bats echo-locate; they do not determine position by sight and touch, as we humans do. Due to bats' very different sensory apparatus and behaviour, we human beings cannot extrapolate sufficiently to understand the inner life of a bat. There is something that "it is like" to be a bat, and this "something" cannot be grasped by human beings, who are non-bats. For a human being to grasp what it would be like to be a bat, it would not be enough to understand what it would be like for that person to behave as a bat behaves, or to imagine either additions or subtractions from present experience. Nor would it suffice to imaginatively reconstruct what it would mean if he or she were gradually to be transformed into a bat. These approaches would be sidelines and not the real thing. The issue is how it feels, for the bat, to be a bat.

There is something it is like to be a victim like Sahar Gul. A person who has not experienced such a thing cannot know this. If we apply Nagel's thinking to the case of victims, the implication is that thinking of how a victim might behave in response to her suffering, or trying to imagine what it would be like to be her, or articulate facts that only she could know, would not convey the specific painful knowledge of what it is like to suffer as she has. Experientially, then, there is a kind of unique personal authority to the experienced suffering of a victim. A person who is not herself a victim cannot possess it.

Discussing the case of the inaccessible experience of a bat, Nagel argues that there are facts, facts accessible by the bat but beyond the reach of human concepts. On Nagel's view, these are facts about what it is like to be a bat; they are humanly inaccessible facts. As facts about the experience of some conscious being, these facts embody, essentially, some point of view. Nagel chose to first consider bats because they are different from human beings in their sensory structure and behaviour, and their differences would lead us to expect profound differences in awareness. To form a conception of what it is like to be a bat, one must take up the bat's point of view. But clearly we do not need bats as the basis for such an argument. Nagel's argument obviously extends to dolphins, raccoons, dogs, and indeed all non-human species. Physiological, environmental, and behavioural differences indicate that whatever the subjective quality of non-human consciousness may be, it has qualities very different from those of human consciousness. Animal subjectivity is not human subjectivity: these other creatures have experience very different from human experience and we cannot know—or for that matter even imagine—what that consciousness is like—if by "knowing what it is like" we mean knowing what it would be to experience the world from their point of view. We cannot know what it would be like to be a bat, raccoon, dog, or elephant. We can try to imagine their alien experience by exploring their behaviour and physiology and comparing it with our own, but even when we do that, we remain too different to possess the needed understanding. We cannot lose our human perspective; we experience the world as human beings and cannot know what it is like to be non-human creatures.

Nagel acknowledges that the problem of extrapolating so as to understand "what it is like to be X" does not apply only to inter-species contexts. He acknowledges that this problem exists between any two persons and does not hold only for exotic cases. The problem to which he is referring is that of grasping the specific subjective character of the experience of another. Point of view, Nagel says, is what is fundamental to the internal world. In short, the subjective character of experience is only accessible from one point of view—that of the being whose experience it is. Difficulties in grasping what it would be like to be another subject apply also to human beings and, more particularly, to human beings who have suffered as a result of serious harms imposed upon them. The matter takes us rather far from Nagel's original context, but considerations about subjective viewpoint obviously apply when we consider the experiences of victims and ask to what degree they can be known by persons who are not themselves victims suffering similar harms.

The points of view of some of my fellow human beings are accessible to me; the points of view of all other human beings are not, according to Nagel. If a man was born deaf and blind, and I was not, I will not be able to understand facts about that man's experience. He is so radically different from me, and his experience so radically different from mine, that such facts would simply be inaccessible to me. I cannot know what it is like to be that man. This sort of gulf will apply in the case of many victims and non-victims. I experience the world as myself, as TG, an older Canadian woman who has led a relatively privileged and sheltered life. I might try to expose myself to further information through reading and interviews so as to better understand and describe the experience of another person who has undergone tragedy and suffering in a world radically different from my own. Indeed, to do this would be wise and important for many purposes: I could indeed gain much information and put it to good practical use. If, for instance, I were to be involved in planning funding projects in Afghanistan, I could gain factual knowledge and use it to improve my ability to function in Afghanistan and, hopefully, to interact more sensitively and effectively in that country. I and others could benefit from my efforts. But inevitably something central and fundamental would be left out of the picture, and this is that subjective aspect of "knowing what it is like." This I would never grasp. Sahar Gul knows what it is like to be a tortured young bride in a highly patriarchal culture; I do not, cannot, and never will. There is something it is like to be her, the "something" that was, at the time of her experience, the very subjective centre of her being. And that "something" I will never have. Her point of view and consciousness are hers alone, and the same may be said of every person and, accordingly, of everyone who has suffered.

Nagel maintains that one person can take up a point of view similar to that of another person, provided her experience is sufficiently similar, and there is a sense in which she can come to understand the other's experience on this basis. Arguably, then, I can know what it is like to be my best friend, although I cannot know what it is like to be born deaf and blind or to suffer as Sahar Gul has suffered. And it is because my background and experience are so different from those others that I cannot know what it would be like to experience what they have experienced.

I do not know, and cannot know, what it would be like to experience the world from her point of view. I experience the world as a mature and relatively privileged Canadian woman, she as a young and most severely abused Afghan woman. The consciousness of a victim such as Sahar Gul, her sense of what it is or was like to endure the suffering she went through, involve her own sense of what the world is like from her perspective. My consciousness, that sense of what the world is like when viewed from "within," is subjective and private to me.

Although he is committed to the distinctively subjective character of experience, Nagel does not go so far as to state outright that we conscious creatures have unique access to the character of our subjective experience and only to that. He does not want to endorse the solipsistic idea that I can understand only what it is like to be myself and not what it is like to be any other person. He wants to allow that a human being can grasp the quality of another person's experience if he or she is sufficiently similar to be able to adopt the other's point of view. According to Nagel's account, although I cannot know what it is like to be a bat or a deaf and blind man, I can know what it is like to be another human being who is sufficiently similar to myself. There is a point of view that we share. Because the gap regarding sensory information (visual, auditory) between the deaf and blind man and myself is so large, we are in epistemically different worlds. Relative to my world, his may be said to be epistemically impoverished. The point here is not simply that I have some experiences that this man does not have. Rather, it is that, for fundamental empirical reasons, he does not have whole categories of experience that I have; his lack amounts to impoverishment because these categories are fundamental in human life.

Applying these standards, the reason I cannot know what it is like to be Sahar Gul does not lie simply in the basic metaphysical fact that I am myself experiencing the world from my point of view and Sahar Gul is quite another human self experiencing the world from her point of view. This gap based on the fact that we are two distinct subjects is metaphysical. A second gap is not metaphysical; it is empirical. It is due to empirical facts about our backgrounds and points of view: our circumstances do not have sufficient similarities to be of a type. To use Nagel's language, there are fundamentally important empirical respects in which we are not sufficiently similar for me to be able to take up her point of view.

It appears from Nagel's discussion of sufficient similarities that the gulf between a suffering victim and someone else who has never suffered in just that way is not a gap that is absolute and metaphysical in nature. Rather, it is empirical and a matter of degree. I cannot know what it would be like to experience the world from Sahar Gul's point of view because her situation and cultural background are so dramatically different from my own. For Sahar Gul and myself, this gap comes from age and luck, protection and privilege, and fundamental differences between Afghanistan and Canada. To say that these differences are empirical is not to say that they are *merely* empirical. After all, they have been basic in structuring the contours of our lives, affecting perceptions, values, capabilities, and opportunities. There is a whole dimension of experience that Sahar Gul has had and that I, as a far more fortunate woman, have not had. Whatever their grimly painful character, these experiences will have profoundly affected her point of view and consciousness. These impacts have not been characteristic of my experience; they have not been felt by me, and they would not be wanted by me. One would not likely say that my situation is epistemically impoverished compared to hers, given that her experience has involved so much intense pain and suffering of a character not typical or necessary for normal human functioning. Only relative to the understanding of suffering would one be likely to argue that I am epistemically impoverished by my background.

TWO KINDS OF GULF:
METAPHYSICAL AND EMPIRICAL DIFFERENCES

Nagel's emphasis on the irreducibly subjective and un-capturable nature of conscious experience implies that there will always be a gulf between one person's experience and another's. The first gulf is metaphysical and exists regardless of similarity of background. When Nagel points to this gulf, he is pointing to the subjectivity of consciousness—any consciousness—and the fact that any conscious subject will necessarily experience the world only from its own point of view. In this sense, I necessarily experience the world only from my point of view, and Sahar Gul from hers. Nagel allows that if we could understand how subjective experience had an objective nature, we would understand how subjects other than ourselves, we would understand the nature of subjects other than ourselves. The problem is, Nagel has argued precisely that we cannot understand how subjective experience could have an objective nature. He should, then, admit that on his account one cannot understand what it is to exist as a subject other than oneself. And that point will apply to any two subjects. This is the first gulf: we can never know what it would be like to be another person because, by definition, we can never have that person's experience. Here, in his discussion of the *pour soi* and elsewhere, Nagel seems committed to the conclusion that, with my perspective essentially connected with my experience of the world, and another person's perspective essentially connected with her experience of the world, there is an ultimate sense in which I can never know what it would be like to be that person.[4] My inability to know would be metaphysically grounded in the distinction between one person's consciousness and another's. Clearly, the point would apply to any two people, whether or not these two people have vastly different backgrounds. This metaphysical gap may be important when we try to comprehend what victims have gone through, but it is not, in this context, the important gap.

The metaphysical gulf arises for any two selves and even for highly trivial examples, such as knowing what it would be like to taste Vegemite or smell a skunk.[5] It exists because an experience is not detachable from the point of view on the world from which it is an experience. The metaphysical distinction between self and other is present not only for cases of profound suffering but also for cases of slight practical significance. If my friend has eaten burnt toast, given I do not experience the world from her point of view and I cannot know what it would be like to experience the world from her point of view, I cannot know what it is like to be her, eating burnt toast. I do not, cannot, and could not experience the world from her perspective. That is a logical and metaphysical point. Yes, I too have tasted burnt toast, but what is in question here is my friend's taste of toast—what it is like for her, not my taste and what that is like for me. On Nagel's account, any person's perspective is essential to her experience of the world and inseparable from it. Though Nagel may not wish to draw this conclusion, it will follow from his account that there is a metaphysical sense in which no human being can know what it is like to be any other human being. And this conclusion holds for human beings generally; it is not based on degrees of similarity between their experiences.

In Nagel's account of the subjective and the objective, we find an insistence on an irreducible aspect of a self that is inaccessible to others. In this metaphysical sense, it is not only the awful suffering of Sahar Gul that is inaccessible to me but, rather, the experience of any other self. Any experience is what it is only from the perspective of that self whose experience it is. There are aspects of another's experience, and sense of what it is to be in the world, that are metaphysically inaccessible to me, whether or not my circumstances are empirically similar to those of that person. Call this inaccessible element the raw edge of experience. At this point, philosophers have also spoken of "raw feels," "the intrinsic character of a sensation," "qualia," or "phenomenal aspects of the world." These are felt elements of consciousness impossible to fully articulate. If I know a fact, I can express that fact in words and tell another person what I believe to be the case. If I know what it is like to taste burnt toast or vegemite, to mourn the death of a child, or suffer a torture, I cannot express that knowledge in words and cannot convey it to another.[6]

Because he is committed to the view that there is a unique private knowledge or access to private subjective facts, we find in Nagel a profoundly Cartesian element with regard to these phenomenal aspects of the world. They are private to persons. They are private to suffering persons, accordingly, private to victims. The facts of someone's experience, the sense of what it is like to be her, are available only to that person, only to her. It is in this sense that she is the "owner" of the experience to which these facts apply.[7] There is, then, a form of self-knowledge or self-understanding accessible from only one phenomenal perspective, which is that of the experiencing self.[8] In this sense, I have unique and raw knowledge of my experiences, Sahar Gul of hers, and Nagel of his. For such knowledge, there are metaphysical limits and these limits apply in all cases. I have only mine, you only yours, and so on.

Only Sahar Gul knows what it is like, or was like, to be the victim of the brutality of her forced early marriage because only she experienced, from her point of view, these abuses within this marriage, in this country.[9] Such facts about Sahar Gul's uniqueness do not depend on empirical facts about perceptual or cultural differences or the severity of harm and suffering. They do not depend on suffering, harm, innocence, or responsibility. Rather, they find their basis in the subjectivity of consciousness.

But there are in addition the other sorts of gaps—empirical gaps—between one person's experience and another's. If Sahar Gul has experienced beatings and torture and I have not, I cannot know what it would be like to be her and experience that torture because I live in a markedly different sort of world and have never experienced anything like that. My point of view, from which I experience the world, is not sufficiently similar to hers. There is a vast gap between us and this vast gap is empirical, not purely logical and metaphysical. It is a different gap and in fact a different *kind* of gap. This second gap is experiential and qualitative: there is a vast gulf of experience between us, a gulf established by the differences between my highly fortunate life and her brutally abused one. Given profound empirical differences between her life and my own, she has a range of experience and, from it, kinds of knowledge that I do not share. I do not know the sort of suffering she has experienced: I do not understand her life well enough to have a grasp, even, of what this suffering is like. Reading her story, wincing over its details, I may do my best to sympathize and empathize; my best is all I can do. The gap between her life and mine is experiential and empirical and too wide for me to understand what she has gone through. It is for empirical as well as metaphysical reasons that I cannot know what it would be like to experience her suffering. I will admire her for surviving the horrors of her young life and perhaps wonder whether I myself could do that if I fell into similar circumstances. But there are powerful empirical reasons underlying the fact that I cannot know what she has gone through.

What we must note here is that my case relative to that of Sahar Gul is not that of all other persons. Regrettably, there will be many women in Afghanistan whose experience will be sufficiently similar that they can begin to understand what Sahar Gul has gone through. The metaphysical gap remains and is unbridgeable for them as it is for me, but the empirical gap that exists for me does not exist for them. This is the gap that Nagel describes in terms of sufficient similarities; it is not universal and not absolute. It is a matter of degree and can be lessened by effort.

It is fundamentally important to distinguish between the metaphysical and the empirical in the context of reflecting on the unique knowledge and experience of victims. Metaphysically, every consciousness is utterly distinct from every other;

only victims have their experience, only Nagel his, only Sahar Gul hers, and only I mine. Yet empirically, and importantly, people can have relevantly similar experiences. Other women who have been young brides married into cruel families will have experiences rather similar to those of Sahar Gul, and in virtue of those experiences that are "sufficiently similar" to hers, they will have some understanding of what she has gone through as a victim—of what it would be like to be her. This background of sufficient similarity puts them in a better position than myself to offer sympathy, understanding, solidarity, and support.

BACK TO THE DEFERENCE ARGUMENT

When we take into account the distinction between the metaphysical gap and the empirical gap, the opening premise of the Deference Argument is exposed as ambiguous. This premise is:

1.   Only the victim of a harm knows what it is like to suffer from it.

In the metaphysical sense, this premise is true. In the empirical sense, it is false. If we interpret the premise of deference as referring to empirical knowability it is not true, because someone with a similar background, or acquiring a similar background, can to some extent know what it is like to have the other's experience. Empirically, there are similarities and differences between subjects, and these are more or less relevant to what they know and what they can come to know. The Deference Argument can be understood in two different ways, depending on whether it is based on a metaphysical or empirical interpretation of the subject's knowledge. For the argument to hold universally, for it to be watertight and not open to qualifications regarding subjects of "sufficiently similar" experience, the metaphysical interpretation of the gap between experiencing subjects should be presumed. But the problem with this interpretation is that the "raw feel" or "raw edge" of phenomenal consciousness seems to yield no articulable knowledge that could enter the public sphere. What is known by the subject is an unarticulated and inarticulable "it" or "somewhat" that does not imply any conveyable knowledge that subject might have applied to the responses to harm or wrongdoing.

The opening premise of the Deference Argument is not of practical significance when the unique knowledge attributed to a self is based on the metaphysical distinction between that self and another. On that interpretation, the premise is true but not useful in establishing the conclusion of the argument. On the empirical interpretation, the premise would be useful but does not hold universally. In those cases where persons share sufficiently similar backgrounds, there is a sense in which a person other than the victim can know what it is like to suffer as she has. When the distinction between these two interpretations is taken into account, we see a crucial problem arises for the Deference Argument. It derives its plausibility from an equivocation in the opening premise.

Look again at the argument on the first page of this chapter.

1. Only the victim of a harm knows what it is like to suffer from it.
   So,
2. No one other than the victim of a harm knows what it is like to suffer from it.
   Accordingly,
3. The victim of a harm is the person in the best position to determine what is the right response to it.
   Therefore,
4. No one who is not the victim of a harm is in a position to criticize the victim's response.

The universality in the opening premise to the effect that only the victim of a harm knows what it is like to suffer from it is true if one presumes the metaphysical interpretation, but not true if one presumes an empirical interpretation. The metaphysical interpretation means that the victim's knowledge would be of the phenomenal edge of experience. That edge cannot be put into words or publicly conveyed. It cannot be shared, so it cannot constitute or ground public knowledge about practical matters such as treatment, punitive policy, sentencing, and public entitlements. What this means is that the kind of unique access to experience that can be metaphysically guaranteed to victims does not provide any sort of authority relevant to policy and practice. In those contexts, empirical considerations of access are relevant, and publicly statable beliefs and knowledge are required. These fit with an empirical interpretation of the opening premise. Factors establishing metaphysical uniqueness on the raw edge of consciousness cannot establish authority as to practical matters. Empirically, there are both differences and similarities between the experiences of persons, and there are degrees of similarity and difference. People have experiences that may be quite similar, radically different, or something in between.

Only the victim of suffering can know what it is like to experience that suffering; therefore, no one else can know what that is like. These claims will always be true in the metaphysical sense, but they will not necessarily be true in the empirical sense. Knowledge of the raw edge of experience is available not only to persons who have suffered as victims but to every experiencing self. Only I can know what is the quality of my experiences from my point of view—my experiences, whether those of pain, pleasure, or boredom, are mine alone. Things are otherwise, however, when we shift to an empirical interpretation. At that point, similarities and differences between the lives of experiencing beings are relevant. There are degrees; there are qualifications. From an empirical stance, it is most unlikely that only the victim knows what her suffering is like, because there will be persons of relevantly similar background and experience who are in a position to understand that suffering.

Other Afghan women suffered through abuse similar to that of Sahar Gul; they have been child brides in forced marriages and endured beatings and threats from family members. Having undergone rather similar tribulations in a very similar context, they would have painful and powerful recollections as a basis for empathy and the imaginative understanding of her suffering. They could rightly claim to know how it feels to be her, though they are separate beings and do not experience the world from a point of view exactly the same as hers.

WHAT KNOWLEDGE? WHAT AUTHORITY?

Only a victim knows the raw edge of her own experience; no one else knows it—no one else can know it, or ever could. The point is that, necessarily, this inside grasp of her suffering is something the experiencing self has got and others do not.[10] That is a position about knowledge, a kind of knowledge over which the later Wittgenstein anguished and which he refused even to call knowledge.

In the Deference Argument, the reasoning is that in virtue of the victim's unique knowledge of her experience, she is in the best position to determine how to respond to the harm that has befallen her, and her response should not be criticized by others. It is she who knows best what should be the response to her suffering—what should be done in its aftermath. She has a moral authority based on her status as the only person who knows what it is like to suffer as she has. To say that she is in the best position here is to say that no one is in a better position; thus, the argument proceeds to its conclusion about deference to victims. As a corollary of the victim's (perceived) moral authority, the Deference Argument proceeds to the conclusion that no one else can rightly criticize the victim's response to her suffering. When the claim is made that no one is in a position to criticize a victim's response to suffering, there is a shift in this argument from epistemic to practical concerns about what to do. What sort of authority can a victim rightly claim, based on her metaphysically unique knowledge?

At this point, it is interesting to look back to feminist standpoint theory where issues of the epistemic privilege and authority of persons have been extensively considered. Although few treatments of feminist standpoint theory explicitly mention victimization specifically, it is reasonable to understand that theory as relevant to responses to victims. After all, the original motivation behind feminist standpoint theory was to seek understanding of marginalization and related harm that women (on this view, victims of oppression in a male-dominated society) experience due to their social position. In its original form, feminist standpoint theory claimed that due to their oppressed condition, women were in a position of epistemic privilege with regard to the understanding of social forces and realities. The original conception was that as oppressed persons, women would have direct experience of oppression and would for that reason have a privileged standpoint from which to understand it.

We may define a standpoint theory as one in which certain persons are taken to have an epistemically privileged perspective, due to their experience as oppressed persons in society. Since its origin in the 1970s, feminist standpoint theory has undergone many adaptations. Questions arose and continue to arise concerning the supposed connection between oppression and insight. A basic problem is that "women" do not constitute a unitary group with regard to the nature and interpretation of their experiences: there are too many different women in too many different positions and too many varying experiences in those positions for it to be plausible to speak of what it is, *in general*, to be a woman. Another fundamental problem is that a person's membership in a particular oppressed group is neither sufficient nor necessary for understanding the nature of that person's oppression. (It is not sufficient: clearly, one can be a victim of capitalist competition without understanding any economic theory. It is not necessary: equally clearly, one might understand theories of capitalist competition without being a victim of them.)

In an extensive and detailed article, Elizabeth Anderson states the following requirements for a complete standpoint theory, using in a pivotal role the notion of "privilege."[11] She is referring to what is privileged for knowledge: the privilege is that one is in an especially suitable social location to possess or acquire knowledge. Anderson states that a developed standpoint theory should specify:

1. the social location of the perspective;
2. the scope of the privilege claimed;
3. the aspect of the social location that generates what had been deemed superior knowledge;
4. the ground of the privilege (I take this to mean providing an answer to the question of what it is about the social location that generates the superior knowledge);
5. the type of epistemic superiority claimed—for example, is it greater accuracy in predictions, something that counts as moral expertise, greater competence in articulating fundamental truths...;
6. the other perspectives relative to which that epistemic superiority is claimed;
7. the modes of access to the privileged perspective.

It is helpful to consider these factors when considering the supposed epistemic privilege of victims and the deference that might be due to them on the basis of it. Working through Anderson's points in the context of the Deference Argument, we arrive at the following. The social location is that of victim. For present purposes, we will consider a victim to be a person who has been significantly harmed and has suffered through little personal fault as a result of an unwelcome and harmful event or wrongful action of some other person. On the basis of the analysis here, we should say that the scope of the privilege is the raw edge of experience, the victim's awareness of her own suffering. The aspect of the location that generates the superior knowledge is the victim's own awareness of what it is like to suffer through just this kind of suffering. The epistemic superiority that can be claimed on the basis of this privileged insight is restricted to this domain, and the superiority claimed is over the perspectives of others not identical with the suffering self. The victim has epistemic privilege as compared with these others in the sense that she knows, and they do not, what it is or was like to suffer as she herself did. As to the mode of access, it is through direct awareness—the raw edge of experience.

If we scrutinize the notion of epistemic privilege through these lenses and look back to the question of scope, which is most relevant to issues about the connection between epistemic privilege and moral authority, we will see immediately that the scope is extremely limited. What stands out here is that the raw edge of sensation—knowing what it is like in a metaphysically unique sense—is a narrow edge indeed. The fact that a victim has unique and privileged access to her own consciousness while experiencing suffering does not appear to establish her authority on any moral or policy matter that extends beyond the privacy of consciousness. Victims' unique awareness of their suffering and special metaphysical access to it does not suffice to make them experts on matters pertaining to criminal trials, the justice of punishment, sentencing issues, peace processes, transitional justice, reparations, political reparation, or even, for that matter, issues of their own treatment in the wake of serious harm. On all these topics private experiences cannot establish knowledge or good judgement. Scientific evidence, discussion, criticism, and debate are appropriate. Victims will not necessarily know better than others what are the answers to relevant practical questions.

If there are multiple victims of a single offender or offending group, these points will be particularly obvious, because victims are likely to disagree about issues in the political or legal aftermath. The need for reasoning about what should be done does not disappear in virtue of the metaphysical uniqueness of private consciousness. Uniqueness of knowledge holds only in the metaphysical sense, applies to all persons and not only to victims, and could generate only a limited authority on practical and policy matters. This is not of course to deny that victims deserve respect. Clearly victims, as persons, do merit basic human respect. As experiencing selves who have lived through bitter and often horrific experiences that are (in the sense explained above) unique to them, they merit respect with regard to attention. And as citizens in the public realm similar in various regards and to various degrees to others who have suffered, they merit respect as do others.

EPISTEMIC PRIVILEGE OR SOCIALLY GROUNDED AUTHORITY?

In a recent article, Mariane Janack argues that epistemic privilege and epistemic authority should be distinguished.[12] She considers the granting of authority to be based not on expertise and insight but, rather, on social practice. Janack argues that to have authority in a given context means to be treated in that context as someone who has a right to speak and to be taken seriously on some matter. One is granted authority as a matter of social practice. A fundamental phenomenon motivating feminist standpoint theory in its early days was the fact that women were so often regarded as lacking credibility and as such were denied authority. As a matter of social practice, women were readily dismissed as non-expert, not formally qualified, too emotional, affected by hormones and physiological conditions such as menstruation or pregnancy, and other such factors.

Janack's claim is that both traditional epistemology and feminist standpoint theory seek to base authority on epistemic privilege. She argues that both are wrong to do so. Traditional epistemology is incorrect in this regard because it presumes, contrary to fact, that certain sorts of people are ideally rational and objective, seeking to base authority on those characteristics. Feminist standpoint theory is also incorrect due to its faulty presumption that certain people are ideally situated (due to their oppressed condition) to arrive at valid insights about social institutions. Janack maintains that feminist standpoint theory is (ironically) wrong in just the same way traditional epistemology is wrong: both presume that a certain kind of person is epistemically privileged and should be granted authority on the basis of that epistemic privilege.

Janack maintains that there should be no epistemic privilege that presumes special insights to be recognized as authoritative. Rather, she contends, what should be considered are social practices with regard to credibility. In many contexts, women have been marginalized in the sense of not being heard and not being listened to. They have not been given a voice in conversations and debates about matters of general concern and of profound concern to them. In these crucial social respects, women were not given authority as a matter of social practice. The underlying problem is not one of epistemology but rather one of custom. The issue is custom as to who is deemed credible in the sense in which credibility means worthiness to be believed. Others judge one's sincerity, reliability, objectivity, and trustworthiness, and they grant authority (or not) through social practices. Like persons of colour and (lower) social class, women were often treated as unable to provide their own descriptions of their own experience; they were not able to have their own accounts taken seriously by others who deemed themselves to be more authoritative due to their more highly rated social position. A doctor would be an expert on the difficulties of early pregnancy; a pregnant woman would not.

Such a difference about expertise would make some sense if one were considering discomfort in pregnancy as a general phenomenon, but when it is a matter of the difficulties of some particular woman, her voice needs to be heard and taken seriously. If she has trouble sleeping due to discomforts of pregnancy, she should not be dismissed as having no authority because she is a "mere woman" or "subject to hormones," "emotional," "prone to exaggerate," or whatever.[13] On Janack's view, the solution to these problems of authority denied is not to develop a theory of epistemic privilege based on the notion that women and other oppressed persons have better insights due to their being victims of oppression. Rather, it is to look directly at social practices with regard to authority and correct for those practices that deny authority to women and other marginalized persons. In other words, people should allow women and other persons in less dominant social positions to speak. And when women do speak, others should pay attention and listen to them without presuming their incompetence.

At this point, epistemic and moral issues are intertwined and cannot easily be disentangled. Questions of authority should be understood as questions as to whom we should trust to develop what we consider our best beliefs. Victims who have suffered harm should be heard. People who are disadvantaged and marginalized have often been victims and have not been heard. And the results have been poor, in terms of ethics, law, and politics—whatever one might wish to say about epistemology. On this account, the solutions to the problem of marginalizing oppressed persons lie not in epistemology but in social ethics. We must learn to let previously suppressed voices be heard and pay attention to them when they speak out.

Reasoning along these lines, if we ask why victims should be able to speak and be heard, to be full participants in moral and policy questions, the answers are not to be found in considerations about knowing what it is like to suffer. It lies in the fact that victims are people, people who are affected and will be affected by action and policy, and people whose participation should affect that policy. Victims should have authority in the sense that they should be heard and their accounts should receive attention. To ignore the voices of those who have suffered would be a mistake. It would be a mistake not for any metaphysical reason establishing victims' privileged epistemic access to their own consciousness but because victims are people whose empirical experience makes them concerned in outcomes of processes of therapy, counselling, punishment, justice, and reparation. They are people almost certain to be affected by those processes. And they are members of the community whose responsibility it is to deal with the aftermath of a wrong. Furthermore, often those who are victims are people who, quite apart from their victimization by some specific wrong, found themselves on the margins of society before that wrong ever happened.[14]

When it comes to social authority, our social practices should make room for victims. These needs are fundamentally moral, and the authority in question is not absolute or privileged. The point is not that we should listen to victims because they will, in some absolute sense, possess an understanding unique to them and denied to other people. Their authority is real though not unique, not based on epistemic privilege, and not absolute. Questions about response to wrongdoing and harm cry out for answers, and it is difficult to work out those answers. But difficulties will not be resolved by presuming that, as victims, people have a unique epistemic privilege grounding moral authority. Victims should be respected. As a matter of social practice, their voices should be heard and listened to. They should be deemed credible and granted authority in the sense of significance and importance, but not in the sense of having the final word on matters outside the range of personal experience.

ANOTHER APPROACH: THE IDEA OF TRANSFORMATIVE EXPERIENCE

Recently, the idea of transformative experience has been discussed and developed by several feminist philosophers. They define a transformative experience as one that is radically new and is personally transformative in the sense of being life-changing. An influential account is that of Laurie Paul, who has written about the rationality of deciding to have a child and used the idea of "knowing what it is like" to develop her account.[15] For a person who had never seen colour, coming to see it would be a transformative experience; similarly, for a person who had been born deaf to acquire hearing as a result of a cochlear implant would be transformative. Merely having some new taste sensation would not be personally transformative in the strong way required even though it would be epistemically enriching. It would be new, but not transformative. Nor (it seems) would merely acquiring a new skill such as learning to swim or play an instrument.[16]

Philosophers discussing transformative experiences have been interested primarily in the rationality of decision-making and in the limitations of traditional decision theory in contexts where a person is making a decision about whether to embark on a course of action that would result in transformative experiences. They argue that decision theory does not provide a basis or standard for rationality in such contexts. They have become interested in the idea of transformative experience from that particular background and have developed the notion of transformative experience there, arguing that for some choices, given the transformative nature of the experience that would result, rationality is not possible.

Crucially, Paul argues that a person who does not have a child cannot know what it is like to have a child. If one is deciding whether to have a child, one cannot know or even reasonably estimate what sorts of things one would experience if one had a child. This means one cannot calculate expected utilities. She argues that because one cannot know in advance what it would be like to have a child or what it would be like, comparatively, not to have a child, and because one does not have access to this information, basic to rational decision-making, one cannot make a rational decision about the issue. In deciding to have a child, a person cannot be rational and must instead take a leap of faith. What one would need for rationality would be phenomenal values, the knowledge of what it would be like to be in the various mental states involved in having a child. One cannot know in advance what it is like; one cannot have those phenomenal values; and one's previous experience could not have enabled a good prediction. Because one does not know what it will be like to have a child, Paul argues, one does not know what emotions, beliefs, desires, and dispositions would be caused in oneself as a result of the experiences she would have as a parent. A person choosing whether to become a parent is in an impoverished epistemic situation; she is in a position where she cannot know what she would need to know in order to rationally make the decision she needs to make. Paul says that a personally transformative experience will radically alter what it is like to be you; perhaps even your most basic experiences will be changed.

Given their focus on decision-making and choice, those who discuss transformative experiences do not seem to attend to those experiences likely to be highly negative in character. Paul stresses that one does not know what it is like to be a parent before becoming one and she does acknowledge that, for some, parenthood may bring stress and unhappiness. But she is not discussing the potentially transformative nature of suffering. That, of course, is precisely what we would wish to consider if we were to think about the transformative (or potentially transformative) experiences of victimhood. Typically, one does not choose to suffer; often, one does choose to have a child. But, focusing on choice and the limits of rationality for important personal choices, the discussion of transformative experience does not extend to the context of victimhood. Nevertheless—and the point is clearly important with regard to victims—there are personally transformative experiences that are not chosen. They are not subject to personal decision-making and the question of whether we can make rational decisions with regard to them does not arise. One does not become a victim by choice; there is no question, then, of whether the choice to suffer as a victim could be one that is rational in terms of classic decision theory.

As Paul emphasizes, coming to see colour or becoming a parent may epistemically and personally transform one's life, providing emotions, beliefs, and capacities that one could not have predicted and did not have before. As she emphasizes, one would not have the information to make rational choices in these areas. As a victim, one is harmed by external agents or forces; one is not harmed in virtue of decisions or choices of one's own. As a victim, one is harmed and suffers. As a victim of serious wrongs or harms, one may suffer considerably and in personally transformative ways. One may come to see the world differently and as a result have emotions, beliefs, and capacities that one did not have before. Given Paul's concept of a transformative experience, and given common knowledge about the changes that people often undergo after experiencing serious harms, it is reasonable to suppose that suffering a particular harm may be a transformative experience. One who has not gone through the experience will not know what it is like. This empirical gap between her and others is fully comparable to the gap between a parent and one who has not become a parent. The fact that the victim experience is not chosen (so that reflections on decision theory do not apply) does not affect the validity of this claim. Regarding victimhood, one does not make rational choices that might or might not count as rational, because one does not make choices at all.

Clearly, the context of transformative experience for victimhood is different from that of decision-making. Yet the notion of transformative experience would seem to apply here as well, especially for serious wrongs and serious harms. Without experiencing auditory sensations, a person does not know what that is like. Without experiencing a sleepless night caring for one's own newborn child, a person does not know what that is like. Without experiencing abuse and suffering, a person does not know what that is like. Indeed there are indefinitely many experiences that are inaccessible to us. Some of these may be personally transformative experiences, as discussed by Paul. They may affect our lives in fundamental ways, altering much of our experience and altering even our selves as subjects of experience. We are fortunate if we are in a position to make choices about whether to expose ourselves to such experiences. Notoriously, many people are not, and many of those people are victims of wrongdoing, accident, or disease. If a woman experiences a gang rape, the painful and humiliating experience could very well be personally transformative. If a man loses both legs in an industrial accident, or becomes sterile as a result of medical treatment, those experiences are likely to be personally transformative as well. What has been said about the epistemically new and the conveying of beliefs and emotions not accessible to others can be said here too. There is a new phenomenal realm that these subjects have and others lack. Those others do not know what it is like, having not undergone the personally transformative experiences. Those who have lived it can only do their best to tell the rest of us, and we can only do our best to listen.

NOTES

1   *Globe and Mail* 2 and 3 Jan. 2012. The case was also described in the *New York Times* 12 Aug. 2012.

2   According to the *Globe and Mail* articles cited above, the Afghan government has passed laws against such violence, under pressure from the international community, but such laws are not enforced or even taken particularly seriously.

3   Thomas Nagel, "What Is It Like to Be a Bat?" in *Mortal Questions* (New York: Cambridge University Press, 1979) 165–80.

4   Gender itself might suffice to make the difference. But the point here is more basic; what is at issue is the mere fact that *this other person is not me* and cannot be

experiencing the world from my perspective. At most, he would be experiencing the world from a perspective relevantly *similar* to mine. See Nagel, footnote 14.

5   David Lewis, "What Experience Teaches," *There's Something about Mary*, ed. Peter Ludlow, Yulin Nagasawa, and Daniel Stoljar (Boston: MIT Press, 2004) Chapter 5.

6   The older term here was "knowledge by acquaintance." One might seek to convey through fiction a sense of what it is like to experience the world through the subjective point of view.

7   The later Wittgenstein would object that notions of knowledge and "things" to be known make no sense in this context.

8   Kathleen Wilder, "Overtones of Solipsism in Thomas Nagel's 'What Is It Like to Be a Bat?' and *The View from Nowhere*," *Philosophy and Phenomenological Research* 50 (1990): 481–99.

9   The distinction between "is" and "was" is highly important, in fact, but I am glossing over it at this point, being unable to explore it here. At the time Sahar Gul was undergoing suffering, she knew what it was "like" in the sense that right at that moment she was undergoing it. Later, when she recalls it, she is unlikely to have had just that kind of knowledge; she knows what it was like on the basis of recalling what she experienced at an earlier time, and considerations of the selectivity and accuracy of memory arise.

10   Apologies to Wittgenstein.

11   Elizabeth Anderson, "Feminist Standpoint Theory," *Stanford Internet Encyclopedia of Philosophy*, ed. Edward N. Zalta, Fall 2012 <http://plato.stanford.edu/archives/fall2012/entries/feminism-epistemology/> last accessed 8 Nov. 2013.

12   Mariane Janack, "Standpoint Epistemology without the 'Standpoint'? An Examination of Epistemic Privilege and Epistemic Authority," *Hypatia* 12.2 (Spring 1997): 125–39.

13   My example, which I take to be in accordance with Janack's account.

14   This point should be obvious and examples may be found all too easily. For those in need of further evidence, I offer the appendices of my *Taking Wrongs Seriously*.

15   L.A. Paul, "What You Can't Expect When You're Expecting," *Res Philosophica*, forthcoming 2015. I benefitted also from hearing Laurie Paul speak on the topic of transformative experiences at the University of Calgary in January 2014.

16   I confess to not finding it entirely clear where to draw the line. One might argue that swimming for the first time could be a personally transformative experience if the person who learned to swim developed a whole career and lifestyle based on this new experience.

CHAPTER 5

THE TESTIMONY OF VICTIMS

The fact that only victims know from experience what it is like to suffer as they have does not have the expansive significance that is often given to it. That fact, however, does not deny another important one that we ignore at our peril. We need to listen to victims; to fail to do so is not only inhumane, but dangerous. A common problem for victims is that when they tell what happened to them, they are not believed. Sometimes they are not believed because they are deemed to lack credibility in the sense of worthiness to be believed. They may be thought to be overly emotional or incompetent; they may be members of groups against which subtle or not-so-subtle biases are operating. The claims of victims may not be taken seriously because they contradict what we believe or would like to believe. For these reasons their claims are sometimes rejected because they are judged to be implausible. If victims make claims describing abuse at the hands of the powerful, problems of plausibility may combine with issues of credibility to facilitate cavalier dismissal of their narratives.

Reflections on the testimony of victims must be evaluated in the context of broader knowledge, much of which is itself based on testimony. People need each other for knowledge and transmit knowledge to each other, often successfully. The role of testimony in knowledge is large, and its exploration a fundamental topic in the theory of knowledge. Important aspects of this topic include credibility, trust, and the role of background beliefs in critical scrutiny. These themes are sensitive and important in the context of the claims of victims.

TESTIMONY

Were our knowledge restricted only to things we have subjectively experienced or directly studied, it would be limited indeed and certainly not sufficient even for daily living. We take into account what others have to say, and that is something we need to do. Our inescapable dependence on the knowledge, beliefs, and experience of others should be acknowledged and explored; it is not something to bemoan.[1] Much of what we know, we know because we learn from words, meaning in effect the words of other people. For much routine information ("Where is Green Street?" "Are the banks open today?") we can obtain what we need by asking others, whom we presume to be reliable. These other people know what we need to know; we ask them; they tell us; then as a result, we know. And thus is knowledge transmitted from one person to another. The norms operative in this transmission come from the theory of knowledge and also from ethics. Our acquiring knowledge and reliable beliefs from other people depends on both competence and character: to be a reliable source of knowledge, a person must have competence relevant to the claim he is making and be sufficiently honest to merit our trust that he is truthful. Issues of competence and character become complex when questions are about less routine matters, including those that involve value judgements ("Would you recommend that film to a 14-year-old?") or contestable interpretations ("Was his joke intended as an insult?"). On such matters, we are not relying on others simply to transmit to us their knowledge of straightforward matters of fact. Issues of relevance, judgement, and appropriateness of standards arise. Nevertheless, we still need to take account of what other people believe and have judged to be the case on the basis of their acquired knowledge and experience of the world.

It is not possible to offer a philosophical account showing why in general it is justifiable to rely on the testimony of others, because our dependence on their testimony is too basic. The problem is that any attempt at a general justification of human reliance on testimony would itself rely on testimony in the broad sense that it would rely on what we have learned from other people. Most obviously, any such attempt would be couched in a public language learned from other persons. For that reason, the supposed justification would rely on just the sort of knowledge it purported to justify and would be circular. Thus, it would be unsuccessful. The problem for testimony is analogous to those that arise for deduction if we try to justify by logical argument such basic logical principles as the principle of non-contradiction, and for induction if we try to justify that reasoning by contending that claims based on past experience have been successful in the past. With testimony the underlying philosophical problem is this: to justify relying on what other people have told us, we have to make use of what other people have told us. A completely general justification of testimony will, accordingly, fail in the end. It will be question-begging. Human knowledge is not the knowledge of any single human being; it is the knowledge of human beings and has developed in communities and societies. It is, by definition, shared, and it is shared because in gesture, speech, or writing, we make claims to each other and tell each other things. We are too dependent on testimonial knowledge to be in a position where we can systematically justify its claims.

Questions about specific kinds of testimony can quite sensibly be raised, however. Among the many people whose claims and stories we need to hear and consider are victims, and fascinating practical questions arise concerning their testimony. We need to attend to what victims tell us to understand the realities of this world, including suffering experiences, acts of victimization, their causes and perpetrators, and many other factors. This is not to say that we should deem the subjective experience of victims an authoritative source of public knowledge concerning issues of treatment or policy. Rather, their claims should be carefully considered and not simply dismissed as lacking plausibility or coming from non-credible sources. We owe to victims careful attention, if not wholehearted deference, and we ignore them at the risk of inhumanity and the condoning of crime and abuse. The point is not that when victims' claims extend to matters in the public realm (science, political policy, morality) those claims should be accepted without scrutiny as a matter of deference. Rather, we need to attend to the claims of victims, but we owe such deference to no one.

Let us first consider the reception of a testimonial claim in a rather abstract and neutral case. Suppose a person, call him Henry, accepts a claim on the grounds that another person, call her Sheila, has told him this. Sheila is the speaker, here, and Henry is the "hearer" or listener. Henry may acquire knowledge on the basis of what Sheila has told him, but in listening to Sheila he does need to be alert to the possibility that she might be an unreliable source. She might be trying to manipulate or deceive him, or she might be lacking in relevant competence and honestly mistaken. Henry may simply presume that Sheila is a trustworthy source of relevant knowledge and accept what she has to say, and often he will do this, especially if the claim is about something fairly mundane. But he may have some indication of possible error or lack of reliability. If so, he may hesitate to simply accept what Sheila says and pause to consider it further. To do otherwise would be unwise, the more so the more significant the claim is for Henry. (For instance, he will likely take more care if he is asking Sheila about the safety of his likely travel in a faraway country than about a bus schedule close to home.) We should accept what people tell us only insofar as we have good reason to believe both that they are credible and that the claim they are making is plausible. To reasonably accept a claim on the grounds that Sheila has told him this, Henry needs to believe that she is honest and competent on the subject in question.

As to victims, the same critical scrutiny should apply. If victims are judged untrustworthy or their claims are deemed implausible, their testimony should not be accepted at face value. Such reasoning about victim claims is, in the abstract, proper and correct, but in practice, background assumptions and prejudice lead to flaws in their application.

A person who tells us something is assuring us that what she says is true. However honest and reliable she is, her assertion to us does not provide direct evidence for the claim. She is not simply an indicator of truth, in the way a thermometer is an indicator of temperature or a barometer an indicator of pressure. Rather, she is a person who is telling us something. In her act of telling, she is assuring us that what she says is true and offering us what she takes to be knowledge. If, after critical reflection on her trustworthiness (credibility) and on the content of the claim, we decide to go ahead and accept her claim, we are depending on her competence and honesty. In accepting the claim, we trust her as an informant; we believe her. An absolutely fundamental notion in contexts of testimony is that of credibility, where credibility means worthiness to be believed.[2] Epistemic credibility in this sense is clearly an evaluative notion. A person with a reputation for truthfulness is more credible than one with a reputation for dishonesty; a person known to have relevant expertise and perceptual capacities is more credible than one lacking these attributes. This notion of credibility is centrally linked to that of trustworthiness, which is judged both ethically (regarding honesty and integrity) and epistemically (regarding competency on the matter at hand).

We generally regard other people as credible and trust them as sources of knowledge. This does not mean that we grant credibility all the time and always accept what people tell us. Rather, there is an "unless" in all this, a kind of Default Principle.[3] The normal situation is to simply accept (that is the default); we do not simply accept if we have reason to doubt either the credibility of the person or the plausibility of the claim. We regard other people as reliable and trustworthy sources of knowledge and accept what they tell us, unless we detect or determine that there is some reason not to accept it. We trust the word of others when they tell us things, and we are prepared to learn from them, accepting what they say unless there are reasons not to accept it. Reasons not to accept could come either from our judgements that the person is not trustworthy or from our skepticism about the content of the statements made.

To believe people requires trusting them to be competent and tell us the truth. Such trust can be naïve, as when very young children trust and in so doing believe what their parents tell them. Or it can be a matter of default, something granted other things being equal, given that there is no particular reason to deem the other person untrustworthy in the context at hand. A third possibility is that of critically reflective trust, trust that is granted after examination of relevant facts about the person who testifies and the matter at hand.[4] So far as the claims and stories of victims are concerned, default trust and critically reflective trust are most relevant. If a testimonial claim is implausible, as judged by background knowledge, there will be evidence and reason against it as well as the assurance of the speaker in its favour. The hearer then finds himself having to balance two considerations: credibility and plausibility. A generally credible person has told him something, and the fact that this credible person has made such a claim provides reason to accept it. But if such a claim is highly implausible is just to say that there are reasons not to accept it. That situation poses a need to balance considerations of personal credibility against considerations about the plausibility of the content of the claim itself. The situation of a victim is often one in which credibility is questionable for some reason and the Default Principle—embodying a presumption of competence and appropriate motivation on the part of the speaker—does not hold. A very real problem for victims is that some of their claims are highly implausible, especially when made against perpetrators with greater power and social status.

To reasonably accept Sheila's claim about some topic, Henry does not need to be able to provide a convincing argument to the effect that Sheila is trustworthy on that topic. He merely needs not to have any reason to doubt her when she gives him her assurance about that matter. Credibility and plausibility are both factors. When Sheila tells Henry something, she is inviting him to trust her regarding that matter, and in a standard situation (the default), Henry accepts what Sheila tells him. In believing her, he trusts her and relies on her to tell him what she knows. Credibility, or trustworthiness in this context, itself has itself two aspects: the *integrity* (with regard to motivation) of the speaker and her *competence* regarding this sort of thing.[5] A good informant is one who is competent and willing to tell you what you need to know. If Sheila is a good informant for Henry, and he understands her to be such, she will be both trustworthy and trusted by him, with regard to both competence and integrity. Henry is not in a default position if he has reason to think that Sheila is untrustworthy—if he has (or thinks he has) evidence of her incompetence with regard to the matter at hand or of her dishonesty on this and other topics. Perhaps Henry suspects that Sheila is deficient in the relevant perceptual capacities, memory, and understanding; perhaps he thinks that she has poor judgement or is somehow motivated to deceive him or deceive herself. Nor is Henry in a default situation if what Sheila claims strikes him as highly implausible.

There are many situations in which the Default Principle does not apply and in which we proceed to scrutinize testimony, reflecting critically both on the credibility and the competence of a speaker or writer. We question trustworthiness, evaluating competence and honesty, and in principle it is not erroneous or prejudicial to do that. The problem is that norms that make sense in the abstract may be applied selectively, according to various biases and prejudices. There are interesting ways that this can happen, and the pitfalls involved are especially significant and dangerous regarding the claims of victims.

PITFALLS AND COMPLICATIONS

Not Just One Claim at a Time

Writing about credibility problems, Karen Jones warns that when we begin to distrust one aspect of an account, we become generally suspicions and tend to seek out signs of deception or incompetence, magnifying their significance for the story as a whole.[6] The problem here is one of enlarging the significance of an anomaly and focussing unduly on it when assessing the narrative as a whole. Philosophical discussions about the reliability of testimony tend to be simplified in their presumption that people assert one claim at a time. We have considered the case of Henry and Sheila as though she had simply one thing to say to him. More realistically, people tend to offer their stories or accounts—narratives about what happened to them and how they were affected by it. Most testimonies are narratives of what a person has undergone; they are not claims put forward one at a time. A pitfall in this area is that on finding that one element in a narrative is false, we may too readily become suspicious of the story as a whole. When we do this, there is a risk of allowing attitudes of doubt and distrust to spread too easily.

The "one at a time" approach that characterizes many philosophical accounts does make sense from the standpoint of strict formal logic. Stipulate that the narrative is a logical conjunction of a number of claims. For any conjunction of claims to be true, all of the individual claims conjoined must be true. If any one claim is false, the conjunction of them is false. So if, evaluating the testimony, we discover that one claim in a narrative is false, we can properly infer by deductive logic that the narrative as a whole is false. Thus, the falsity of one or a few elements in a narrative can serve as a basis for judging the whole narrative to be false, given strict logical reasoning. The implication here is that even if the person telling a story were deemed to be maximally credible—and that is often not the case for victim claimants—his testimony would not be accepted. But the apparently impeccable logic masks a problem here: a narrative containing a false claim can nevertheless be substantially true, meaning that it can be true with respect to the aspects relevant to practical deliberations in the case at hand. There are cases in which a claimant who makes a false claim in the course of his narrative should nevertheless be believed when it comes to the story as a whole. An account with one demonstrably false element may nevertheless be generally plausible and reasonable to accept as largely true. An obvious way in which this can happen is that the false element may be a detail not key to the plausibility and importance of the whole story.

To see how this works, consider a case in which a Tamil refugee making a claim for asylum reports that he fled civil war in Sri Lanka, never having fought for either side in that struggle, and had made his way to Thailand, where he then paid $55,000 for passage on a boat from Thailand to Vancouver. A government official investigating matters finds that this story checks out in most respects, except that the standard fare in Thailand for such a trip was $50,000, not $55,000. It would appear, on information from good sources in Thailand, that the claimant was incorrect in what he said about the fare. There is, then, reason to believe that one claim in this man's story is false. By deductive logic we can infer the falsity of the conjunction of claims that constitute his whole story. But other elements, central to his case, seem to be true: there was a civil war, many Tamils were persecuted in its immediate aftermath, there is medical evidence that this man is too frail to have been a fighter, and there are "people smugglers" in operation between Thailand and Vancouver. There is, then, a clear sense in which the anomaly about cost does not undermine the man's whole story. He is in all central respects describing his situation with regard to his need for asylum in Canada. Should his whole narrative be rejected on the grounds that it seems to contain a factual error with regard to boat fare? Should the person himself, telling his story, be deemed to lack credibility on the basis of having made this one false claim? And when we come to draw together judgements of plausibility and those of credibility, should they be allowed to infect our acceptance of the story as a whole? The answer to these questions should be negative in each case.

If we find ourselves inclined to judge the whole narrative implausible, and the man untrustworthy, on the basis of a single anomaly in his story, we should pause to examine the basis of our own judgements. There are, after all, alternative explanations for the false claim about the fare, and these explanations do not support either the hypothesis that the entire story is false or the hypothesis that the claimant is untrustworthy. This man may misremember; there may be confusions about currency transactions; the government investigator may have been deceived or made a mistake; the man may have been cheated and charged an unusually high fare; the difference is relatively small in proportion to the total. The point is not that we should trust claimants to the point of ignoring warning signs about credibility and plausibility but rather that even when we deem ourselves to have some basis for some distrust, we should pause to examine our own grounds for doubt and take care not to exaggerate their significance. We should take care not to prematurely reject accounts that should be taken seriously. Such hastiness may come at great cost to victims among others.

Judgements of Trustworthiness, Judgements of Plausibility

It is possible for the considerations of credibility and those of plausibility to point in opposite directions. A person deemed generally credible may make a highly

implausible claim, and at that point it is unclear whether to accept her testimony. Such cases are easy to imagine: suppose, for example, that a competent and
respected teacher were to claim that the principal of her school sent her messages
with descriptions of bestiality. She would be a believable person making a claim
that was, in itself, implausible and hard to believe. The Default Principle does not
give an easy verdict on this sort of case.

A person need not testify to a supernaturally caused event to make an astonishing, or highly implausible, claim. In her exploration of credibility, Karen Jones
carefully and interestingly considers this situation.[7] She notes that the aspect of
being astonishing is subject to degrees; it is also relative to the background beliefs
of the person making judgements about it. Obviously, people with different experiences and variations in their background knowledge may find different sorts of
claims astonishing. Astonishing claims range from reports of the miraculous, events
that contradict the laws of nature so far as we know them ("when the priest prayed
over him, he came alive again, even though his heart had stopped for three days"),
to reports of events that are merely surprising ("I was cheated by my former English
professor when I met him in Lhasa, Tibet").

Jones argues convincingly that there is a problem when judgements about the
trustworthiness of a person are too closely entangled with judgements about
the plausibility of that person's claims. These two strands need to be kept distinct. Doing that is not always easy, a fact that is of considerable significance in
contexts of victimization. Consider, for example, the case of a man who is a gang
member and has been arrested and accused of murder.[8] He claims to have been
beaten by police after his arrest. As a criminally accused gang member, he will be
regarded with some suspicion and will lack credibility with regard to integrity and
motivation. Furthermore, to many people, his claim to have been beaten by the
police may seem implausible in its own right; for instance, the people evaluating
his claim may themselves have experienced only benign and appropriate behaviour
on the part of the police. Many people will judge that this is not a situation in
which we can go ahead and trust as a matter of default; the Default Principle does
not arise. And, indeed, there are problems both with regard to credibility and with
regard to plausibility. If this man claims to have been a victim of police brutality,
he is rather unlikely to be believed. (Note: this is not to say that his claim is false.
It is, rather, to say that many people will not accept his testimony.) People will be
apt to question his claim to have been victimized, insisting either that the alleged
beating did not happen or that, if it did happen, he must have done something to
provoke it and bore some responsibility for the attack.

Jones argues that what is fundamentally important in such a case is to separate judgements about personal credibility from judgements about plausibility. She
argues, persuasively, that we mistakenly count the same thing twice if we fail to
do that. We might begin from our sense that the claim of police brutality itself is

implausible and then infer from that that the man must have been lying and thus lacks credibility. Or we might allow our judgement of low credibility to affect our judgement about plausibility of the claim ("look at the sort of person who is making this claim; he is a gang member; what he says about the police must be false"). Jones persuasively argues that both lines of reasoning are incorrect and for the same general reason: they too closely tie considerations about the credibility of a person to considerations about the plausibility of his claims. Though both sorts of considerations bear on the issue of whether this man's claim should be accepted, they should be kept separate. The question of whether someone might as a matter of fact have been beaten by police is distinct from the question of whether he is a person of good reputation and character. The first issue is about what police are likely to do or not do, and the second issue is about the personal qualities of the claimant. It is one thing to make judgements about the content of a person's claim and another to make judgements about his honesty and competence.

If we do not observe this distinction, we may too readily dismiss surprising or astonishing reports from persons we regard as untrustworthy. If credibility is inferred from plausibility, or plausibility from credibility, a needed separation of considerations is missing. We will, in effect, count the same factor (whether lack of credibility or lack of plausibility) twice and in so doing make a mistake. Clearly, this sort of mistake can be harmful in contexts of victim testimony. In fact, the case considered here is one of victimization: the man claims to have been the victim of a beating.

Facile dismissal of claims will be especially likely if persons seeming not credible put forward unwelcome information. A convincing and regrettably common example is that of a young and highly emotional person claiming to have been sexually abused by a person in authority. So often we are told things that we do not want to believe by people whose credibility we can question. We may (mis)apply the Default Principle and, by doing that, spare ourselves uncomfortable news. If vulnerable people claim that powerful people have perpetrated cruel and unusual acts against them, there is a dynamic of factors that can too easily lead to dismissals of the claims and narratives. We would not like to believe that persons of power and authority do such things. It is all too easy to mingle what should be distinct lines of appraisal, reasoning that since the claim made is implausible and unacceptable, it could not be that a reasonable and sensible person would make it. This dynamic of non-acceptance can easily lead to premature and damaging dismissal of the claims and narratives of victims.

To counter tendencies in this direction, we should be prepared to question our own judgements in cases where we depart from the Default Principle. We should carefully distinguish issues of credibility from those of plausibility. Furthermore, we should reflect carefully on the reliability of our own judgements and be prepared to examine the background beliefs and assumptions that we employ when making them.

Prejudice and Diminished Credibility

A fundamental problem concerning judgements about trustworthy sources and believable testimony is that they may be affected by stereotypes and prejudices. Some persons are commonly deemed to be more credible than others—in the Western world, advantages tend to go to those who appear middle class or upper class, white, dress well, speak well, and seem rational and unemotional. This issue was, notoriously, illustrated in the hearings regarding the suitability of Clarence Thomas for a position on the US Supreme Court. A law professor, Anita Hill, had worked as an intern for Thomas and her testimony at the hearings was startling. She claimed persistent sexual harassment, maintaining that Thomas had bragged to her about the size of his penis and described pornographic films of women having sex with animals. Though a law professor, Anita Hill was in this context considerably less powerful—and apparently less credible—than Thomas. Her claims dealt with her own experience, recounted as she remembered it. But Thomas denied them. Though covered extensively by the media, Hill's testimony was apparently not taken seriously. Thomas defended himself by seeking to shelter under the mantle of blackness, claiming some kind of extra believability for himself based on his being an African American man needing to struggle against prejudicial dismissals of black people. (Somewhat ironically, Anita Hill is also African American.)

As I argued in a 1993 article, this case illustrates Hill's rhetorical disadvantage as a woman testifying to the occurrence of what (on standard assumptions about Supreme Court nominees) would have been most unusual behaviour.[9] Her claims seemed highly implausible. On a ladder of credibility linked apparently to social status and gender, Hill did not rank as high as Thomas. As events unfolded, it appears that her claims about his behaviour were dismissed. Stereotyping and prejudice can result in the marginalization of certain persons and groups, who are deemed to be lacking in credibility, unworthy of being believed, and even, in extreme cases, unworthy of being listened to. The problem illustrated in the Hill/Thomas case is that of misapplication of what is itself a reasonable principle. The Default Principle about testimony, though couched in universalistic terms, may be applied selectively and prejudicially, as apparently happened in this case. People may be judged to have less credibility on the basis of stereotypical assumptions about their competence and integrity, assumptions incorporating biases regarding social class, race, age, gender, accent, ethnic affiliations, and other matters.[10] Such assumptions, whether purely individual or socially acquired, may influence our judgements concerning the credibility of others, and the result can be premature dismissal of their testimony.

People in certain marginalized groups may have a considerable rhetorical disadvantage, a disadvantage extending even to the point where others fail to grasp that such persons are making assertions at all. We may not understand their speech acts: they may strike us as mumbling and muttering, making up stories, fantasizing, being overly emotional or not emotional enough in context, joking, and so on—as distinct from making assertions and trying to tell us things. If, as seems to have been the case with Hill, a person is not taken seriously and not believed partly because she is an African American woman speaking in a high voice and making implausible claims about her higher status boss, there is an important sense in which that person suffers from discrimination as to credibility. The bias easily extends to judgements about plausibility; the claims may be astonishing to those who hear them in part because the hearers have not been in the position of the speaker and cannot easily envisage going through this sort of thing. In fact, many of Hill's claims about Thomas did strike observers in this way.

Drawing together such factors, consider now a situation in which a person deemed lacking in credibility tells us something we regard as implausible or even astonishing. We are unlikely to accept her claim or claims; in fact, we may refuse even to listen and hear out her story. We are told something by someone deemed not credible, and what we are told we regard as implausible, so we do not accept what this person says. Given our lack of acceptance, we will not acquire knowledge from what such a person tells us. We can reason that our dismissal is based on an application of the Default Principle on testimony. It is, indeed, an application of that principle, which as far as it goes is a correct principle. The problem is, it is a flawed application of a fundamentally correct principle.

We reflect: "Here is a person rather lacking in credibility; furthermore, she is making a claim that is implausible; given what I already know, I simply don't believe it. I don't accept what she is telling me." In such a case, the rhetorical disadvantage of the speaker will result in epistemic loss for listeners. Considerations of credibility and plausibility seem to have been mingled together in ways contrary to the admonitions urged by Karen Jones. Arguably, the outcomes of the Hill/Thomas case was a long-term deficit for the US Supreme Court. Obviously, this sort of dismissal can adversely affect our readiness to attend to the testimony of victims. In the Hill/Thomas case, Hill was, after all, testifying as a victim of sexual harassment. This sort of case points to worrisome aspects of the application of the Default Principle as to testimony. We seem to proceed reasonably according to that principle, but we fail to apply it with sufficient care. We may allow stereotypical assumptions to dictate facile verdicts on credibility and plausibility. Often, in doing so, we protect ourselves from unwelcome news.

In her widely cited book *Epistemic Injustice*, Miranda Fricker raises similar concerns about the effects of stereotyping and prejudice on the evaluation of testimony.[11] She argues convincingly that our sensitivity with regard to the accuracy and reliability of testimony is subject to various biases of a personal and social nature, and these provide the major theme for her work. Miranda Fricker developed a philosophical account of testimonial knowledge from the standpoint of *virtue epistemology.* Virtue epistemology can be explained by analogy with virtue ethics, within which the normative study of ethics is approached from the standpoint of character. According to virtue ethics, to determine what would be the right thing to do in a situation, we should consider what a person of good character would do in that kind of situation. Following in the tradition of Aristotle, proponents of virtue ethics put questions of good character prior to those of right action. Presuming for the moment the correctness of Miranda Fricker's analogy between virtue ethics and virtue epistemology, to evaluate the credibility of a source, we should consider how a virtuous knower would evaluate its credibility and monitor the source on that basis. What would this virtuous knower do? Of course, this question points immediately to a still more basic question about the qualities a virtuous knower would have.

On Miranda Fricker's account, a person who is a virtuous knower will be aware of the need to be a responsible and careful listener, sensitive to reasons counting for and against the trustworthiness of the source. She will be aware of various signs of unreliability in a speaker. A person who is a virtuous knower in this sense has an ability to monitor a source for aspects relevant to credibility. He or she will also consider the plausibility or implausibility (based on background knowledge) of the claim the speaker is making. To bear properly on the case, these originally distinct considerations of credibility and plausibility need to be considered together and, in some cases, balanced against each other. So far, Miranda Fricker's account is in accord with the Default Principle. We trust a person putting forward claims unless we sense that something is awry. We have a testimonial sensitivity in the sense that we are alert to potential problems relating to the credibility of the source and the plausibility of her claim.

Presuming no adverse judgements about credibility or plausibility, we accept what others tell us. But things can go wrong, and they often do. The presumptions we make with regard to credibility and plausibility are themselves based on background assumptions and judgements. Clearly, that can be a problem. We are open to the prejudices and stereotypes of our society with regard to such matters as age, social class, accent, race, gender, appearance, and ethnicity. We need to consider relevant aspects pertaining to competence and honesty when we assess the credibility of a source, and problems arise because our personal and social limitations (in the form of prejudices, stereotypes, and faulty information) can adversely affect our estimations of credibility and plausibility. We can discriminate and fail to take some worthy informants seriously. What results, according to Miranda Fricker, is epistemic injustice: we unjustly deny to some persons a fair hearing and, when this is done repeatedly, deny them even the status of knowers who have something to tell us. The denial of this status is enormously significant for interactions and is no trivial matter.

Miranda Fricker argues convincingly that people who are denied credibility on the basis of prejudicial stereotypes are seriously harmed as a result. Because people do not take them seriously, they are undermined as givers of knowledge. To fail to accept another person's claim with regard to her own experience of the world is to dismiss her as untrustworthy in a fundamental regard. It is to presume that she is lacking in basic competence regarding perception and memory and in fundamental integrity regarding honesty. To treat a person in these ways and to systematically dismiss what she has to say on these grounds constitutes a profound insult. The dismissed person is, in an important sense, dishonoured. For such a person, the results of persistent epistemic injustice are likely to be a lack in confidence and courage, an unstable sense of what the world is like based on one's own experience, inhibited intellectual performance, and significant inhibitions in conversations about fundamental matters such as one's own social identity. To be unfairly dismissed regarding testimony is to be wronged as someone who can provide knowledge to others, and this is profoundly disturbing to one's sense of humanity and personhood. It is a long-standing assumption that rationality is what lends humanity its distinctive value. Thus, being undermined as a giver of knowledge is something that can cut deep. Miranda Fricker states that victims of testimonial justice become isolated because they cannot engage in trustful conversation, which could assist them to steady their thinking and resolve issues of identity. In addition, prejudices that undermine a person's credibility may have a self-fulfilling quality: persons who are not listened to, not taken seriously, and not believed may come to have diminished capacities for observation, description, and reflection. Such persons may come not to trust their own judgement.

It is difficult to propose a complete remedy where epistemic injustice is concerned. But one thing can be urged. To be fair when assessing credibility, we need to be critically reflective about our own beliefs. If we find ourselves failing to take seriously a person who has a facial deformity, is fat, or speaks with an accent, we should examine our own attitude and assumptions that lead to our judgements about credibility and plausibility. To acquire reliable beliefs based on what other people tell us, we need critical openness to other people, a receptiveness to what they have to say. We need to be receptive to what they have to tell us, but not so receptive as to be gullible or naïve. We do have to monitor; we do have to scrutinize.

Let us apply these ideas to the abstract example of Henry and Sheila. Henry will accept what Sheila tells him and accept it quite spontaneously unless there is something alerting him to the fact that something is awry. If he does regard Sheila as unreliable for some reason, he is unwilling to apply the Default Principle in this case and should ask himself why. He should reflect on his grounds for making these judgements and be open to the possibility that his judgements about her are unfair. To the extent that he does this, Henry has a testimonial sensibility, on Miranda Fricker's account, and this means that he has an intellectual virtue essential for the acquisition of testimonial knowledge and beliefs. But his estimations are just that, and they may be flawed.

We are not always as open or as critical as we should be; we do not always listen as we should or assess testimony as we should. As a result, we may accept claims that we should not accept. But we may also fail to accept claims that we should accept. Certain persons—and whole groups of persons—do not enjoy the credibility they deserve. And this applies particularly to victims. Yet these discussions of rhetorical disadvantage and epistemic injustice do not explicitly mention victims. From what has been said, it is apparent that persons whose claims are systematically dismissed for faulty reasons are victims in one significant respect. They are victims of at least one kind of discrimination, discrimination with regard to their believability. Such persons are likely to be victims of other wrongs as well. Victims are typically less powerful than those who have harmed them; consider, in this context, women, children, the poor, persons with disabilities, and the elderly. They are often vulnerable and marginalized. These factors suggest what is statistically clear: many who are victims of wrongdoing are disadvantaged in various ways within society. Insofar as they are further rhetorically disadvantaged and not believed, they have little chance of receiving proper acknowledgement and care. And yet it is important that (with due care) the voices of victims are heard and that we learn from what they have to tell us.

Presumptions of Credibility Excess

Miranda Fricker does not take seriously the phenomenon of overestimating credibility, which she regards as relatively harmless. This element of her account has been criticized by Jose Medina, who offers a powerful analysis of credibility excess.[12] Medina points out that if speakers are systematically given more credibility and authority than they deserve, they may become dogmatic and arrogant; furthermore, others may hesitate to question them, becoming intimidated and gullible as a result. Thus, the accounts of persons with credibility excess may come to have an undue impact on public deliberations, to harmful effect when such claims turn out to be incorrect.

Medina observes that credibility has an interactive nature and is often comparative or contrastive. We can see this: in many contexts to be judged credible to some degree is to be regarded as more credible than some and less credible than others. This is not to say that there is always some kind of credibility pie to be distributed in such a way that when persons of one type get "more," persons of another type get "less." But, as Medina argues, there is a close relationship between credibility excess and credibility deficits. It often happens that one group dominates another and members of the dominant group enjoy many advantages with regard to status and recognition. Differences in power and status mean that members of one group generally enjoy more credibility while members of the other group enjoy less. So far as credibility is concerned, there is a disproportion.

Strangely, Medina does not explicitly consider particular clear, and rather common, "he said/she said" cases in which the testimony of one speaker explicitly contradicts that of another and the person presumed to have higher credibility is presumed to be correct. Because there is outright contradiction of one person's claims by another, there appears to be a fixed quantity of credibility that is to be divided. If one person gets more, the other will have less, in a zero sum fashion. If A is to be believed, what B says must be false; if B is to be believed, what A says must be false. When it is a matter of he said/she said, more for him is less for her. If she says a wrongful deed happened and he says it did not, there is an outright contradiction between their claims. At most one of them may be believed. Suppose that someone coming forward to make a claim is a member of a low-credibility group at a rhetorical disadvantage. As such, she is unlikely to be believed. Her claims may receive little attention and may be dismissed out of hand. In fact, her voice may not be heard at all. Now add to this supposition the further supposition that what this person has to say is contradicted by a member of a powerful group whose members are granted credibility in excess of what they merit. That person—be he a successful doctor, affluent executive, police officer, or priest—is very likely to be believed, and because that is the case, the person who contradicts him will be disbelieved.

Credibility deficits and credibility excesses work together in this sort of case, which clearly illustrates Medina's claim that credibility excess can be harmful. A person lacking power and prestige is disadvantaged; another, possessing them, is privileged; the elevated status of one person works to reinforce the diminished status of the other. Within this dynamic, unequal status, credibility deficit and credibility excess function together to buttress unfairness. Closed-mindedness and an unwillingness to be open to new information and alternative perspectives and explanations will serve only to aggravate the syndrome. All too often, the dominant perspective will seem plausible precisely because it is dominant, and voices that could challenge its dominance and moral power will not be taken seriously.

Thinking of such cases, we may be inclined to focus first on courts, asking who is testifying, who is accused, and so on. Contexts of formal justice are, of course, important, but they do not exhaust the contexts relevant to victims. Apart from criminal justice, there are issues about how the claims of victims are properly received by family, friends, teachers, doctors, and society more generally. If a person has been seriously wronged and harmed, it will be fundamentally undermining to have her claims of suffering denied. What we face here is not simply an issue of believability in a court of law. What is heard and accepted in the broader society also matters and matters enormously.

THE VOICES OF VICTIMS

If we do not attend to the voices of victims and seriously entertain the possibility that what they are telling us is true, we will not understand suffering and wrongdoing. Denials of credibility to victims can have terrible effects. All too many powerful illustrations of this point can be found, such as the case of the sexual and physical abuse and economic exploitation of tens of thousands of children in Catholic institutions in Ireland. These amounted to grave, systematic human rights violations.

According to the Amnesty International report *In Plain Sight* (itself a summary of three other reports), over many years there was little attention in Ireland to the welfare of children in church-run institutions.[13] Between 1936 and 1970, some 173,000 Irish children were placed in industrial schools and reformatories. When there was a Commission to Inquire into Child Abuse, some 30,000 people complained to it, and 14,448 of those applied for redress. But only 11 of those complaints were forwarded to the Director of Public Prosecution. Of those 11 cases, there was a decision to prosecute in only three. According to Carole Holohan, main author of *In Plain Sight*, given the sheer number of victims, there were circles in which people knew about serious abuse of children in Catholic institutions. Power was used to protect power, and there was no accountability. But people did know and were complicit in the abuse, given that voices were raised and many letters were written and ignored. There were clearly strong veins of knowledge about such abuse within Irish society more generally. Some victims had written about it: Holohan mentions novels by Mannix Flynn and Paddy Doyle, published in 1983 and 1989, respectively. But generally people did not attend to the claims and stories of children.

What were the causes of the abuse suffered by children in these institutions? According to the Amnesty International analysis, they included lack of accountability mechanisms, the low status of staff, a lack of resources, the transferring of abusers to other institutions and geographic areas, and the ignoring of complaints. This last factor was highly important. The Irish case was of course not unique: the transferring of perpetrators and suspected perpetrators has become notorious and a decried feature of the handling of sexual abuse cases by clergy and teachers in North America and Europe. The Church in Ireland was typical in that its concern was to protect its own reputation and those of priests, rather than to protect vulnerable children. The Church saw itself as a sacred institution above the law, and a victim in its own right. Church officials did not believe they were accountable to civil authorities. An absolutely crucial factor in this appalling situation was the absence of the voices of children. Institutions were often isolated. The testimony of children was simply disbelieved. Child victims were invisible in law, policy, and public debate. And yet there were mass violations, including physical, sexual, and emotional abuse and also gross neglect in very poor living conditions.

The list of wrongs is extensive. There was gross neglect with regard to food, clothing, heat, hygiene, bedding, health care, and education. The Amnesty International report lists as examples of cruel and inhumane or degrading treatment such things as smacking, beating (perhaps with clothes removed), punching, flogging with or without implements, assaults, bodily attacks, and the inflicting of injuries to the head, genitalia, or kidneys. One offence for which such treatments could be inflicted was left-handedness. Another was illegitimate birth. Children might be hosed down with cold water before being beaten, physically assaulted by more than one person, set upon by dogs, or burned and scalded. These punishments could be inflicted in response to bedwetting, talking at meals, complaining of feeling unwell, or for no reason in particular. Sexual abuse included forced masturbation, digital penetration; vaginal, oral, and anal rape by individuals and groups; penetration by objects; and forced public nudity. Emotionally, children suffered fear, humiliation, loneliness, denigration, rejection, hostility, criticism, verbal abuse, intimidation, bullying, and a lack of family contact.

Holohan writes as an Irish woman. Poignantly, she asks, "Why didn't we listen?" Her answer is summarized here. The general attitude to children in Ireland (as in many other places) was that they were not persons deserving status under the law. Those children whose fate led them to be placed in reformatories, training schools, or orphanages were deemed to be even less deserving than others. They were working-class children; their parents were typically uneducated and lacking in social power, and the children themselves were thought to be defective and unreliable due to their poor moral background, immaturity, and vivid imaginations. Children who had been placed in institutions were perceived as liars and persons not to be trusted. Their credibility was deemed to be very low. They were typically afraid to tell adults about the abuse they suffered. The standard approach was to disbelieve what these children said about abuse and to punish them for saying it. This approach was so standard and led to such hopelessness that many said nothing at all. Their personal experience was so at odds with official views about the Church that their claims were deemed implausible, even astonishing.

These children were subject to torture, to cruel, inhumane, or degrading treatment. They were victims who were deemed not credible because of social class, age, and social position. As children, they were at an enormous rhetorical disadvantage for basic credibility. Then there was the surprising nature of the claims they were making when they (or others on their behalf) did speak out. To say the least, claims that priests or nuns had committed sexual assault against boys and girls in their care contradicted standard assumptions about the moral merit of persons working within Church institutions. Stories of such abuse were regarded as highly implausible. Their content was surely something that people did not want to believe. It was far easier and more comfortable to simply dismiss such claims as lies or imaginings. This is a paradigm case of the powerless trying to speak truth about the powerful. What efforts they did make were nearly always futile.

According to Holohan, during the years in which these phenomena were studied, the Church in Ireland had power extending beyond that of the government and police. In Ireland generally, there was a deep fear even among police and government officials of offending the powerful Church, and a culture of secrecy prevailed. The state had granted it virtually absolute authority. Church officials were most concerned to protect the reputation of the Church itself; they defined the Church, rather than children, as the prospective victim in the case. There were a few whistleblowers, but no one listened to them. People later said they had not reported their abuse because they would have been made outcasts. Holohan comments that reports on abuse in Church institutions show a consistent absence of the voice of the abused child. Boys were assumed to be criminal; girls were regarded as actual or potential sexual deviants. Her interpretation in the end was that there was a sense in which many Irish people did know something of abuse within these institutions but had chosen not to listen to the testimony of victims. As a result, they "knew" and "did not know"—they had evidence to which they could have attended, but they dismissed it because it came from low credibility persons and alleged misdeeds of an astonishing nature committed by high credibility persons. Unwelcome claims were dismissed; had it not been so, the nature and extent of the abuse would have been known earlier. The case powerfully illustrates both the inhumanity and the danger of ignoring the claims of victims. Had they been taken seriously, many later victims could have been spared.

The children in these Irish institutions were victims of very serious wrongs. They had information crucial for their own welfare and development and, indeed, for the well-being of Irish society. And yet they were not listened to. Shocking stories of brutality and abuse were mostly not heard and, when heard, mostly not believed. Credibility judgements and prevailing assumptions about trust and moral character did not provide anything like a reliable testimonial sensibility. The effects were disastrous, allowing serious abuse of children to go on unchecked for decades. One may have doubts about the stories of victims, but this case shows, appallingly and powerfully, that we dismiss such stories at our peril. The Default Principle of testimony is sensible enough, but it needs to be applied with care.

Central themes of the Irish reports were echoed in a February 2014 report by the United Nations (UN) Committee on the Rights of the Child. This report noted that tens of thousands of children worldwide had been molested by Catholic clergy and that in response bishops had imposed a code of silence. Crucially, the report stated that children should be able to express their views and should be heard, urging that parents and guardians should listen to children and give weight to their views. Rather than seeking above all to protect its reputation, the Church should be guided by the interests of children and make their protection the top priority. The report urged that the Vatican ensure abuse was reported and that offending clerics were removed from office, police alerted, and victims compensated. It decried the failure of the Church to acknowledge the depth and extent of the problem and to protect children and prevent abuse. The report claimed that the Church had "adopted policies and practices which have led to the continuation of the abuse by, and the impunity of, the perpetrators." The report urged the Holy See to open its files on pedophiles and on bishops who had concealed their crimes and facilitated transfers from parish to parish. It criticized Catholic teachings on homosexuality, abortion, and contraception, which it understood as contributing to the contexts of sexual abuse, and it urged changes in canon law to ensure the protection of children's rights and access to health care. Noting the hierarchical power structure of the Church, the report gave responsibility for the protection of children and ending of impunity to the Pope himself. It blasted the code of silence persisting in the Church. Notably, no Catholic bishop had ever been sanctioned for sheltering an abusive priest, and it was not until 2010 that the Vatican directed bishops to report abusers to the police in countries where the law demanded that.[14] Compensation should not be made contingent on keeping the abuse and subsequent negotiations confidential, as had been common. The problem of abuse was not due simply to clergy who had mistreated children. Rather, a whole system had functioned so as to enable these crimes.[15]

Attending to the voices of victims would be a fundamental step in work toward change.

NOTES

1   Trudy Govier, *Social Trust and Human Communities* (Kingston and Montreal: McGill-Queen's UP, 1997) Chapter 3. A summary of my account is offered by R.C. Pinto in "Govier on Trust," *Informal Logic* 33.2 (Spring 2013): 263–91. There are many accounts of testimonial knowledge. An especially thorough one, early but still influential, is that of C.A.J. Coady in *Testimony: A Philosophical Study* (New York: Oxford UP, 1992). See also John Hardwig, "The Role of Trust in Knowledge," *Journal of Philosophy* 88 (1991): 693–708; and Elizabeth Fricker, "Secondhand Knowledge," *Philosophy and Phenomenological Research* 73.3 (2006): 592–618.

2   There is also a sense of credibility related, more descriptively, simply to persuasiveness. We may speak for instance of someone being more credible when he is tidily dressed.

3   The idea of default as explained here is quite standard. See, for instance, Jonathan Adler, "The Epistemology of Testimony" *Stanford Internet Encyclopedia of Philosophy*, ed. Edward N. Zalta, Spring 2014 <http://plato.stanford.edu/archives/spr2014/entries/testimony-episprob/> last accessed 13 Aug. 2014.

4   Trudy Govier, "Needing Each Other for Knowledge: Reflections on Trust and Testimony," *Empirical Logic and Public Debate: Essays in Honour of Else M. Barth*, ed. Erik C.W. Krabbe, Renee Jose Dalitz, and Pier A. Smi, *Poznan Studies in the Philosophy of the Sciences and Humanities* 35 (Amsterdam: Rodolphi, 1993) 13–26.

5   These distinct strands appear in Hume's essay on miracles, where he comments both on the likely low competence of witnesses and in the implausibility of the content of reports to the effect that miracles have occurred. David Hume, *Enquiry Concerning Human Understanding*, 2nd ed., ed. Eric Sternborg (Indianapolis: Hackett, 1993).

6   Karen Jones, "The Politics of Credibility," *A Mind of One's Own: Feminist Essays on Reason and Objectivity*, ed. Louise Anthony and Charlotte Witt (Boulder, CO: Westview Press, 2002) 154–76.

7   Jones, 156.

8   My example.

9   Trudy Govier, "When Logic Meets Politics: Testimony, Distrust, and Rhetorical Disadvantage," *Informal Logic* 15.2 (1993): 93–104. See also Jamie Stiehm, "Remembering Clarence Thomas and Anita Hill, Twenty Years Later," *US News* 31 Oct. 2011 <http://www.usnews.com/opinion/blogs/jamie-stiehm/2011/10/31/remembering-clarence-thomas-and-anita-hill-20-years-later> last accessed 24 June 2014.

10   Only some of these aspects are relevant to the Hill/Thomas case.

11   Miranda Fricker, *Epistemic Injustice and the Ethics of Knowing* (New York: Oxford UP, 2007). Miranda Fricker is always referred to here with her full name, due to the fact that there is another Fricker, Elizabeth, who also writes about issues of testimony.

12   Jose Medina, "The Relevance of Credibility Excess in a Proportional View of Epistemic Injustice: Differential Epistemic Authority and the Social Imaginary," *Social Epistemology* 25.1 (2011): 15–35.

13   Carole Holohan, *In Plain Sight: Responding to the Ferns, Ryan, Murphy and Cloyne Reports.* Amnesty International, Ireland <www.amnesty.ie/sites/default/fles/INPLAINSIGHT(WEB_VERSION).pdf> last accessed 14 Nov. 2012.

14   "U.N. Panel Criticizes the Vatican over Sex Abuse," *New York Times* 5 Feb. 2014. Other information is taken from the editorial, "UN Report on Child Rights Challenges Vatican to Mend Its Ways," *Toronto Star* 9 Feb. 2014 <http://www.thestar.com/opinion/editorials/2014/02/09/un_report_on_child_rights_challenges_vatican_to_mend_its_ways_editorial.html> last accessed 24 June 2014.

15   It should be noted that the spokespersons for the Church offered criticisms of the report and of the U.N. and groups within it. The Church stated that it had no intention to bow to the wishes of the U.N., which had many credibility problems of its own. Spokespersons argued that the U.N. committee had exceeded its mandate when criticizing Catholic positions on abortion, contraception, and homosexuality as harmful to children's health. They argued as well that the U.N. committee had been "soft" on such countries as Saudi Arabia, Iran, and North Korea, where children had come to very serious harm as a result of government policy. See, for example, Agence France-Presse, "Vatican Claims UN Child Sex Abuse Report Is 'Prejudiced' Against Catholic Church," 7 Feb. 2014 <http://www.rawstory.com/rs/2014/02/07/vatican-claims-un-child-sex-abuse-report-is-prejudiced-against-catholic-church/> last accessed 24 June 2014; and Deal W. Hudson, "United Nations Demands the Catholic Church Drop to Her Knees," Catholic Online, 7 Feb. 2014 <http://www.catholic.org/news/national/story.php?id=54141> last accessed 24 June 2014.

CHAPTER 6

WHEN TESTIMONY GOES WRONG

Credibility excess is a real phenomenon: people are sometimes deemed to have more credibility than they merit. As a result their testimony may be given insufficient scrutiny. The costs to accuracy, truth, fairness, and sensible action can be considerable. Rarely is it true that the sorts of people likely to become victims are granted excess credibility, but that can happen, leading to serious problems.

TOO READY TO BELIEVE?

Ironically, one source of this problem may be a growing awareness of the risks of denying credibility to victims whose accounts of suffering and wrongdoing have been dismissed. Premature and cavalier dismissal has led to prolonged suffering and abuse in a number of contexts, and public understanding of that fact has led to an awareness that victims' voices need to be heard. That understanding is profoundly important, but it may result in exaggerated deference to the extent that people feel embarrassed and somehow on the wrong side if they raise questions about victims' accounts. The conviction that victims have been harmed and have suffered through no fault of their own leads to respect for them and, indeed, for those claiming victimhood. With no clear notion of just what that respect should involve, it can easily extend to the granting of excess credibility, based on a sense that these people have been wounded, are vulnerable, and should be protected from harsh treatment. The need for care and protection is real, but respect in the sense of abstaining from critical reflection about victims' stories goes too far. Respect in the sense of listening attentively is compatible with close scrutiny of victims' stories and careful reflections on their accuracy and meaning.

A common feeling with victim stories is that we should simply accept them, out of sympathy and a desire not to repeat errors of dismissal. We may feel that to do less would be to expose ourselves as lacking in sensitivity and willing to inflict discomfort on damaged persons who have suffered from painful experiences. Another factor supporting excess credibility in some contexts of victim testimony is the sense that knowing what it is like to undergo such experiences conveys a special kind of moral authority. We may grant credibility or plausibility or both out of a sense of political solidarity with the vulnerable and downtrodden. Such solidarity is enormously valuable in many contexts—but not if it furthers injustice and inaccuracy.

A striking example of this problem is the case of the Martensville sex scandals of 1992. Martensville is a small town near Saskatoon, Saskatchewan. There Linda Sterling and her husband Ron ran a small daycare centre in which they cared for some 30 children. When a child of two was found by her mother to have diaper rash, the mother saw additional redness in the little girl's genital area. Speculating that her daughter might have been sexually abused at the centre, she reported that situation. Investigations found that the daycare had been operating without a licence. When social workers and police questioned the girl and other children, they were told of fondling, "something poked into my bum," being forced to perform sexual acts, being put in a cage, being taken to Devil Church, being forced to drink blood, and other horrifying things. A highly disturbing aspect of the case was that Ron Sterling had worked for the local police and had friends and connections in the police force. People in the town became highly suspicious that police were involved in a terrifying ring of Satanic sexual abuse of children.[1]

Six police officers, Linda and Ron Sterling, and their 23-year-old son Travis were charged with sexual offences. In 1993, Travis Sterling was found guilty on eight counts of fondling and touching. Six of these counts were later overturned on appeal. Ron and Linda Sterling spent five months in court and were eventually found not guilty, as were the six police officers. One of these, John Popowich, was deemed innocent when children who had named him as an abuser could not pick him out of a courtroom line-up. Popowich was a Saskatoon officer who had visited Martensville only a few times in his life and had no connection with local authorities there. A suspected perpetrator whose career and reputation were ruined, he had a breakdown, was hospitalized, and never returned to his career. When he was accused as a perpetrator on testimony that was insufficiently examined, he became a victim. As judicial proceedings dragged on, he experienced enormous stress as a defendant. Popowich later sued and received $1.3 million in compensation and an apology from the Saskatchewan government.

The problem with the case against these eight people was that the court found no reliable evidence that they had committed the acts in question. The only evidence available came from interviews with children, and it was shown that there were substantial doubts regarding those interviews. One crucial problem was that the children had been asked leading questions. Another was that they had been rewarded for giving answers of the sort the interviewers wanted to hear. Their testimony implicated accused persons, nearly all of whom were found in court to be not guilty. The verdicts were issued only after the accused had gone through considerable anxiety and emotional and financial stress—to say nothing of the damage to their reputations. The developments clearly indicate the need to be careful when interviewing child witnesses and not lead them into providing answers of the sort the interviewer wants to hear. In the aftermath of the mismanaged scandal, policies about such interviews were articulated and training was provided to avoid encouraging false testimony.

The notoriously mismanaged Martensville case illustrates the obvious: false testimony can be very damaging. In cases of alleged wrongdoing, the testimony of victims or alleged victims may name perpetrators, whose lives are gravely affected when the testimony is accepted. In the Martensville case, there were eight accused people eventually deemed by the courts to be innocent on all counts against them. Lives, careers, and reputations were damaged—often for years—because flawed testimony was uncritically accepted. Some of those charged reported, years after the events, that they had not fully recovered and remained suspect in their dealings with children even after the legal verdicts in their favour. Popowich lost an eye when a member of the public attacked him in a Saskatoon restaurant after the verdict. He never returned to police work.

The Martensville case developed in a context of what is now regarded as a moral panic in the 1980s and 1990s in North America about sexual abuse of children allegedly committed by persons belonging to Satanic cults. A popular and widely read 1980 work entitled *Michelle Remembers* described horrifying ritual abuse at the hands of a cult called The Church of Satan.[2] A psychiatrist co-wrote the work, which had considerable influence and came to be used as a guide by social workers and prosecutors. The idea was that during therapy persons could retrieve memories of horrific events that they had previously not recalled out of a desire to protect themselves and that these were real memories of events that had actually occurred. Yet Federal Bureau of Investigation (FBI) investigations were not able to find evidence of any underground network of Satanic cults. In California, there was an especially notorious case. Six members of the McMartin family were charged with 115 counts of sexual abuse at a preschool. A trial dragged on for years, and eventually all charges were dropped. As in the Martensville case, it was determined that testimony from purported victims was not credible due to suggestive questioning, children being led to endorse statements generated by an interviewer, and false memory syndrome. Another well-publicized instance was that of the Hosanna Church in Ponchatoula, Louisiana, where nine people were alleged to have committed ritual rape. Eventually all those cases were dismissed.

As these cases powerfully illustrate, an important reason to scrutinize the testimony of victims is that other persons may be wrongly implicated as perpetrators. Consequences to accused persons may be lasting and profound. These problems are most obvious in legal contexts, but there are broader social contexts (family, friendship, community, medical) where they are profoundly important as well. It was in a restaurant and not in a court of law, after all, that Popowich lost his eye.

Accused perpetrators may be innocent and, though innocent, seriously damaged in reputation, health, and quality of life by persons telling their stories of victimhood. This highly important fact is perfectly obvious from a commonsense point of view. What may be less obvious, however, is the harmfulness of a binary lens at this point. We too often have a tendency to think of victim and perpetrator in either/or terms, as though we have to support either one or the other, so that questioning the testimony of a victim or supposed victim will indicate support of perpetrators or accused perpetrators. Often we face emotional and social difficulties if we suppose ourselves to be taking a stand against an innocent and suffering person. We will not want to be in that position or to be seen by others to be in it, and as a result, there is a risk of presuming the guilt of an accused perpetrator. It is too easy to fall prey to the conviction that we either side with a victim or side with a perpetrator. We will not want to benefit a perpetrator by attacking a victim, and so we will too easily reason "this person appears to be a victim and as a victim he will be innocent and thus reliable and truthful; therefore the one whom he accuses must have guiltily harmed him." We carelessly assume that either the accuser or the accused is guilty and the "opposite" party is innocent, with no space in between. We too readily believe the one who appears as a victim, because we feel that we must be on the "right" side in an either/or dispute. Clearly there are logical and emotional pitfalls in such reasoning, which is grounded on a presumption of an exclusive victim/perpetrator opposition. Given that there are many cases in which that presumption is incorrect, the exclusive dichotomy should not be assumed at the outset. To scrutinize the details of a victim's testimony does not amount to siding with a perpetrator.

Even a person who is truly and fully a victim, and innocent with regard to the harm inflicted on him, may nevertheless be incorrect about significant aspects of the events through which he was harmed. He may not know just who did what to whom or how, why, and where that harm was inflicted. Additionally, there may be aspects of a perpetrator's situation that he may not understand and that are relevant to issues of that person's blameworthiness. The victim may also be mistaken about the nature of the harm or even whether putatively damaging events happened at all. We need to remind ourselves that victims can make mistakes—innocently or non-innocently.

We rightly sense that there is something—there *must* be something—that the victim of serious harm knows and others do not. But it is very difficult to put into words just what that "something" is and what its significance is in practical contexts. If a victim has suffered a painful experience, we are inclined to reason that through his experience he understands what it is to suffer harm, whereas we do not. The victim has personal experience not shared by others and has, apparently, insight stemming from that experience, insight not shared by others. What are the nature and scope of that insight? Is there something here that is ineffable? Or is there nothing at all? Could someone put it into words or perhaps express it in some artistic form? As argued earlier, it is hard to articulate those aspects.[3] We feel doubt and are unable to articulate presumptions that would describe the presumed authority. As a result of these sensed limitations and the imponderable nature of the area, we may come to extend victims' authority too far. We become reluctant to scrutinize a victim's claims about matters beyond that raw edge. Granting that the victim knows something we do not know (true, for the raw edge of experience), and being aware of considerable harm done when people have failed to listen to victims, we may be inclined to grant excess credibility.

In both legal and non-legal contexts, accuracy is important. The Default Principle should not be applied too easily: credibility and plausibility have to be examined when there are indications that things could be wrong. In the Martensville case, such indications were many and were initially ignored, with great damage to the community and individuals. We encounter again here the very basic problem of recounting personal experience. Typically, the victim will tell his story about the harmful experience, an experience that is by definition foreign to us in the sense that he has gone through it and we have not. The metaphysical uniqueness of that experience and the fact that no one else has had just "this" may lead us to grant a kind of moral authority to the experiencing subject. In the case of children, such a deferential attitude is unusual, unless background cultural factors such as moral panic about ritual Satanic abuse existed to support it. But an attitude granting excess credibility may obtain in the case of many victims or potential victims. We grant, often on the basis of compelling evidence, that persons have been harmed and have suffered from events or actions externally imposed upon them. Regarding them as victims and knowing that their experience is unique to them, that they have undergone suffering that we have not, we feel that we should defer to them. We too easily reach a condition of exaggerated respect wherein we come to suppose that it is inappropriate to question or carefully scrutinize what victims tell us.

When people tell stories as victims, we should listen and attend to them, of course. But emotional dynamics may come to play in ways that encourage gullibility. Awareness of the vulnerability of victims and the dangers of ignoring or dismissing what they have to say can facilitate carelessness, as can feelings of pity and compassion that stories of abuse and suffering are likely to arouse. It will feel heartless to critically question such tales, the more so in contexts where public awareness of the risks of silence has been exposed. We may feel guilty even at contemplating the prospect of questioning the testimony of a victim; we may fear costs to our own reputation (and offenses against norms of "political correctness") for doing that. Respect for persons is a central ethical aspect in human relationships, and conscientious persons will be aware of that. However, while it is easy to accept that persons merit respect, all the more so if they are suffering from harm imposed on them, it is difficult to explain just what that respect involves. To respect someone with a narrative to tell requires listening to that narrative and refraining from rude and unnecessary interruptions. It requires treating that person as someone with normal competence in perceiving the world, understanding human interactions, and describing what he has gone through. It does not presume believing everything that person says, even to the limit of holding back from questions with regard to implausible facts of evidence or personal lack of credibility in the context in question. And yet a fairly common, but incorrect, assumption is that to respect someone is to hold back from doubting that person's claims or questioning her about them. We may feel that respect compels us to hold back. In fact, respect should imply the opposite: if we think of a person as capable and truthful, we should suppose that she will be willing and able to answer questions, especially in contexts where the well-being of other persons will be affected by her testimony. That point holds even with regard to claims about personal experience of harm and suffering.

Respect means that doubts should be carefully expressed but it does not mean that they should not be expressed at all. In many contexts of harm and victimization, it is dangerous to accept testimony uncritically. By failing to scrutinize, we facilitate false accusations and harm to accused perpetrators. Sympathy and compassion, while admirable in themselves and deserved by victims, are compatible with critical attention to details, especially when these affect attitudes and actions toward other people.

THE IMPORTANCE OF ACCURACY

One might feel that it is not necessary to pursue questions of accuracy when people offer accounts of suffering based on tragedy or wrongdoing, that it is inappropriate to push critical questions at damaged people or to insist that they account for anomalies and implausible elements in their stories. Deferential attitudes to victims support such ideas. Indeed, one of the early motivating elements behind the South African Truth and Reconciliation Commission was that testifying victims should be spared the sort of tough cross-examination they might encounter in courts of law. Given that many testifying victims might remain emotionally vulnerable due to the terrible things that had happened to them, this motivation is entirely understandable. Early in its proceedings, however, the commission had to admit lawyers to proceedings of victims' testimony because some victims named perpetrators. There had to be some way of protecting such named persons from false charges and even from the inferences based on true charges. A prime reason for scrutinizing carefully the testimony of victims and alleged victims is just this: avoiding injustice for others accused as perpetrators.

The claims of victims contribute to understanding history and society, but only do so insofar as they are correct. Persons who have been seriously harmed in institutions such as reformatories, orphanages, or residential schools have important stories to tell about what happened there, and those stories are ignored to great peril. The same can be said of victims of sexual abuse, domestic violence, war, colonialism, apartheid, and totalitarianism. These persons have seen and experienced appalling harm in circumstances of conflict. Conflicts cannot be understood without understanding what has happened to such people; it will be insufficient and dangerous to attend only to the accounts of the victors or "top layers" of a society. It really matters to get things right, and to do that, we have to attend and listen to victims and putative victims. But we cannot uncritically accept every account they have to offer. Whether by accident or by intent, false stories of suffering abound, and the stories that are heard often merit probing about their accuracy.[4]

Victims may contradict themselves or contradict each other; they may also make claims inconsistent with known facts or plausible knowledge. Several outstanding examples of such problems are reported in a recent paper that describes several persons claiming to have survived Holocaust events due in part to protection by wolves. It is surely difficult to scrutinize critically the claims of a person who identifies himself or herself as a Holocaust survivor. Yet, a man proclaiming himself to be a Holocaust survivor may know that he is not so but may wish to exploit public interest in the Holocaust for monetary gain. For instance, Binjamin Wilkomirski published a best-selling memoir in which he claimed to have lived as a child in a concentration camp.[5] Journalistic and historical investigations found that his highly implausible claims were false: he was not a Jew and had grown up safely and comfortably as an adopted child in Switzerland. At that point his book, which had won prizes and been translated into 12 languages, was withdrawn by his publishers. Wilkomirski had described surviving as a Jewish child alone in Nazi camps. Scenes were described in detail, and the book was described as beautiful and displaying a poet's vision. In fact, the book was fiction. There was some evidence that Wilkomirski believed his own stories, or elements of them. His birth mother had given him up, and he had spent time in an orphanage before being adopted. Perhaps he was a man psychologically disturbed by the details of his own past and in particular his abandonment by his mother, and so he had invented a Holocaust history for himself to replace his true history.[6]

The point here is not that the perceived implausibility of claims proves their falsehood. After all, many highly implausible claims deserve to be considered, and some of them—even some that are really astonishing in character—turn out to be true. The point is that the implausibility of such claims provides a reason not to simply accept the testimony of a putative victim but rather to investigate and seek corroborating or disconfirming evidence, so far as that is possible. We are not in situations of default acceptance of testimony in such cases. Even one whom we suppose to be a victim may turn out to be dishonest and motivated by a quest for fame and fortune.

Sad though it is to say, there are many examples of false "memoirs." The attractiveness and marketability of the genre presses authors and publishers to favour the memoir form in contrast to straightforward fiction or non-fiction. Why does the memoir narrative have such appeal? One likely factor is that it will seem direct, forceful, and personal in contrast to other forms of literature. The storyteller seems to be revealing to the audience his suffering soul, and the apparently close relationship will invite a sense of intimacy and trust. When fraud is exposed, those who have believed the narrative are likely to feel betrayed. Apart from cases of outright fraud, a supposed victim may be honestly mistaken about some matters. He or she may have been vulnerable to suggestions by authoritative persons including therapists or sufficiently disturbed to have dreams and hallucinations that cannot be distinguished from memory.[7]

However much we may wish to be sensitive to the needs of victims and however much we may wish to respect them, it is obviously not reasonable to adopt an epistemic strategy of granting acceptance to every story of every victim. Issues of textbook accuracy and public memorialization reinforce these considerations; clearly, the needs of victims and alleged victims are not the only factor in these contexts. Acceptance of erroneous accounts needs to be avoided; the need for accuracy, coherence, and social truth are too important to be dismissed out of sympathy and deference. The value of truth is not only for itself but because law, policy, and scholarship will be led astray if they are founded on untruths buttressed by careless acceptance.

A CONTESTED POLITICAL CASE

A highly contested political case is that of Rigoberta Menchú, a Mayan Guatemalan woman whose work as an activist and author gained enormous attention for the plight of her people. Menchú fled a civil war in her country for the safety of Mexico and was first known as the daughter of a Mayan grassroots activist. She was highly articulate and had a pronounced ability to tell a good story and influence an audience. During a visit to Paris in 1982, she told her story to Elisabeth Burgos-Debray, an ethnologist well-connected to publishing houses in France. This interview resulted in the book, *I, Rigoberta Menchú*, which won an award as the best testimonial narrative for 1983. Within a few years, the book began to circulate in Guatemala, where it was much discussed. Anthropological scholars, concerned about the tragic circumstances of many villagers and activists, met Menchú to discuss the issues raised by her stories. She gained symbolic status as the representative of her people, and in particular of downtrodden and denigrated Mayan women. In 1988, Menchú (sometimes referred to as Menchú Túm after her marriage) returned to Guatemala as part of a delegation that included three other prominent exiled figures.[8] She was arrested and briefly detained. After her release, she became the symbol of abused and brutalized people fighting against the military to preserve democracy and served as a spokesperson for all Mayan peoples because of her reputation and ability to participate in the discourse of scholars and activists. Menchú led a strong movement for recognition of indigenous people in Guatemala and was awarded the Nobel Peace Prize in 1992.

Menchú was an indigenous author representing the point of view of poor people in a post-colonial context. Her book was a highly readable and deeply moving account that provoked discussion not only among educated persons in her own country but on university campuses around the world. It was used as an illustration of the importance of studying the perspectives of the non-elite. It served in discussions of key themes of post-modernism and of history as told from below— including the testimony of persons typically subordinated in society and scholarship, referred to as sub-alterns. These factors made *I, Rigoberta Menchú* a staple for many university courses, a status it retains. The book was often used as a class text, particularly in courses in anthropology, Latin American history, indigenous studies, and literary studies.

Problems arose in 1999, when a *New York Times* article by Larry Rohter described questions raised about Menchú's story in a book by anthropologist David Stoll.[9] Stoll had argued in a previous work that the horrific civil war in Guatemala was not an inevitable result of the struggles of the poor but was, rather, a conflict between left and right political factions, spurred by Cold War politics and the US government's support for the country's military. Stoll did not side with the Guatemalan army, but he did seek to complicate standard war narratives of "poor versus rich." He believed that villagers did not wholeheartedly support the guerrilla movement, as implied in Menchú's account. Stoll argued that although most atrocities had been committed by the army, guerrilla forces had also committed some serious violations and villagers were sometimes afraid of them and supported guerrilla forces out of fear. He maintained that Menchú's account embodied romantic ideas about indigenous people and their support for guerrilla warfare and that her memoir was not accurate with regard to problems regarding land ownership that had been faced by her family before the intensely violent events of the civil war. While not denying that Menchú's writing and activism had achieved much for her people, Stoll concluded that her work could not be the eyewitness account it purported to be, because it described experiences that she had not had. Yet there had come to be an air of sanctity around her work, so that it was highly controversial to criticize it.

Researching the Guatemalan civil war and guerrilla activities as they affected village people, Stoll had encountered a number of anomalies based on interviews and archival research. He concluded that *I, Rigoberta Menchú* contained significant false elements. Examples of statements that even Menchú and her defenders have acknowledged to be untrue include the following:

1.   Menchú had said that she was uneducated, having never gone to school, and could not read or write in Spanish. However, it turned out that she had been educated up to middle school level at private boarding schools operated by nuns.

2.   A land dispute was central to the struggles of Menchú's family, as described in the book. This struggle was described as one between wealthy landowners of European descent (Ladinos) and Menchú's father. In fact, the struggle was between her father and some in-laws, who were also peasants. Wealthy landowners were not involved, and there was no class struggle in the case.

3.   In the book, Menchú claimed that she saw her youngest brother Nicholas die of starvation. But Stoll found that her brother Nicholas was alive and well.

4.   Menchú described seeing another brother die; on her account, he was burned alive by army troops while she and her parents were forced to watch. Through research, Stoll concluded that that brother had been killed by the army in entirely different circumstances, and the family was not present when he was killed.

5.   Given that Menchú was for much of her youth in boarding schools, Stoll concluded that there would not have been time and opportunity for her to have worked on coffee and cotton plantations and as an underground political organizer as she described in her book.[10]

These matters were by no means small and incidental anomalies. They were central to the narrative presented in testimonial form in *I, Rigoberta Menchú*. Stoll did not deny Menchú's importance or even dispute that she had deserved to receive the Nobel Prize. (Her Nobel Prize was for Peace, not Literature.) What

Stoll questioned was the first-person nature of this chronicle of victimhood. It was Menchú's claim to have personally witnessed and personally suffered through the horrific events she described. Stoll argued that Menchú should not have represented herself as having been an eyewitness to events that she did not see or that did not happen at all. He argued that such misrepresentations made her account unworthy of acceptance and that she did not qualify as a reliable witness to all of the events described in her book, which was written as testimony. Stoll did not deny that the Guatemalans had suffered terrible things, or that the Guatemalan army was guilty of committing atrocities, that Menchú's writings and activism had served positive purposes, or that she deserved the Nobel Peace Prize. His point was, rather, that some events that she claimed to have personally experienced she could not possibly have experienced—either because they did not happen at all or because she could not have been there. It was not that the Mayan people were undeserving of compassion and expressions of solidarity; it was not that there were no powerful stories to tell. Rather, the point was that an account of one supposed eyewitness should not be idolized in such as way as to avoid critical scrutiny.

Of special interest here are aspects of the controversy that focus specifically on the role of a victim in testimony. Menchú did not devote a lot of energy to the task of responding to Stoll. She said that many people had used her book and commented on it, and it was not her job to reply to all of her critics. But some of the responses she offered did focus specifically on victims. The scandal about the book hurt her because "it humiliates the victims. It wasn't enough to kill them, to leave them dead. It wasn't enough that my mother was killed, my father, my brothers, but they even want to build a polemic around the dead."[11] This response assumes that if victims are critically questioned, they are humiliated—obviously, an overly general comment that goes nowhere towards offering any substantive rebuttal of Stoll's arguments. To question an account is not even an expression of disrespect, much less an initiative that goes so far as to humiliate the person questioned. Perversely, the one who claims to be humiliated is bullying the other by placing his questions in a category where he cannot raise them except at cost of personal disrepute.

One defender of Menchú said that as a victim, she showed courage and as a courageous spokesperson for her people, she was entitled to assume the atrocities that her people lived through as her own personal story. On this account, the people who were killed in the civil war were dead—an undeniable fact not disputed by Stoll and other researchers. Details about whether such persons were burned alive or died by some other atrocious method are not important. That the dead are dead is a truism, and it is trivially obvious that questioning factual anomalies as Stoll did will not make these people come alive again. The presence of questionable claims in Menchú's account does not prove that people did not die, and Stoll did not claim that. The questions he raised concerned the circumstances of their deaths and the identity of the persons who witnessed them. To be sure, for some purposes and for some details, errors that are merely incidental do not matter, as these defenders of Menchú and critics of Stoll allege.[12] But then again, for other purposes and for other details, errors do matter, and they matter very much. Stoll allowed that many thousands of people were cruelly killed and cruelly suffered during the Guatemalan civil war. He did not deny facts of death and suffering. If someone such as Menchú offers a compelling first-person account alleging details that turn out to be false, doubts about her accuracy and credibility will arise and should not be stifled.

One could argue that it does not matter whether someone was burned by kerosene or by white phosphorous, and that argument could have force in some context. However, when a person claims to have witnessed an event, it does matter whether the event occurred and whether she was there to witness it. In addition to issues of fact, important issues of trust and emotion arise here, especially for those who were deeply moved by the special qualities of effective first-person narrative. A statement by the Rigoberta Menchú Túm Foundation said that no one has the right or the authority to deny the pain felt by Menchú in her heart. On one interpretation this is true. In view of her suffering and considerable losses, Menchú no doubt does feel pain. What her feelings are, their intensity, how long they will endure, and how they affect her life—these are aspects known only by her or known best by her. She has endured suffering, and only she knows what it was like to suffer as she did. Menchú was and remains a victim of horrific violence in Guatemala. Her whole family was dispersed; her father, mother, two brothers, and many friends were killed. But from her suffering, as experienced, it does not follow that what she claims about specific events within the war is beyond question. If she claims to have witnessed a death and there is ample evidence that the death did not occur as she described it because the person is alive, or that she could not have been there as a witness because she was somewhere else, there is a problem. To state that doubts arise is not to deny suffering. Issues of fact can be explored and discussed without denying Menchú's pain. It is unquestionably true that she and many other Guatemalans suffered enormously, and that fact is highly important. But it does not warrant deference to testimony if there are reasons to question specific details.

Some who took Stoll's side accused Menchú's defenders of being anti-Western and, simply as a result of that fact, of having faith (beyond critical rationality) in Menchú as a narrator. One commentator, Daphne Patai, asserted firmly that it should not be supposed that when one of the oppressed—and, in particular, a third-world woman of colour—tells her story, she is the authority on the described events in the sense that what she says is beyond challenge. Emotionally and politically, it may seem difficult to raise questions, but to allow that is not to deny that they should be raised.[13]

Given the validity and importance of the Mayan cause and Menchú's role, first as a victim, then as a key leader and later a Nobel Peace Prize winner, many on the political left were reluctant to seriously consider Stoll's critique. They did not want to blame the victim; still less did they wish to side with perpetrators in the Guatemalan army. Indeed *ad hominem* and trivializing responses to Stoll's criticisms were abundant, alleging racism on the part of white people against brown; attacking the "outsider" status of critics, calling them imperialists and colonialists; alleging cultural misunderstanding; and charging that critics were siding with the wrong people in a struggle over land and social justice.[14] A silencing lingered, a fear that to deny aspects of Menchú's account would be to deny the brutality of the Guatemalan army. But such reluctance is founded on mistakes characteristic of exaggerated deference. In this case and many others, we can acknowledge the suffering of a victim while questioning details of her account, and we can doubt the claims of a victim without thereby siding with a perpetrator.

Given the role that *I, Rigoberta Menchú* had played in US university courses and in the formation of public opinion, it is unsurprising that larger themes about methodology, culture, and social science were embedded in the controversy over Menchú's work. Stoll was branded by his critics as a simplistic empiricist, one who naïvely emphasized facts over interpretation, values, and political solidarity. Defenders of Menchú and the teaching of her text alleged that Stoll and other objectivity-oriented anthropologists had failed to grasp the correctness of post-modern deconstructions of truth and method. In so doing, it was alleged, her critics had deliberately or inadvertently worked to preserve the distinction between the elites and the people, failing to properly commit themselves to solidarity with the downtrodden and oppressed. General questions about objectivity and post-modernism became part of the disputes about Menchú's work. It was alleged that persons insisting on factual accuracy in testimony about atrocities did not understand that post-modernism had established the "collapse" of the supposedly great narratives of Western progress and enlightenment. Wittingly or not, it was alleged, her critics were defending an outdated canon based on the work of dead white men. They were on one side—the wrong side—of the culture wars in North American education. Disputes expanded to include the nature of multiculturalism, the meaning of the presumption of the equal worth of peoples and cultures, and ultimately relativism about knowledge in general.[15]

Menchú's defenders maintained that the factual anomalies were not as significant as the broader truth about the civil war and the suffering of Mayan people. This point merits consideration. Granting that one or two factual anomalies in a narrative of victimization should not be judged as sufficient grounds for rejecting the narrative as a whole, we must recognize that a victim account may be substantially correct even when there are false claims within it, if those false claims are incidental to the whole story and can be explained away.[16] There is a distinction to be drawn between incidental errors and fundamentally disruptive falsehoods, though precise grounds for such a distinction would be hard to establish and the matter is somewhat context-dependent. Even in the absence of a general theory, however, it is fair to say that the errors and contradictions identified by Stoll and subsequent investigators were not purely incidental. The falsehoods they found in Menchú's book concerned family history, education, and the witnessing of horrific events passionately described and pivotal to the persuasiveness of her account. It is not plausible to judge these matters as slight anomalies.

Was Menchú testifying as an individual about events in her own life? Or, given her identity as an oppressed Mayan woman, was she testifying about experiences common within a collectivity? Does it matter? If so, why?

The *Testimonio*

The most interesting defences of Menchú's work urged that it should be understood as a *testimonio*, a literary form with characteristics of its own.[17] Appearing in the 1960s and 1970s in the wake of social movements in South and Central America, the *testimonio* permitted the emergence of hitherto suppressed voices such as those of women, gay, black, indigenous, and proletarian peoples. It expresses a collectively experienced reality, where the narrator is an indistinguishable part of a whole. It tells a story that needs to be told, challenging traditional assumptions about what constitutes knowledge. The *testimonio* is to be "read metonymically," meaning that it is to be read as a part that stands for a whole.[18] The "I" that invites empathy in a first-person narrative is, properly understood, a "we."

In this form of literary expression, an individual narrator, author of the memoir and speaking in the first person as though she herself went through the events described, is actually speaking not only for herself but rather for the whole community of which she is a member. As a narrator in this role, she is entitled to take onto herself the experience of the whole community because she is part of the whole and shaped by it. (The part is shaped by the whole and properly represents the whole, so can take on characteristics of that whole; hence, metonymy.) If some community members experienced an earthquake or a plague when a narrator was far away, she would on this view be entitled to describe their experience as hers, because she is always with them, as a member of the community. She is identified with the community, and when the community suffers, she will suffer also, as a member of it. The *testimonio* form is intended to allow for the identification of a person with the community of which she is a member and with which she stands in solidarity. In this form, the identification can properly be employed as a literary device, enabling the appeal of the first-person voice to render powerful the communication of experiences of various members of his or her community. The community, for this purpose at least, is understood as sharing experiences and as one.

The *testimonio* can in this sense be understood as an extended metonymy. It amounts to a sort of oral history expressing solidarity with a suffering people, based not on book learning, but rather on the lived experience of the people. In this literary form, there is an expressive leniency with regard to what one can claim to have experienced, but there is also a strong appeal to what it is like to be there, to go through it. It is a strange combination. In this literary form there is no implication of deception or even of fiction if one relates an experience as if the writer were there when she was not. In effect, there is an implicit appeal to the authority of the sufferer with the amendment that one can suffer as a member of a community. The first-person element provides a sense of the oral; it is as though the victim is right there, telling her story.[19]

The *testimonio* provides knowledge as a strategy of cultural resistance or survival. Its characteristics are that it is told from an individual perspective, based on traumatic historical or social episodes, and that it is a political statement against oppression. Thus, Menchú's story falls into the category of a *testimonio*. She is an example of a communal, indigenous narrator who has and is expressing in her memoir a collective identity. Menchú said, "I have my own truth of what I lived for twenty years. The history of the community is my own history"; and also, "Everything, for me, that was the story of my community is also my own story. I did not come from the air; I am not a little bird who came alone from the mountains, from parents who were isolated from the world. I am the product of a community, and not only the Guatemalan community."[20] Another characteristic of the *testimonio* is to displace intellectuals as authorities. A central issue in the Menchú case is whether anthropologists correctly see themselves as authorized to represent indigenous peoples. Stoll, her critic, is a Western anthropologist. Those supporting Menchú stated that the anthropologists were wrong if they thought they could appropriately represent indigenous people.

If Menchú's book was never intended to be a factually accurate autobiography or memoir in the Western sense but was, rather, written as a *testimonio*, it would not be open to the criticisms Stoll raised. This defence is problematic since it was made rather late in the debate over her work and may for that reason seem rather *ad hoc*. When her work was first published and publicized, and when it had made a considerable impact, there was no claim that it was a *testimonio* and not a memoir. No one acknowledged that experiences written as first person were not necessarily those of the author in person.[21]

There are broader questions about the *testimonio* itself. If an event did not occur, no one can witness it, and this fact will remain true even if similar events have occurred and there are people who have witnessed them. If a key event did occur, one cannot have witnessed it if one was not there. Furthermore, the logically minded will certainly question the aspect of metonymy, which will strike them as encouraging the fallacies of composition and division. In the fallacy of division, we infer that a property of a group applies to every individual member of that group. That is a mistake: groups can be described by statistically common or structural features that do not apply to every individual within them. (For example, a society can clearly be tolerant without every individual within it being tolerant.) In the fallacy of composition, we infer that a property of some individual within a group applies to the group as a whole. That is also a mistake: individuals can have properties that logically could not apply to groups. (No group, as a group, can be tall, although individuals can be tall.) Division and composition are recognized logical errors. The *testimonio* seems to embrace both. First, the experience of some is deemed to be the experience of a collective all (composition). Then, the experience of the collective all is deemed to be the experience of every single separate one (division).[22] Both steps underlie the writing of experiences of some within the group as the experiences of one group member who did not go through those things personally. (The experience of some is taken to be the experience of all; then the experience of all is taken to be the experience of one in particular—the author of the *testimonio*.) To have a part represent the whole is a recognized rhetorical device, but recognition of part/whole shifts as rhetorical devices does not establish the logical cogency of those shifts. The fact of naming a literary form intended to conflate individual and group experience cannot avoid the errors identified in the fallacies of composition and division.[23]

In defence of the representative aspirations of the *testimonio*, one could appeal to collective narrative and memory. There is a sense in which a historical event told and commemorated may become part of a collective consciousness; its occurrence, then, can be inferred from the products of that culture. As a Guatemalan Mayan, one might claim to experience massacres that one had never witnessed. But this sort of experience as a member of a collective in solidarity remains different from that of a firsthand witness. It does not deserve the same persuasive force.

To many outside observers, the form of a *testimonio* will seem a rhetorically effective exploitation of the power of the first person, though it is not cogent from a logical point of view. For many, the form has a special emotional power conveyed through the narrator's seemingly honest and moving account of what she has gone through and revealing her personal feelings about that. We sense that this person is revealing to us something intimate and true about experiences that she has had, and it is in her own first-person voice that the story is told to us. If we are aware, instead, that the author is using the first person as a literary device to tell of the experiences of others, our sense of revelation and intimacy is lessened. If we discover that these were not her personal experiences but rather those of others in her community, the power of the account will be weakened. For many, the finding of falsehoods in *I, Rigoberta Menchú* considerably diminished the force of the narrative.

If we know that a victim account is in the *testimonio* form, the force of the narrative will be somewhat diminished and will not have the power of the first person.

Our response will be: "This is awful; someone went through it; that person must have suffered a lot; such things should never happen." But we will not identify with the personal voice of the victim, even though the writing may be grammatically in the first person. If we do not understand the flexibility of "experience" described in the first person in a *testimonio*, we will believe that these are the writer's real experiences. Yet our conviction and the persuasive force underlying it will be based on an illusion. We will feel deceived and perhaps even betrayed by this person who had seemed to call for a relationship of trust in confessing to us intimate truths about his or her life and striking experiences of suffering.

If Menchú's account was in the form of a *testimonio*, readers should have been told that from the beginning. The genre should have been made clear at the start. It was not. The indigenous cause was eminently defensible and could have been defended without deception. The determination, energy, and power of the narrator are eminently real and could have been conveyed without deception. That victims need a voice and should have a voice is undeniable; that they did genuinely suffer and experience pain should not be disputed. But to say that much is not to say that the testimony of victims should be beyond critical scrutiny.

NOTES

1   I rely here on research by Erica Messenger, Haile McBride, Jeremy Altman, and Kayla Robbins, as presented in their essay, "Martensville Scandal." See also "Martensville Scandal," *Starphoenix* (Saskatoon) 24 June 2006 and transcripts for the CBC, The Fifth Estate, "Hell to Pay," 12 Feb. 2003 <http://archive.today/2bNa> last accessed 26 June 2014.

2   Michelle Smith, *Michelle Remembers* (New York: Pocket Books, 1989).

3   In Chapter 3 of this book.

4   Sue Vice, "False Memoir Syndrome in Holocaust Testimony," lecture, University of Sheffield, 14 Dec. 2011; Elizabeth Loftus, "Make-Believe Memories," *American Psychologist* 58 (2003), 864–73; and Paul Faulkner, "On the Rationality of Our Response to Testimony," *Synthese* 131.3 (2002): 353–70. See also Debbie Nathan, *Sybil Exposed: The Extraordinary Story Behind the Famous Multiple Personality Case* (New York: Free Press, 2011).

5   Binjamin Wilkomirski, *Fragments: Memories of a Wartime Childhood*, trans. Carol Brown Janeway (New York: Schocken Books, 1997).

6   "Fragments of a Fraud," *The Guardian* 15 Oct. 1999 <http://www.theguardian.com/theguardian/1999/oct/15/features11.g24> last accessed 26 June 2014. See also Philip Gourevitch, "The Memory Thief," *New Yorker* 75.15 (14 June 1999).

7   The case of Sybil provides a compelling example. See Nathan.

8   Arturo Arias, "Introduction," *The Rigoberta Menchú Controversy*, ed. Arturo Arias (Minneapolis: U of Minnesota P, 2001) 3–28.

9   Larry Rohter, "Tarnished Laureate," *New York Times*, 15 Dec. 1998 and Arias 58–65. David Stoll, "I Don't Seek to Destroy Menchú," Arias 66–69. Stoll's 1999 book is *Rigoberta Menchu and the Story of All Poor Guatemalans* (Boulder, CO: Westview Press, 1999). His earlier book is *Between Two Armies in the Ixil Towns of Guatemalans* (New York: Columbia UP, 1994).

10   Larry Rohter, "Tarnished Laureate," Arias 58–65.

11   The Rigoberta Menchú Foundation, "Rigoberta Menchú Túm," Arias 103–06.

12   A narrative can be substantially and importantly true, even though it is false in a few details, provided these details are about comparatively minor matters. The point is, Menchú's personal witnessing of the events described was not a minor matter.

13   Daphne Patai, "Whose Truth?," in Arias 270–87.

14   These ideas appear frequently in *The Rigoberta Menchú Controversy*.

15   Clearly such issues are too broad to be addressed here.

16   As explained in Chapter 5 in this book.

17   Use has been made of Kalina Brabeck, "*Testimonio*: A Strategy for Collective Resistance, Cultural Survival, and Building Solidarity," *Feminism and Psychology* 31.2 (2003): 252–58.

18   In the figure of speech, metonymy, a part stands for the whole, as for example in the expression "all hands on deck."

19   As a literary form, the *testimonio* also will permit incorporations of selections from other texts.

20   Juan Jésus Asnárez, interview, "Rigoberta Menchú: Those Who Attack Me Humiliate the Victims," Arias 109–17. Quoted phrase is on p. 113.

21   Rather, Menchú and her defenders initially alleged that her interviewer, Burgos-Debray, had made mistakes in transmitting her narrative.

22   For a detailed discussion of the fallacy of composition, see Trudy Govier, "Duets, Cartoons, and Tragedies: Struggles with the Fallacy of Composition," *Pondering on Problems of Argumentation: Twenty Essays on Theoretical Issues*, ed. Frans van Eemeren and Bart Garssen (The Netherlands: Springer, 2009) Chapter 7.

23   These considerations raise broad questions of culture and relativism as to standards of logic and evidence. It is sometimes argued that "Western" logic should not be employed to cast doubt on accounts of persons from non-"Western" cultures. I would dispute the claim; obviously, though, the issue is too large to discuss here.

CHAPTER 7

VIGILANCE

Dangers exist both when victims' testimonies are dismissed and when they are taken at face value. Balance has to be achieved, and there is no easy recipe for doing that. Victims may tell us what we do not want to hear, and we may dismiss it to protect ourselves from unwelcome news. Or, being aware of the frequency and dangers of that mistake, we may come to an overly deferential attitude to victims and uncritically accept their narratives out of respect and sympathy. Very serious mistakes can be made in our responses to victims. An especially prominent consideration is this: if we are reluctant to question victims and investigate the truth of their accounts, we may create new victims in those falsely claimed to be perpetrators.

About victim testimony, and indeed all testimony, it can, of course, be said that we should neither too readily dismiss nor too readily believe. So much is obvious and no more than a Goldilocks statement. The goal is to get this "just right," deliberating about all the correct factors and proceeding to accept what is true and dismiss what is false. But little guidance is to be found in the Goldilocks truism: clearly difficulties arise because we do not know how to determine what the "just right" approach and acceptance would be. It is difficult to provide useful general standards; to a considerable extent, these matters will have to be judged on a case-to-case basis. Plausibility and credibility (trustworthiness as to competence and motivation) have been cited as two basic factors bearing on the acceptability of testimonial claims and accounts and have been explained to some extent. What more can be said?

JUDGING PLAUSIBILITY

We can begin with statements of common sense. Clearly an account containing logical contradictions cannot be true: at least one of the contradicting statements must be denied and explained away. Nor can claims that refute themselves be true as, for example, when someone says, "I cannot speak" or responds to a question by saying, "I am not aware of what is going on." Obviously, neither can we accept accounts containing statements that violate established scientific knowledge. If a narrative contains claims that someone flew across a room, was tortured by aliens on a flying saucer, or saw a trained unicorn in the streets of Toronto, that story will rightly be received with the greatest skepticism. As Hume argued in his essay on miracles, even impeccable credibility on the part of the person offering such an account serves only to balance out the tremendous unlikelihood of such claims, yielding in the end a net probability balance of zero and indicating non-acceptance (at most charitable in the form of suspended judgement) as the most rational response.

Most often, though, matters are less straightforward. Issues about plausibility involve neither outright contradiction nor denial of physical laws but rather, claims that are surprising or even "astonishing" to the audience. As in the case of the Irish children recounted in Chapter 5, many victim accounts are amazing to listeners because the narratives do not fit well with audience experience and established beliefs. They seem irreconcilable with listeners' views about the world. An adult woman claims to have been raped by a highly reputable member of a community; a man claims to have been raised by wolves; a former child soldier admits dismembering relatives, drinking blood, and committing further acts of astounding barbarity. In such cases, plausibility will be low from the point of view of listeners who may never have imagined that such things could happen. For such audience members, these stories will contain astonishing claims, claims they will be reluctant to consider. As is colloquially said, such claims will be "unbelievable," a term that can be interpreted quite literally in this context. One's own past experience and background knowledge are obviously relevant to judgements about plausibility. Nevertheless, their bearing on the "astonishing" account requires careful reflection because they may lead to premature rejection of unwelcome claims.

Accounts of events that are extremely rare though not incoherent or impossible are likely to be regarded with skepticism. Examples come easily to mind—a householder claiming insurance after testifying that an elephant, escaping from a zoo, crashed through his living room window; a woman seeking divorce testifying that her husband of many years was a bigamist and had a second family in another town; a college student telling how a professor shocked and upset her when he urinated in class to make a point. Hearing such stories, many will be inclined to reject them out of a powerful sense of their great implausibility. If we do, we have to remind ourselves that these claims could be true—unlikely events do happen. (The strange events described actually have happened.) We should do our best to check further, especially if much is at stake.

Interestingly, so far as frequency is concerned, a contrary problem also arises. In some contexts, the fact of great frequency should itself evoke suspicion.[1] Taken together, a number of claims may seem highly implausible. Suppose, for example, that allegations about the institutional functioning of residential schools result in such common claims of sexual abuse that it seems every single resident was abused and every single staff member an abuser. At that point, the collective narrative will begin to seem implausible and scrutiny is appropriate. A skeptical careful listener will wonder whether this sort of abuse could actually happen to every resident. Here, as elsewhere, we need to consider the assumptions underlying our own reasons for non-acceptance if we do not believe a victim's story. As listeners and readers, we should carefully examine our own responses, our reasons for doubting claims that strike us as astonishing and implausible. A crucially important aspect of considering testimony is to question ourselves about the assumptions and beliefs underlying our doubt.

The same may be said if testimony contains statements that turn out to be false in the light of independent testimony from other credible persons. Some anomalies are incidental and do not fundamentally upset a person's narrative. For instance, a minor falsehood may appear with regard to an incidental matter, as in the case where an applicant for refugee status tells a story incorporating an honest mistake about a boat fare. In other cases, factual anomalies may be significant and serve as a kind of "alert" sign, signifying the need for corroborating evidence, as when a person claimed to have died a gruesome death turns out to be alive and has been encountered by several reliable persons, or a massacre said to have happened on one date has, by consensus of credible local inhabitants, happened at another time. Few are the events that literally happen to only one person, and plausibility questions will arise when different persons, appearing to be equally credible, testify as to different details on important matters. Whatever is the case, it is clear that not all of their claims can be accepted at face value, and some explanation for the contradictions will be needed.

Such checking is routine in legal contexts, but it is not only in law that scrutiny is needed. Issues of belief are as relevant to responses to victims in medicine, social work, and peace processes as they are in family and community relationships. To provide genuine assistance and support, we need to understand the reality of what happened to someone. It is important to recognize that a person may tell an untrue story without intending to manipulate or deceive: he may be self-deceived and honestly think things happened in the way he remembers. This phenomenon was suggested in the case of Binjamin Wilkomirski, the man who made fraudulent claims of Holocaust experience.

The work of Elizabeth Loftus is well-known as having established not only the unreliability of eyewitness testimony but the possibility of people being misled with regard to their own memory claims. Especially when people have experiences when under conditions of fatigue, alcohol consumption, or hypnosis, they may seem to remember events that did not happen at all. Such pseudo-events can be made to seem particularly real if stories about them are often repeated or if they are reported as remembered by family members.[2] The fact that exaggeration and false memories are real tells us nothing about their frequency and should not encourage the quick dismissal of victim testimony. Nevertheless the possibility of someone being honestly misled about what has happened to him or her is a real one. Especially in cases where the testimony of a victim implicates another person as perpetrator, caution is required, lest the alleged perpetrator become a victim of false accusations. Checking for confirming or disconfirming witnesses is important, as is seeking physical evidence. We should not be moved by deference to victims to avoid it.

In addition to the work of Loftus, several other findings by social psychologists merit consideration here. They have described two errors in thinking that bear importantly on our reflections about testimony. The first is confirmation bias; the second is the fundamental attribution error.

Confirmation bias is the human tendency to seek out and favourably consider evidence that confirms our views while ignoring or dismissing evidence that goes against them. For example, if we believe that a public official is respectable and doing a good job, confirmation bias will work against our acceptance of an anecdote that he swore at a taxi driver or refused to pay a housekeeper. If, on the other hand, we think the official is a crass and incompetent bumpkin, we will be more likely to follow and repeat every news story alleging misdeeds on his part. Welcoming confirming evidence and tending to ignore disconfirming evidence is a general human tendency and obviously not one that is restricted to reflections on victims, perpetrators, and their circumstances. But the biases of confirmation apply in these contexts as they do elsewhere, and they merit serious consideration. When we deliberate as to whether to accept testimony, we have left the context of the Default Principle. We are no longer in a position where we simply presume that people are honestly and competently offering us information likely to be correct. We have arrived at the stage where we need to consider and evaluate various strands of evidence.

In doing that, however confident we might be about our own capacities, we need to be aware of a confirmation bias in ourselves. We are, after all, considering testimony by resorting to our own background beliefs—many of which we take to constitute knowledge—and we should be willing to question the plausibility and correctness of those beliefs. We need to acknowledge that there are things we would like to believe, supportive of our values and those beliefs we already hold, and that there are also things we would not like to believe, tending to disturb our values and disconfirm beliefs we already hold. Obviously, the confirmation bias can affect plausibility assessments. In the Irish case, people did not believe, and did not want to believe, that priests and nuns had committed serious violations of children. Evidence that they had done so was ignored, as were the further conclusions that would have been implied if people had taken the children's testimony seriously. Here, as elsewhere, we need to scrutinize those of our own beliefs that lead us to reject victims' claims as too astonishing to be true.

In such considerations, we are likely to be influenced by our attitudes toward institutions, professions, and related roles. These factors can cause overestimations or underestimations so far as our judgements about plausibility and credibility are concerned. Confidence in an institution and in people working within it will make us likely to credit testimony that supports it and to deny claims imputing incompetence or wrongdoing.

JUDGING CREDIBILITY

As well as judgements of plausibility, confirmation bias can affect our judgements of credibility. We will be more inclined to make favourable assessments of a person, or a kind of person, whom we have found believable on other occasions. This person may be a colleague, friend, family member, media personality, or recognized expert. He or she may be a respected community figure or member of our own ethnic group. These people may be granted credibility in excess, as argued by Jose Medina.[3] The fact that people are in authoritative roles and have professional credentials is genuinely relevant to the assessment of their testimony, but there are contexts in which it can result in excess credibility. Lack of confidence, or even animosity, towards professionals or institutions may have the opposite effect. For example, a person might have experience with one aggressive lawyer, whom he judged to be over-charging and unhelpful; on the basis of that experience, he might cultivate a general distrust in lawyers. (Clearly, this would be a hasty generalization, but people do often think in these ways.) There is no recipe for successful scrutiny of testimony; this example is offered to illustrate the point that we need to carefully reflect on our own attitudes to avoid such pitfalls affecting our judgements.

As Miranda Fricker has emphasized,[4] there are persons we are inclined to regard with disfavour when it comes to credibility. We may simply presume that such people are ill-informed, unintelligent, or lacking in integrity based on our own antecedent beliefs and assumptions. Some of our own beliefs may reveal themselves to be quite irrational, as when we assume that an overweight person is less intelligent than a slim one or that someone with a hard-to-understand accent cannot be a competent expert. Such dismissals based on personal attributes that have nothing to do with perceptual and epistemic capacities are purely *ad hominem* and not relevant to credibility in contexts of testimony.

But to point out irrelevance in some contexts is not to deny that personal considerations may be highly pertinent in others. To the extent that we accept the account of another person and could not have knowledge of the relevant facts without it, we are trusting that person; we are depending on his competence and integrity in providing us with information, and we may act on the basis of his testimony. We are allowing ourselves to be vulnerable to him. Where the facts and feelings of victims are at stake, their vulnerability may be considerable, and sometimes ours is considerable as well. If we are relying on a person's honesty and competence insofar as we trust him for the truth, claims that are relevant in supporting or disconfirming those characteristics need to be considered as relevant to our judgements about his testimony.

Whether we can properly trust a person's testimony depends on facts about that person regarding his past record, competence, honesty, and situation. If we know that someone has lied about similar matters in the past, is highly partisan or dogmatic, or has vested interests in one side of a story or another, those are reasons to question his credibility and not to take his testimony at face value. The Default Principle does not apply in such cases.

There are many questions to ask regarding our own beliefs when we are reflecting on a person's credibility. Could we be granting too little when we do not accept the account of such a person? Or too much when we do accept it? And why? Once we depart from the Default Principle concerning testimony, we begin to reason about acceptance. Is a victim more emotional than would be plausible, given her situation? Is she less so? Is her emotionality fluctuating from one situation to another, making her seem, somehow, insincere? If emotionality makes her seem insincere, should it really do so? Is that fair, in the context? If a person has to repeat an account of a troubling event, there is every likelihood that her degree of emotionality would vary from one situation to another. And, too, we need to acknowledge that different people may be very differently affected by events. For instance, one victim of a burglary might become fearful to the point of moving away from a neighbourhood while another becomes defiant and resolves to stay to organize some sort of community response. It is important not to impose our own standards about the "correct" emotional response to harmful events. Factors of culture, age, and gender are relevant, affecting both effects felt by victims and expectations of others as to what the "appropriate" reactions to a tragedy might be. Reflection should unearth background assumptions, which merit examination. There are pitfalls here, and risks of false dismissal of accounts.

Social norms and moral commitments have a bearing on acceptance. Elizabeth Anscombe once said, "It is an insult and an injury not to be believed."[5] In the essay from which this remark is excerpted, Anscombe was emphasizing the fundamental role of interpersonal relationships and assumptions in conversation and information exchange. Philosophical accounts of knowledge have generally emphasized believing propositions, as in such statements as "John believes that his lecture was successful" or "Susan believes that her bicycle is in the garage." In these cases, the object of the belief is a proposition. One is believing that something is the case, and in the description of this belief, there is no reference to persons who might have conveyed the idea. One may discuss the evidence for the proposition in question. (For example, on what grounds did John believe that his lecture was successful? On what grounds did Susan believe that her bicycle was in the garage?) One can ask whether the supporting evidence is sufficient to merit saying that the proposition in question is known to be true, and not just believed. Indeed, these have been standard questions in classical epistemology, which has not been construed as dependent on sound personal relationships. Believing that a proposition is true, and having an evidentiary basis for one's belief, have been standard topics in the theory of knowledge, whereas the credibility and trustworthiness of persons have been less standard, at least until recently. That was part of Anscombe's point. She stressed that we acquire knowledge and information from others because we believe *people*, not propositions. In human interactions, it is normal for us to believe each other, and believing people is prior to believing propositions. Our very ability to speak depends on interpersonal interactions, which are fundamental in human life. It is because they are so fundamental that it is an insult and an injury not to be believed and it may seem a matter of etiquette not to question someone's testimony. We can feel when we do that that we are terribly rude, and this sense may make us hold back. It is especially likely to make us hesitate when someone is offering an account of his own injury and suffering. To avoid insulting people, we may defer too much, especially when they make claims about highly sensitive matters.

Anscombe's essay was written in the 1970s. More recently, a related point has been stressed by Miranda Fricker, who agrees on the importance of believing people. Miranda Fricker maintains that if a person's claims are frequently questioned, she may even lose the ability to think for herself. She will question her own thoughts and attitudes, looking elsewhere for a sense of what is happening and what is going to happen.[6] In extreme cases, there is almost a literal sense in which a person "loses" her mind. She will find it difficult or impossible to rely on her own ideas when they are frequently challenged or denied by someone whom she deems to be in authority. She is insulted as an experiencing, conscious being. If she is questioned systematically and discounted, about even mundane matters such as daily conversations or household affairs, the implication is that she does not have the competence needed to understand even her immediate surroundings. A more "authoritative" person, presumably better equipped, will step in to fill the role and do it for her. This dynamic is fundamentally undermining, especially when it appears in intimate relationships such as that between husband and wife.

In one case, an elderly woman developed memory problems, and her husband repeatedly questioned and contradicted what she said, even when the claims were about mundane matters such as the timing of telephone calls or the menu for supper. His behaviour lowered her confidence to the point, even, of affecting her ability to chat with family members. When the husband began to develop his own memory problems, and recognized that, he lost some of his previous confidence in his own judgements, and he held back on his contradictions of his wife's claims. After a few months, she regained some confidence, which was apparent in her interactions with other family members.[7] Sometimes she corrected him.

Acceptance is based on trust as to competence and motivation. Non-acceptance, accordingly, implies distrust, which could be based on lack of confidence in competence or motivation or both. To suggest that a person is not sufficiently competent to recall and describe what happened to her is insulting; to suggest that she lacks the capacity to offer a reliable account is similarly so. These reflections bear out Anscombe's remark about the insult implied when one does not believe another person. Not wishing to insult, we may find it difficult to inflict the injuries of insult on others, especially when talking with them face to face. The challenge is likely to be especially felt when we are hearing the accounts of family members or close friends. We will not wish to inflict injury and not wish to insult and as a result may feel a reluctance to openly question what we are told. Our instincts are commendable, but they may lead us to exaggerated deference. Stories of supposed victimization are especially sensitive in this regard, as we feel pressed to offer sympathy and support. We may feel pressed by a kind of obligation to believe, or at least try to believe, what a victim tells us. We may be influenced by felt moral commitments, resulting in exaggerated estimates of credibility.

The situation points to a more general question. How much should factors of loyalty and prior trust count, when there is also evidence regarding competence and honesty about the topic at hand? How important is it to arrive at an accurate judgement about what occurred? (For the time of a mail delivery, probably, it is not very important. For a statement of diagnosis by a medical specialist, probably it is very important.) How far do obligations to family members extend? Should we hold back from questioning their claims out of solidarity or consideration? These questions may be debated. Here, as elsewhere, the likely truth of claims made remains of central importance. Some basics are clear. If a family member has a shaky general record, being known to be in the early stages of dementia or to have been untruthful and manipulative in the past, the mere fact that he is a family member does not support an overwhelming obligation to accept what that person says. Loyalty goes only so far.

A fascinating article by Gloria Origgi explores such issues. Origgi maintains that there are many factors underlying our acceptance or non-acceptance of the claims made by other people. She allows that Miranda Fricker was correct in emphasizing how prejudices may lead us astray but argues that there are other important elements as well. In addition to assessing for plausibility of content and the reliability of the person testifying, we consider other aspects; we employ institutional norms of authority and reputation, emotional reactions, and moral commitments; we adopt cultural attitudes and values and will not pause to criticize them unless there is a special need to do so. John Locke famously discounted testimony as an inadequate basis of knowledge, describing its effects as ideas merely floating about in our minds. Like most philosophical writers on testimony, Origgi rejects accounts of this type. Reflecting on Locke's negative account of testimony, Origgi states poetically that what he disparaged as the mere floating of other people's words in our minds is the price we pay for thinking.[8] We do evaluate many of the things people tell us, and we do so with regard both to the plausibility of the claims and to the credibility of the people. In circumstances where the Default Principle does not apply, we have to rely on our own thinking. But this is a tricky and complex matter: after all, our own thinking in turn is likely to employ social and cultural norms that merit scrutiny. It would surely be incorrect to judge that all such norms are faulty due to prejudice. We cannot extend vigilance to everything, although we need to be aware both of our need for it and of the fallibility of the mechanisms we employ.

The fundamental attribution error identified by social psychologists is relevant to credibility assessment. This error concerns explanations on the basis of character; the attribution error occurs when relevant situational factors are not taken into account. Ignoring relevant situational factors results in a double standard, one that is often exhibited when we blame people for misdeeds or mistakes. When we make mistakes ourselves, we tend to attribute them to some feature of our circumstances; for example, "I drove into that wall because my new medication makes me inattentive." But when we seek to explain comparable actions of others, we attribute them to faults in character; for example, "he drove into that wall because he is such a careless person." The fundamental attribution error allows us to favour and excuse ourselves on the basis of circumstances, while blaming others on the basis of character. It is a kind of my-side bias: we overestimate the significance of character in our explanation of (other people's) actions while underestimating it in the explanation of our own. They are careless and make mistakes, while we are victims of circumstance.

Suppose that a professor needing funding for his program is denied it by the dean. Complaining, he blames the dean for this decision, maintaining that the dean is a number cruncher who manages university issues solely in terms of the lowest common denominator—money. After some period of time, the dean resigns and this professor becomes the new dean. Now, he is likely himself to consider the budget as a whole, see areas where money might be saved, carefully consider the needs of a number of different programs, and so on. He does this because this is the sort of thing deans do: the role of dean demands it. This example should not suggest that either faculty members or deans are victims. Rather, it illustrates the point made by psychologists who have studied the fundamental attribution error. They maintain that the explanation of the behaviour lies in role and circumstance as distinct from personal character.[9] When this man had to appeal to the dean, he found the dean to be a number cruncher. When he became the dean, he crunched numbers himself. He failed to distinguish person characteristics from attitudes and actions required by a professional role, thereby committing the fundamental attribution error. Many studies question attributions to character, supporting instead the overwhelming significance of situational factors in explanations of behaviour, whether it is us or them.

Studies of the fundamental attribution error need not concern actual or potential victims, but they apply in this context as in others. If such people are telling their stories in contexts where they are tired, ill, frightened, under the glare of media, fearing prosecution, or in the presence of powerful adversaries, those circumstances are likely to have significant effects on the accuracy of their accounts. Errors and inconsistencies attributable to circumstances may arise, and such errors do not establish that the person is dishonest or manipulative as a matter of character. He or she should not be regarded as generally lacking credibility. A generally dishonest person may be honest in a circumstance that would encourage honesty; a generally inaccurate person may be accurate in a circumstance that favours accuracy. One would hope that being in a court of law, or before a public inquiry, is a circumstance that will encourage honesty. But notoriously, that is by no means guaranteed.

Could situation be more important than character, so far as credibility is concerned? Could the claims of a victim properly be dismissed because he or she was a person of "bad character" and not an ideal victim?[10] Some who have written about action in trying circumstances go so far as to dispute the very idea of character. There are just people, making decisions in circumstances that are sometimes very trying and extraordinary. To reflect on the credibility of anyone offering a claim or account, we consider what we know about that person's competence and motivation. This much is standard in accounts of testimony. Aspects of character and credibility mainly concern the factor of motivation. Is this person trying honestly to tell us something? Is she trying to help us out? Is she trying to sell us something? Is she seeking to manipulate and deceive?

Suppose that, due to the overwhelming influence of circumstances, there were actually no such thing as character. On that radical hypothesis, it would not make sense to assess the credibility of a person by considering evidence about character. Credibility assessments would need to be dropped or reinterpreted. If we were to drop the notion of character altogether, then we would not try to assess personal trustworthiness as an aspect of character. Taking situational analysis with utmost seriousness, we would conclude that that there should be no such question as to whether a person is generally trustworthy or not. General trustworthiness would be an aspect of character, and character, on a fully situational account, would not exist. If we wanted to preserve a characteristic linked to that of trustworthiness, we could interpret it entirely as a matter of the likelihood of certain behaviours.

Trustworthiness on this sort of account would not be personal; it would have nothing to do with personal character or motivation. Rather, it would be inductively grounded in generalizations about how people behave in this or that kind of situation. If we pursued this option, relevant evidence would be about what people generally do in this sort of role or situation and not about what this person has said and done in other situations.

Any claim to the effect that, for credibility, situation is even more important than character, would be bold indeed. A claim to the effect that "character" is so overwhelmed by circumstance that it does not even exist would be bolder still. There is no proposal here that we should shift our thinking to this extent. To omit considerations of personal credibility runs contrary both to everyday practice and to standard accounts of testimony. We will not endorse that claim. Suffice it to say that considerations of credibility should at least consider situational factors when considering behaviour to be evidence of a flawed character.

THE TEMPTATIONS OF STORIES

The idea of telling one's story and being heard with respect is attractive and highly important. A person may have a powerful sense of ownership of his story, coming even to ground in it his very identity. Sometimes a person is even socio-economically dependent on having his story accepted as true. He may react very negatively if his account is challenged and insist that no one has a right to question his personal memory of details of his own suffering. In the stories of victims, as in other stories, events can be misinterpreted, misremembered, exaggerated, or even entirely invented. Reasons for false elements vary, but in the end, inaccurate results may be dangerous to accused perpetrators, the public at large, family members, and even victims themselves. A person may honestly be deceived by the story she tells herself, especially if it is vivid, intensely felt, and oft-repeated. Accounts incorporating significant errors are unlikely to be helpful in the end, even when the goal of "sharing stories" is community building, reconciliation after conflict, or the prevention of further tragic alienation of persons. Even though there may be enormous difficulties in raising questions, so far as emotion and etiquette are concerned, these factors have to be taken seriously. Challenges are often relevant and necessary, for obvious reasons. If workshop, therapeutic, and truth commission processes license victims to tell their stories and yet make no provision for respectful questioning and criticism, they are flawed.

The narrative form itself has considerable charms insofar as it displays a kind of fit, coherence, and memorability. These qualities may discourage questions because the story itself is so "good." Diverse elements draw together in a meaningful way, and there is a development of events toward an ending. That sense of meaning, as well as the vividness characteristics of many stories, serves to make many narratives memorable. Often a narrative account is of tremendous interest, especially when told in the first person. Published as a memoir, it may generate valuable attention and funding for an important cause. The narrative of a person who has suffered terribly and somehow come through it to survive receives considerable attention and sympathy. Its coherence and appeal may gain it credit, and if the author has an attractive personality, his credibility and his story will be hard to attack. Often such accounts are useful for healing, history, policy, and much else. But they may receive more credit than they deserve.

The fact that first-person "memoirs" often contain errors and even deliberate falsehood is both important and fascinating in this context. It points to considerable temptation, for publishers and authors, to favour first-person accounts and even to amend details so as to make a "better" story. The first-person account of suffering suggests by its form that the writer is exposing himself or herself to the reader—that she is trusting the reader with this account of her deep-felt emotions and responses. What is conveyed is a message to this effect: "I know what it is like to experience these terrible things, and I am telling that to you." Responding to that sense of being given access to a deeply felt story, the reader will come to trust the writer for an honest telling of events and feelings. If it turns out that the events recounted transpired in other ways or did not happen at all, the reader is likely to feel exploited and betrayed.[11] The reactions of the public to such exposures indicate the powerful attraction of the first person—our sense that someone who has undergone profound suffering is sharing his tragic experiences, which provide to trusted others a valuable lesson about life. Disappointment, even fury, come from learning that the author has invented many events and did not experience these things at all. (See the discussion of I, Rigoberta Menchú in Chapter 6.)

Sadly, the fabricated victim "memoir" has almost become a genre in its own right. Wikipedia treats the matter and lists many examples, including accounts of surviving the Holocaust, emerging from drug cultures, and suffering under "honour" practices in the Middle East. In fact, publishers' resource limitations and background cultural attitudes serve to encourage the genre. There is considerable public interest in someone who has "been there," suffering horrifying and tragic events, and has then manage to "survive," willing to tell all. That interest often leads to considerable attention, exaggerated deference, insufficient fact-checking by publishers and potential financial rewards for both authors and publishers. Given current shifts and difficulties in the publishing industry, there is a strong temptation to cut corners in the editing process, and many publishers have been left with limited provisions for fact-checking. Examples of false Holocaust memoirs include *Angel at the Fence* (2009), in which the author really is a survivor but falsified details to make a more dramatic love story. Another false memoir is that of Margaret Seltzer (M.B. Jones), who wrote *Love and Consequences* (2008). Norma Khouri achieved considerable success with *Forbidden Love* (2003), a story of honour killing based on claimed experiences in Jordan. She never lived there. And, of course, there is the Wilkomirski case (see Chapter 6).[12]

Ishmael Beah is a former child soldier from Sierra Leone and (as of 2007) official UNICEF Advocate for Children Affected by War. Rescued from a UNICEF camp in 1995 and assisted by a US aid worker who became his surrogate mother, Beah now lives in the United States. He is the author of a highly successful memoir of his experiences as a child soldier in the brutal Sierra Leone civil war (1992 to 2000). That memoir, *A Long Way Gone: Memoir of a Boy Soldier*, was published in 2007. Beah has also written a second book *Radiance of Tomorrow* (2014), in the form of a novel about persons returning to a village devastated by civil war and incorporating returning child soldiers who had used machetes to attack fellow villagers during the war. The second book is a novel rather than a memoir. Beah did not return to live in his village when the war was over but went to the United States where he completed high school and university and became a best-selling author. Reviews of Beah's second book are mixed, but it seems unlikely that it will gain the attention and sales of the first.[13]

Concerning the first book, some provocative questions have arisen. Beah claims to have been a child soldier for two years, but a number of sources from his village Mattru Jong agree that such an attack as the one described at the outset of his memoir occurred in 1995, not in 1993 as he claimed. Had this been the case, Beah's experience of child soldiery would have been quite short; the plausibility of a claim central to the factual credibility of his narrative would be undermined. It was the experiences of Bob Lloyd, an Australian mining engineer based in Sierra Leone, that led to investigations by journalists for the newspaper *The Australian*. On arriving in Sierra Leone to work at a mine, Lloyd met a man who claimed to be Beah's father. That claim turned out to be incorrect; the man was a distant cousin. But in posing questions about the matter, Lloyd was so frustrated by responses given by Beah's publisher and agent that he contacted Australian journalists who took up the story. Peter Wilson was among them. Travelling to Sierra Leone to investigate details of Beah's account, Wilson found a number of credible witnesses who contradicted some fundamental points. These included the timing of the attack on the village, Mattru Jong; Beah's whereabouts between January 1993 and January 1995; whether Beah had been shot three times in the foot; and whether a deadly fight, described as killing six and happening in a UNICEF camp in Freetown in 1996, had even happened at all.[14] The matter of chronology was crucial, since if the attack on Mattru Jong had happened in 1995, Beah would have been a child soldier for only a few months. In fact, given that he was 15 in 1995, he would not have qualified as a child soldier at all, according to some definitions of that term. Because Beah claimed to have a photographic memory, the excuse that a child drugged and in highly traumatic circumstances might well confuse some details was unavailable to him when he sought to defend his claims. Notably, he had begun to write his first book as a novel and shifted to the form of a memoir.

Beah, his agent, his publisher, and his surrogate mother all rejected criticisms, avoided questions, and refused to revise details of his account. Wilson did not wish to deny that Beah had suffered hugely and recovered amazingly, but he did present considerable evidence of distortion of chronology and some facts. He was attacked for criticizing a person who had suffered so much and had done so much for the valid and important cause of child soldiers. It felt like "shooting Bambi," he said.[15]

The response to David Frey's *A Million Little Pieces*[16] provides just one of many further examples of disputed memoirs. This work was originally submitted to publishers as a novel and rejected in that form. It was then submitted as a memoir of the author's struggles with substance abuse, illness, crime, and poverty. In the form of a first-person memoir, the book was accepted. The publishers had sensed in the public a thirst for memoirs of suffering and survival; as a memoir, the work told an inspiring story with stunning details about the horrors that he experienced, his responses to them, and what he went through to survive. Frey was a victim—of social circumstance, of illness, and of wrongdoing. His account offered vivid and astounding details about vomit, injury, sexual failings, root canals done without anesthesia, a period spent in jail, and the death of a girlfriend who committed suicide by hanging herself. The publishers wanted a work that could be marketed as the story of an individual who suffered enormously and somehow recovered from highly damaging circumstances. They did not check the facts before publishing it as a memoir. Oprah Winfrey had publicized the book on her popular television show and contributed greatly to its market success. She was horrified and publicly called Frey to account when the errors were exposed after *The Smoking Gun* did extensive work attempting to confirm the books' claims against police reports.[17]

With regard to Frey (and not Beah), questions can be raised as to whether this is actually a case of false testimony offered by a supposed victim. The book presents a tale of suffering in the voice of a narrator supposed to be the author. To a large extent, according to his own story, Frey was harmed by his own actions rather than by externally imposed events or the actions of others. The Frey "character" was harmed by addiction and ill-treatment. The memoir is more one of lurid misadventure and suffering than of victimhood, and, indeed, Frey did not exactly claim to have been a victim. This case is clearly an instance of a falsified memoir, but it is somewhat less clearly an instance of an author's exploitation of his victim status. Perhaps his flawed memoir indicates only our interest in suffering as told in the first person and less clearly our deference to victims. Central to any debate about the victim status of the (fictional or non-fictional) narrator are issues of accountability in contexts of addiction. It is extremely likely that alcoholics, drug addicts, and jailed persons are harmed by life events and that some of these lack responsibility. To some extent, then, it makes sense to think of addicted persons as victims.

Regardless of the victim status of Frey's narrator, his case illustrates other phenomena that are highly important when considering stories in the first person.

There is a temptation to tell a vivid story of suffering because such a story is likely to attract attention and, when published, may enhance sales. Indeed, a narrative popular as a memoir might have comparatively little importance when conveyed as fiction. Ishmael Beah published a novel in 2014; whether it will attract the attention of his first book cannot yet be known. The phenomenon of Beah's book on his soldiering experiences indicates both the attractions and the perils of the first-person memoir and the ways in which these can be enormously enhanced by support from media outlets and personalities. Yet the public is likely to feel sense of deep betrayal when what is presented as a memoir of suffering and recovery turns out to be fiction rather than fact.

But even if excuses can be found, they will not suffice to defend a genre of false memoir. A memoir, after all, presents itself as non-fiction. There is a literary vehicle through which to express emotionally significant claims in accounts of invented circumstances and events. That vehicle is fiction. If a writer wants to write fiction in the first person, in a form similar to that of a memoir, so be it. But it remains dishonest for writers, with the encouragement or collusion of publishers, to present fiction as a memoir of personal experience. If it is a good story, fine. As such it may merit a wide readership and public attention. But to say this much does not provide a sound defence of the false memoir. A memoir, after all, presents itself as non-fiction. A good story can, after all, have much to offer without being a true and accurate memoir. It can be a good story.

If we feel deeply on reading an account that purports to be true but is discovered to be false, and are moved to sympathy and compassion, perhaps that account is false only about incidental facts and is in a deeper sense true. Perhaps it contains a sort of emotional truth, or has some kind of authenticity distinct from truth. Perhaps it preserves some sort of fictional integrity. (The issues here recall the case of Rigoberta Menchú discussed in Chapter 6.) The argument may be that people do, after all, experience such things as this and when they do, their feelings are likely something like this, and it is important to understand such feelings, which have a kind of authenticity.[18] Elusive concepts such as "authenticity" and "emotional truth" may seem to avoid the problem of central inaccuracies. In fact, they leave it unresolved. The point remains that a non-fictional account of moving experiences, told in the first person, presents itself as true and appeals to the trust of the audience. Substantive inaccuracies or downright fraud undermine that appeal, as they should.

An argument sometimes offered is that a person should believe what her feelings "tell" her. Reflection reveals this advice to be more than a little obscure. For one thing, we do not always know what our feelings "tell" us. For another, we should need to acknowledge the possibility that our memories are flawed. It is not only the stories told by others that we need to scrutinize. We need to take the same approach to our own memories and stories of our own victimization, especially when we suppose it to have been at the hands of others. We need to be aware that we may really have been harmed through no fault of our own and that we are not to blame, that we really are victims who appropriately occupy the victim role. But we need, as well, to recognize the temptations of the victim role and the temptations that a vivid victim story may offer. Clearly, there is a sense in which no one wants to be a victim. Nevertheless, the victim role does carry with it social status and privilege. Its benefits are deference, sympathy, and support. Victim narratives portray innocent suffering and moral desert. When these aspects are added to the attractions of a meaningful story of suffering and recovery, the temptations are many. A good victim story is one in which the key figure (often a first-person narrator) suffers greatly and then rises to the challenge, conquering obstacles to emerge as a successful and admirable human being. Such narratives have enormous appeal and are favoured by motivational speakers. Some are true and inspiring, and rightly so, and have served to support important social causes. They deserve to be told and deserve to be believed, albeit with some caution.

A good narrative provides a sense of direction and meaning. It comes to a satisfying end. Life itself often does not. A story may work too well, and when it does, we should reflect carefully, whether it is our own story or that of another. We need to keep in mind the possibility that the story makes more sense than real experience would warrant. We need to trust others for their testimony; we need to trust ourselves, for our memories and values. In neither case should trust be unreflective.

NOTES

1   See, for instance, David Roberts, "Martensville Redux," *Globe and Mail* 17 June 1995.

2   Loftus. See also Meredith Maran, *My Lie: A True Story of False Memory* (New York: Jossey-Bass Wiley, 2010) and "Did My Father Really Abuse Me?," *Guardian* 9 Oct. 2010 <http://www.theguardian.com/lifeandstyle/2010/oct/09/meredith-maran-father-abuse-false-memory> last accessed 26 June 2014.

3   Medina.

4   Miranda Fricker, *Epistemic Injustice: Power and the Ethics of Knowing* (Oxford: Oxford UP, 2007).

5   Elizabeth Anscombe, "What Is It to Believe Someone?," *Rationality and Religious Belief*, ed. C.F. Delaney (Notre Dame, IN: U of Notre Dame P, 1979) 141–51.

6   I think here about the early stages of dementia.

7   My example. Based on personal experience of the interactions within this family.

8   Gloria Origgi, "Epistemic Injustice and Epistemic Trust," *Social Epistemology* 26.2 (2012): 221–35.

9   See L. Ross, "The Intuitive Psychologist and His Shortcomings," *Advances in Experimental Social Psychology*, ed. L. Berkowitz (New York: Academic Press, 1977) 173–200; Daniel T. Gilbert and Patrick S. Malone, "The Correspondence Bias,"

Psychological Bulletin 117.1 (1995): 21–38; and Lee Ross and Richard Nisbett, *The Person and the Situation: Perspectives in Social Psychology* (Toronto: McGraw-Hill, 1991).

10   I have discussed skepticism about character in Chapter 7 of *Forgiveness and Revenge* (London: Routledge, 2002). Thorough application of the debunking that would emerge from accounts employing the fundamental attribution error will reduce the role of character to a minimum. See also Robert D. Stolorow, "What Is Character and How Does It Change?," *Psychology Today* 12 March 2012. See Chapter Two in this book for a brief description of the "ideal victim."

11   Some may insist that despite inaccuracies, the account is authentic or conveys a kind of fictional truth.

12   Herman A. Rosenblat, *Angel at the Fence* (New York: Berkeley Books, 2009); Margaret Seltzer, *Love and Consequences* (New York: Riverhead Books, 2008); Norma Khouri, *Forbidden Love* (New York: Random House, 2003).

13   Ishmael Beah, *A Long Way Gone: Memoirs of a Boy Soldier* (New York: Farrar, Strauss and Giroux, 2007); *Radiance of Tomorrow: A Novel* (New York: Penguin, 2014).

14   Peter Wilson, "Beah's Credibility a Long Way Gone," *The Australian* 2 Feb. 2008 <http://www.theaustralian.com.au/news/beahs-credibility-a-long-way-gone/story-e6frg6n6-1111115457775?nk=46d7b321e61f345771e1ae8d49af9e4f> last accessed 26 June 2014. See also Simon Caterson, "Sting in the Tale a Breach of Trust," *The Australian* 2 Feb. 2008.

15   Peter Wilson, quoted in Marcus Baram, "Does Best-Seller Bend the Facts?" ABC News 25 Jan. 2008 <http://abcnews.go.com/US/story?id=4184154&page=4> last accessed 26 June 2014.

16   David Frey, *A Million Little Pieces* (New York: Anchor, 2004).

17   "A Million Little Lies: Exposition James Frey's Fiction Addiction,". *Smoking Gun* 4 Jan. 2006 <http://www.thesmokinggun.com/documents/celebrity/million-little-lies> last accessed 26 June 2014.

18   Arguments for some sort of emotional truth will seem more cogent only insofar as their proponents can articulate what emotional truth is.

THE NEEDS
OF VICTIMS

Exaggerated and even false claims to victimhood do exist, as do temptations to identify unproductively with a victim role. But the fact remains that there really are victims of serious wrongdoing. Injured and wounded, often both physically and psychologically, these persons have been harmed, have suffered, and may still be suffering. We are called to respond.

VICTIMS AND PERPETRATORS

In the sense in which the term is used here, a person may be a victim of disease, natural disaster, wrongdoing, or a combination of all three. Colloquially, the word "victim" is often used both for those damaged by disease or disaster and for those damaged by wrongdoing. It is only in the latter context that there are perpetrators. Perpetrators may be simplistically understood as standing in a relationship of clear opposition to victims. On such an understanding, a victim is in no sense a perpetrator with regard to the act of which he is a victim, and a perpetrator is in no sense a victim with regard to the act of which he is a perpetrator. Victim and perpetrator represent passivity and agency: the victim an innocent recipient, the perpetrator a guilty agent. Given that some persons may be both victims and perpetrators, even (as in the case of child soldiers) with regard to the same act, such a paradigm is too simplistic to be generally applicable. However, though complications arise and qualifications are necessary for some cases, there are more straightforward instances in which victims are harmed by the wrongful actions of others and different people, perpetrators, are responsible for clearly wrongful acts. In those cases, which we might deem standard, many issues arise about the appropriate response to wrongdoing. Logically, what is required is to reflect on responses to victims, perpetrators, and the affected community.

At this point, we often find a shift away from victims despite the fact that it is they who are the innocent and harmed persons needing sympathy and assistance. It seems that victims should receive some kind of repair and satisfaction and that perpetrators should suffer some kind of hard treatment. Perpetrators are guilty persons, agents of wrongdoing, in need of punishment and reform. It has seemed, to many theorists that victims should be provided some kind of satisfaction that they will receive precisely because perpetrators are made to suffer. We arrive, then, at questions of penalties to be imposed on perpetrators. Western societies have penal rules and institutions; we have such a thing as punishment, which is legally imposed hard treatment as a way of expressing censure of one who has committed a wrongful act. What can societies justifiably do to perpetrators of wrongdoing? What can they effectively do? There are long traditions of theorizing about punishment. Legally instituted punishment may be rationalized retributively, when people look backward at what convicted perpetrators did and why, and seek to give them what they deserve in the form of punishment. Or they may be rationalized from various perspectives having to do with public utility or rehabilitation, looking forward to the effects of sentences with regard to the prevention of similar wrongs or the rehabilitation of the perpetrator.

Forward-looking approaches seek to justify punishment by its beneficial consequences—for the public at large, in the case of utilitarianism; for the improvement of the offender himself, in the case of rehabilitation theories. For several decades (between the 1960s and the 1980s at least) these forward-looking approaches were generally favoured by theorists. But thinking has changed, for various reasons. Two themes stand out. First of all, the intended consequences, whether in benefits for public safety or in the moral improvement of offenders themselves, do not emerge as expected. Empirically, they cannot be reliably demonstrated: deterrence and rehabilitation do not seem to result from punishment. Secondly, there is a problem regarding autonomy and respect for persons. An offender who is used as a means in efforts to ensure public safety or whose autonomy is not respected within a treatment program is not treated as a person in his own right. In utilitarian theory, the problem is one of using an offender as a means, not properly considering his autonomy and moral status when he is treated harshly on the grounds that this treatment will contribute to the safety of others. In rehabilitation theory, the problem appears insofar as those who aim for the rehabilitation of an offender seek to shape that person to their own ends, using treatment instead of reasoning and moral persuasion.

It is an understatement to say that tough questions arise about justifications of punishment. These forward-looking approaches, seeking good consequences of treatments to which offenders are forcibly exposed, by no means exhaust the possibilities. Punishment may be understood and rationalized as expressive in the sense that the hard treatment of a convicted perpetrator amounts to a communication to him or her that society does not accept acts of this kind. It may be understood as retributive, giving to offenders what they deserve. And it may be understood as restitutive, giving back to victims what they deserve. There are, in addition, complex combinations of these views. There are also abolition views denying any moral justification for institutions of legally authorized punishment.[1]

RETRIBUTION

Baldly construed, justice after wrongdoing should give assistance to victims and penalties to perpetrators. There is an obvious asymmetry here: victims are likely to welcome assistance, whereas penalties imposed on perpetrators are not likely to be welcomed by them. If state power and resources are to be used to impose hardships on people, a good justification is needed, and it is that fact that underlies theorizing about punishment. An explanation for the theoretical and practical preoccupation with perpetrators lies in the asymmetry between the supplying of benefits and the imposition of penalties. Errors and injustices are felt to be—and typically are—more serious when state power is used to impose penalties. It would be a more serious injustice to imprison a falsely convicted person than to provide a supposed victim with benefits that she did not really deserve. Imposing sentences on legally convicted perpetrators is imposing hard treatment on them, and if we are doing this due to faulty theory, it is a serious matter. Hence, the problem of punishment.

An argument with some psychological appeal is that the hard treatment for perpetrators is legitimate because it satisfies the retributive feelings of victims. The idea is that those who are victims of wrongdoing feel anger and resentment about the way they have been treated by perpetrators. Primary victims have typically felt physical pain and anguish and considerable subsequent mental discomfort in forms such as fear and anxiety—unless they have been deprived of life itself and hence feel nothing whatsoever. Secondary victims will have felt grief and rage, often experiencing serious emotional loss and hardship in altered economic circumstances. Moral anger and a determination to do something back, to make the perpetrator pay for the wrongful deed with his own suffering, are common results of these harms. And thus we find a line of argument from victims' feelings to the punishment of perpetrators. Putting it simply, seeing that perpetrators get what they deserve in response to their wrongdoing will relieve the angry emotions of victims. On this account, perpetrators deserve hard treatment because of what they have inflicted on victims, and victims, knowing perpetrators have received it, will be emotionally soothed and relieved.

Harmed persons need attention, sympathy, and support; in addition they are likely to have strong negative emotions that should, if possible, be relieved. That much is readily granted. But the unintended effect here is that thought about the rationale for retribution in terms of what perpetrators deserve (given the seriousness of the offence and the degree of responsibility for it) shifts attention away from victims to issues of due process, legal representation, monitoring of conditions in prisons, and other matters pertaining to perpetrators. Retribution requires us to consider what should happen to a person who has been lawfully convicted of a crime; on retributive theory that person is being subjected to hard treatment at the hands of the state and is so subjected on the grounds that he deserves that hard treatment for what he has done. Beginning with an argument about the emotional needs of victims, we have moved to considerations about process and treatment of perpetrators. One might suppose that victims want perpetrators to suffer the hard treatment they deserve and that when victims know perpetrators are getting this, they will feel satisfied that "justice has been done." But things do not always work out this way. Given that we cannot simply assume that all accused perpetrators are guilty as accused and fully responsible for what they have done, the rights of accused persons need to be taken into account. In fact, they have to be taken with the utmost seriousness. Victims almost disappear from the picture once due process, issues of guilt, proper sentencing, prison conditions, parole, and so on enter the scene. Indeed, the frustration of victims and their advocates about their slim judicial role has been one of the prime impulses behind the victim movement over the past several decades. Innovations such as victim impact statements and the consideration of victim views as to appropriate sentences are problematic from the standpoint of legal justice and, for that matter, unlikely to soothe the emotions of victims.[2]

According to retributivism, punishment is justified because it imposes on offenders hard treatment that they deserve because of what they have done. Perpetrators have committed wrongful acts and those acts are rightly resented by victims and others; as guilty, perpetrators deserve to suffer; seeing them get what they deserve will satisfy victims. Reasoning along such lines, we arrive at an argument that links the retributive punishment of perpetrators to the emotional needs of victims. The core of retributivism lies in the notion of "desert," but an important supporting strand connects with the feelings of victims. A common supposition is that victims will want penalties (preferably harsh ones) inflicted on an offender and will be satisfied and relieved if they see that offender suffering as they did themselves. These emotional needs on the part of victims are found in common experience. They are often defended as natural and therefore "right" and socially fundamental.

Andrew Oldenquist offers an account appearing to emphasize the feelings of victims, asserting rather hyperbolically that

> After every conviction the victims, or their relatives, applaud and cry with relief, and otherwise indicate that the world can never be right again until the one who hurt them so terribly received his due.[3]

But as he develops his account, it becomes clear that Oldenquist does not defend punishment on the grounds that victims are emotionally satisfied and relieved by it. Rather, he argues that hard treatment of deserved punishment expresses *community values* defining the wrongful act as a violation. By punishing a perpetrator, we hold him or her accountable for wrongful actions while expressing at the same time the message that he or she is still within the community. Punishment, defined as the legally imposed hard treatment of one convicted of a criminal act, is on this account "a move in the social practice of retributive judgment," which is "essential for human social life as we know it."[4] Imposing punishment, the community expresses a moral message not only to the perpetrator, but to itself. Legal process tames sentiments of revenge in a system that inhibits vengeful parties from imposing wildly inappropriate punishments. For Oldenquist, punishment is a kind of sanitized revenge, one that avoids giving licence to indulging private and variable sentiments of retaliation. Oldenquist maintains that a moral community exacts retribution to articulate and emphasize its own values. Although this account suggests that it is the feelings of victims that justify retributive punishment, in the end there is a shift to public values and public reasons for law and policy.[5]

Problems arise concerning this line of reasoning, though. One central difficulty is that victims vary in their responses to wrongdoing and their feelings about perpetrators. To be sure, many feel intense moral anger and think they would benefit by seeing the perpetrator put down either by incarceration or even by execution. However, not all victims seek the suffering of a perpetrator as a means of achieving satisfaction and vindication. Some focus more directly on their personal needs for sympathy and material assistance, deeming the question of how a perpetrator should be treated as a side issue. Some may advocate the incarceration of perpetrators not on grounds of desert, but as a matter of deterrence, in the interests of public safety. Others may advocate mercy for perpetrators on the basis of mitigating circumstances. Victims may argue for forgiveness on various grounds including, often, religious principles. This variability of victim attitudes makes them a shaky basis for policy on matters of punishment.

That such persons do not agree in their emotional responses and requirements is one point against such rationalization, but it is not the only problem. Suppose that victims did agree in their sentiments. Suppose, contrary to fact, that every surviving victim and every family member of murdered victims were in accord as to the nature and degree of their moral anger at convicted perpetrators. Then suppose, again contrary to fact, that the same level of hard treatment for perpetrators would relieve the moral anger of all these victims to just the same degree. Let us give that type and level of hard treatment a name: call it H. Even on the strong suppositions introduced here, emotional responses would not be justified as a punishment, for three fundamental reasons. In supposing a uniform H, we do not allow for consideration of relevant particular circumstances in the lives of various offenders.[6] These emotional reactions might not take into account psychological facts logically relevant to the perpetrator's degree of moral responsibility. A still more fundamental difficulty is that law and penal institutions express the values of a whole state and society, not only those of the significant subgroup of victimized persons. This is a highly significant subgroup, and one whose needs and interests are highly important. But it is not the only group to be considered.

Defending what he calls "the varieties of retributive experience," Christopher Bennett argues that retribution can be understood as a means of communicating to wrongdoers our reactive attitudes in response to their deeds, showing them why they deserve to suffer hard treatment and why they should repent and reform.[7] A wrongdoer who has violated the criminal law by committing such an act as assault, burglary, or murder has, after all, acted against the values of his or her community. When the community censures such a person by withdrawing its solidarity with him or her, it expresses the message that it is offended by the behaviour and disapproves. Bennett advocates retribution and maintains that it can provide a route to reconciliation. On his account, it is a good thing for persons who have done wrong to undergo certain forms of suffering. This, purportedly, is a good thing for reasons that have to do not so much with the emotions of victims in particular but with the articulation and enforcement of community values. Rejecting any idea that retributivism is primitive and as such an instinct of which we should be ashamed, Bennett defends the fundamental intuition that it is appropriate and fitting for wrongdoers to suffer because of what they have done. The wrongdoer will be blamed for it, properly blamed. Blame looks backward to what a perpetrator has done, as do retributive theories.

Blaming behaviour is a behaviour of the community, and it is both expressive and purposive. It is expressive in the sense that it conveys that the behaviour is wrong according to community values and the perpetrator was at fault in engaging in it. It is purposive in seeking to amend the values and actions of the perpetrator so that he or she can re-engage with the community. A community that blames a perpetrator does in a sense isolate that person. But that isolation is the isolation of someone who is, after all, a member of the community and will continue to be so and may return, even though he or she is temporarily in a state of alienation from that community. Bennett maintains that our reactive attitudes are fully and appropriately retributive and that expressing them in the form of appropriate punishment will lead the perpetrator to do what is needed to move from rupture to reconciliation. A wrongdoer will need to repent and do what is possible to remove the bad consequences of the wrongful act, to restore the situation to what it was before the wrongdoing.[8] That will include alleviating the hurt feelings of victims, repairing damage to their persons and property, and ending alienation from the community.

This account, and a similar one offered by Anthony Duff, represent current philosophical defences of retributivism. Several things stand out in the context of victims' issues. First, it is clear that this account is one of the perpetrator's alienation from and return to his or her moral community. It is not an account of what should be done in response to the emotional or other needs of victims. Still less is it an account in which the retributive treatment of perpetrators is defended on the grounds that it will satisfy the feelings and wishes of victims. Considerations about blame, alienation, rupture, and possible reconciliation with the community by perpetrators are entirely different from considerations about what is felt by victims and how their feelings might be relieved. In retributive theory as carefully understood, it is not the satisfaction of victims' feelings that is taken to rationalize retributive punishment. Rather, the retributive treatment of perpetrators properly involves the communication of blame with the hope and anticipation that it will result in perpetrators' understanding of wrongdoing, offering to victims what symbolic and material amends are possible, and reconciliation with victims and communities. Victims' emotional needs and perpetrators' reform do intersect at the point of possible remorse and apology by perpetrators. If perpetrators come to appreciate the wrongfulness of their actions and are able to apologize to victims, effectively conveying their remorse and sincere intent not to re-commit offences, victims' needs for acknowledgement may be met. When they are, satisfaction is likely.[9] If there is emotional relief for victims at this point, it will stem from recognition, remorse, and reform on the part of the perpetrator and not from satisfaction with hard treatment itself.

In short, it is not plausible to understand retributively grounded punishment of offenders as a practice intended to satisfy the feelings of victims. Correctly understood, theories of retribution are not about victims. Whatever their merits or deficiency, they deal with the attitudes and treatment of perpetrators and their place in communities. Victims' alleged satisfaction with the hard treatment of perpetrators does not provide a satisfactory understanding of retribution. Nor does it offer an account of responses to the symbolic and material needs of victims themselves.

The perspective of restitution seeks to more closely link what happens to perpetrators with what benefits victims. Some theorists have urged that restitution replace the penal institutions of states. Their accounts shift the perspective away from perpetrators to the needs of victims. Though the shift is in many respects welcome, it reveals important problems.

RESTITUTION AS A SUBSTITUTE FOR STATE PUNISHMENT?

We speak of compensating, repairing wrongs, or even of righting them. We speak of restitution when a person who has perpetrated a wrong against a victim gives back to that victim something to make up for his loss. Such talk needs to be taken seriously and has important practical implications. But it can be seriously misleading. If we inquire as to how restitution can make up for a victim's loss, an initial theoretical response is to think of the perpetrator giving back to the victim something that he took away when he committed a wrong against her. The model seems to apply readily, and quite literally, in some cases involving material loss. Suppose that Jones takes $5,000 from Smith and is caught and said to owe Smith restitution. What should that restitution involve? In this case, we are likely to think first of Smith's personal monetary loss and say that Jones should pay Smith $5,000. That would be restitution; the victim's loss would (apparently) be made good, and the person who committed the theft would be the one doing it.

But even in this apparently simple case, there are complications. It is highly unlikely that Smith's loss is entirely financial and captured in the monetary quantity of $5,000. Even on the assumption that Jones could provide him with that amount as a way of making amends, there would remain other matters, including that of Smith's diminished financial status during the interval when he did not have his money. The deprivation would likely have resulted in some inconvenience, particularly if Smith is a person of modest means. Furthermore, the loss likely resulted in a sense of vulnerability and anxiety on Smith's part. These elements of the harm, its psychic costs, would not be covered by the monetary restitution. As well as effects on Smith as an individual, there would likely be psychic costs and inconvenience for family members. If we proceed to consider the case in the context of a society with lawyers, judges, police, and court proceedings, there are further costs. Given all these matters, it would take considerably more than $5,000 for Jones to make full restitution to Smith. Measurement difficulties regarding inconvenience and psychic costs, and some aspects of social cost, would obviously arise. And yet the case of financial damage is simple compared to others where serious injury or trauma is involved. If Jones had attacked Smith and injured him so seriously as to render him incapable of earning a livelihood, or if Jones had killed his children or in some other way seriously traumatized him, the costs of repairing the damage would be enormous, even if it could be done at all.

Some libertarian theorists have gone so far as to argue that restitution could be so full and complete that, after it, both direct victims and family members would be as well-off as they were before the wrongdoing. Amazingly, some even maintain that restitution could be so complete that victims would be indifferent if asked to choose between the situation in which they were not victimized and one in which they were victimized and fully compensated. These libertarian advocates of restitution would construe such full restitution as putting the victim in a condition of indifference between being robbed and fully compensated on the one hand and not being robbed at all on the other. For the sake of considering the restitution view, we might suppose that Smith as a primary victim of a burglary, his family members as its secondary victims, and the surrounding society as tertiary victims could be fully compensated by Jones. But the suppositions are problematic, even for the apparently simple case of financial crime and a high monetary compensation. Suppose, for instance, that after being robbed of $5,000, Smith were to be compensated by $50,000 and six months of vacation leave during which he could take his family on a luxurious holiday. On this supposition, would Smith choose to be robbed, if he did have the choice? Would he be indifferent as to the choice between being robbed with full compensation and not being robbed at all? Perhaps that is possible, although likely not, if anxiety and trauma for family members are substantial and family convenience needs to be taken into account. Additionally, if he were to choose the generous compensation over the robbery, the choice in itself would suggest an argument that the compensation payment was too large.

An additional practical problem is that as restitution costs rise, the likelihood of an individual perpetrator being able to pay them will be diminished. Despite these complications in theory and practice, the example of compensating for a burglary is comparatively simple. For most people, the financial loss of $5,000 would be trivial compared to the losses experienced by a primary victim of rape, torture, or beating—or secondary victims whose family members were killed in a bombing or murder. In these cases, damage is likely to be profound and long-lasting. It is implausible that money at a later time could compensate pain and injury, loss, fear, and anxiety.

Consider, for example, the case of the Boston Marathon bombings of May 2013. In these attacks, some 260 people were injured and three were killed. At least 10 people lost limbs, and two became double amputees. Jeff Bauman was one of these. He had been present at the finish line, awaiting the arrival of his girlfriend, when a bomb went off at his feet. Bauman, a young man, will be living out his life as a double amputee. He will need extensive and expensive prosthetics and medical treatment and will have to adapt his career and personal relationships on the basis of his radically revised personal health. It is not easy to understand what full restitution would mean in such a case. And if we did understand it, it would be most unclear who would be able to provide it. Certainly not a primary perpetrator. One of the suspected bombers is dead; the other, recovered from injuries, will stand trial and likely receive either the death penalty or life imprisonment if convicted. If we try to apply notions of restitution to such a case, two problems stand out immediately. One is that it is unclear just how the young man likely to be convicted could gain the resources to make restitution to even one of the many direct victims. A more fundamental problem returns us to the question of what full restitution could even mean in such a situation, given the impossibility of providing Bauman with his own two legs and no need for prolonged medical interventions.[10]

In writing about restitution, some theorists have endorsed the notion of complete restitution which, in a criminal context, would involve the convicted perpetrator "making good" all the losses ensuing from his crime.[11] Defending a conception of restitution, Mane Hajdin argues that it would require a convicted perpetrator to compensate fully for all losses to these victims and for the costs of investigation and judicial process. In explaining his account, Hajdin uses his own terminology for victims. Primary victims he refers to as direct victims; secondary victims he refers to as indirect direct victims; and tertiary victims he refers to as indirect indirect victims. Total amounts required for restitution to all of these, in cases of serious injury or death, would be large. Direct victims would be the main recipients of restitution except in cases where they were killed, wherein indirect direct victims would be the main recipients. Considering the case of Bauman using Hajdin's terms, Bauman of course is the direct victim; his close family and friends are indirect direct victims; and the Boston community is the indirect indirect victim. Hajdin argues that if a convicted perpetrator could repay to victims at all three levels all the costs associated with his crime, then there would be full compensation. He maintains that if restitution in this strong sense were provided, then punishment, jails, prison guards, and the like would be rendered unnecessary. Full restitution would be a substitute for punishment as we presently know it.

Many questions arise in theory and in practice. A theoretical problem is that of definition. It is implausible to think of restitution as completely replacing punishment because it will have to be imposed and for that reason will require something very similar to the institutions that enforce the hard treatment that constitutes punishment. If a convicted perpetrator had to work full time for 30 years to make up the estimated costs of his crime, and had to be compelled and supervised to do so, there is a sense in which the labour itself would amount to punishment. Clearly, it would amount to coerced hard treatment and the state would be involved in its monitoring and the required enforcement. Advocates of restitution by perpetrators to victims often advance it as a way of interpreting wrongs done against a victim as a matter between victim and perpetrator (omitting the state) and would have the perpetrator "make good."[12] But it is by no means obvious how an offender could be made to do years of labour to offer restitution without the involvement of properly conductive supervisory institutions.

Defending restitution as a response to wrongdoing, Joseph Ellin makes the following bold claim:

> There are two conditions. In one, the crime does not occur; in
> the other, the crime occurs but is fully compensated. Since the

> conditions are of equal value, for you to demand that the law
> . prefer one condition over the other would seem irrational.[13]

When he made this claim, Ellin was considering a case of car theft. He was not considering a case such as that of Bauman, in which serious physical injury necessitated double amputation. Ellin did admit that his view would be more problematic in cases of physical security and death, but goes on to advocate that if all victims of crime are compensated, there should be nothing to fear from crime.

Ellin seems to ignore that people would not wish to suffer physical brutality even if they had every reason to believe that after that brutality, they would be fully compensated. Would you not fear being raped, or having your jaw bashed in and teeth destroyed, just because you believed that later, after you had gone through all this, you would be "restored" (probably by a being given a large sum of money in addition to needed medical treatment which might fix the damage after many painful treatments)? Would you willingly give up both your legs on the grounds that in the aftermath, you would be "fully compensated"? The prospects seem implausible at best, offensive at worst. In his account, Ellin refers to all the direct victims of a crime. On his view, direct victims must be individuals and cannot be groups. His terminology differs from that used here and from that of Hajdin. He would say that all individuals harmed by a wrong are its direct victims. He does not employ the distinction between primary and secondary victims, nor does he allow community victims.

One obvious practical argument against the idea that offenders could make full restitution to all who are in this sense victims is that most of them would simply not have the means to do so. To this objection, Ellin responds:

> It is not true that criminals have nothing of value. Everyone,
> whatever his or her financial condition, owns twenty-four hours
> of potential labor time each day. Allowing eight hours for sleep-
> ing and eating, this amounts to 5,480 hours per year, which at a
> wage of ten dollars per hour, would allow the criminal to earn
> $584,000 in ten years. This is a not-inconsiderable sum, even
> at reduced wages and making allowances for Christmas and
> New Year's holidays and church every Sunday.[14]

It has to be admitted that many persons serving time in prison do so at great cost to taxpayers and are not doing productive labour despite being fit for it. This point is emphasized by Ellin and provides much of the rationale for his account. Those costs merit attention. Yet it is an over-statement to say, as Ellin does, that everyone owns 24 hours of potential labour time each day. In fact, no one owns 24 hours of potential labour a day: people need to eat and sleep. In addition, some

153

persons are ill or disabled and not fit to work; nearly everyone is ill at least some of the time. Other details of Ellin's account can surely be questioned; he fails to consider medical and dental appointments and has no time allotted to those household tasks (shopping, cooking, cleaning, laundry) that are necessary for a person to remain alive and functioning.[15] But these problems concern incidental details. Running contrary to Ellin's commitment to getting rid of prisons and minimizing the role of the state in enforcing the criminal law is the more fundamental point that considerable enforcement would be needed to ensure that these convicted persons laboured for many years in order to provide restitution to their victims.

An even more fundamental difficulty concerns the very idea of full compensation for serious wrongs. What would it mean? Within weeks of the Boston bombings, a substantial fund of $30 million had been raised through charity. One early report on compensation for the bombings offered an account of categories for compensation.[16] Compensations paid through this fund would not be established or provided through courts; hence, victims who accepted them would not waive any right to sue. The awards would have the legal status of gifts, and income would not be a factor in establishing eligibility. Four categories of victims were proposed. The first category was comprised of double amputees, families of persons killed (including the family of the police officer killed during a manhunt after the bombing), and persons suffering permanent brain damage. The second category was those who had lost a single limb; the third, those who required overnight hospitalization; and the fourth, those treated as outpatients.[17]

To insist that costs in cases of serious injury and trauma can never be reasonably estimated would be an exaggeration. After all, such estimations are in fact made, though not in the contexts envisioned by libertarian theorists. Estimations are made by insurers, in mediated settlements and courts, and according to the traditions of tort law.[18] Obviously, the details of such settlements can be disputed. And they are disputed. It is not the details of such disputes that will be discussed here. Nor will the fact that, realistically, many perpetrators will not have the resources to make restitution or the fact that many such payments are needed and are appropriate. Rather, the issue is what full restitution could mean in theory and practice. As the case of Bauman indicates, it is often simply impossible to restore the victim of a serious wrong or illness to his condition prior to the severe damage. He would have to be fully restored physically and financially and suffer no psychic damage from memory, anxiety, or distrust. The impossibility of the full restitution of what was lost by victims of serious wrongs does not argue against restitution as a highly significant symbolic gesture. Nor does it count against the offering of restitution by perpetrators in the context of seeking restored relationships with victims. What it does argue against is the notion favoured by some libertarians claiming that there is a kind of full restitution that can give back to victims everything that had been taken away from them. In theory and in practice, the idea that punishment as a legal institution could be replaced by full (and coerced) restitution does not hold up.

THE PERSPECTIVE OF RESTORATIVE JUSTICE

Given their quest for the healing of persons and relationships, restorative jus-tice advocates recommend restitution as an expression of acknowledgement and remorse. Without maintaining that restitution itself is a substitute for punishment and without defending any notion of complete restitution, they maintain that resti-tution provided by the perpetrator to the victim is desirable as symbolic recognition and a gesture of amends.

It is an understatement to remark that the perspective of restorative justice theorists differs from that of libertarian theorists. In restorative justice, restitution is advocated as an expression of healing and restored relationships, not as some-thing valued for its potential for reducing the role of the state in social life. Within a restorative justice framework, the value of restitution is in large part symbolic— an expression of respect and solidarity, an effort by a perpetrator to restore dignity and offer symbolic and (where feasible) practical amends to his victim. Advocates of restorative justice share with restitution theorists the belief that the immedi-ate and true victim of a criminal offence is not the state, but rather the injured and damaged individual. They insist that it is not the state as such that is harmed when an offender violates a victim; the state on this view does not "own" the con-flict between an offender and a victim. When the state presumes through policing, courts, and prisons, to take over the resolution of a conflict in which one individual has wronged another, the state has moved into territory where it should (at least ideally) not be. Restorative justice theories emphasize the healing of persons and relationships, contending that when an offender harms a victim, these two persons are involved, as is their community. (By "community" here we must presume, to preserve consistency in the theory, that a more proximate collective than the state is intended.)

The ideas of restorative justice differ significantly from retributive ideas. In particular, restorative justice advocates emphatically deny that the healing of one person (the victim) will be furthered by imposing hardship on another person (the offender). They contend instead that restoration and healing require the allevia-tion of the suffering of a damaged person, rather than imposition of suffering on another person. They argue for understanding, repentance, reintegration, and sup-port. Restorative justice theory and practice share important elements with some Aboriginal traditions, within which offenders were held accountable by their com-munities and integrated within them.

Advocates of restorative justice do not seek to relieve the state of its respon-sibility for criminal law, policing, courts, and the imposition and administration of punishments. Even though they deny that the state should "own" conflict, they do not take this stance from an individualist perspective. Emphasizing relationships between persons and within communities, they do not require that it is reasonable or necessary to maintain that things are *fully* "made good" for the victim, whether that would be achieved by satisfying retributive emotions or by providing resources sufficient for "complete" compensation.

Restorative justice practices include facilitated meetings between offenders and victims; family conferences at which family members of offenders and victims are included; and community circle sentencing. Meetings typically include community members as well as families. The nature of these meetings is likely to vary depending on the context. At the meetings, there is typically an encounter between the victim, the offender, and other affected persons with the goal of reaching mutual understanding and empathy. Victims often find it more satisfying and empowering to encounter offenders and hear from them directly than to be exposed to the proceedings of a court. Offenders meet with their victims and hear directly about the effects injurious acts have had on them; for them, such an experience is usually painful, having a more immediate and personal impact than the proceedings of a court. The circumstances and causes of the offence are explored; for example, if drugs or alcohol have played a role, the proposed resolution will likely include measures to address such problems. Hearing stories of childhood abuse or hardship on the part of offenders, victims may gain sympathy for them; and offenders, seeing the pain and suffering of victims, may in turn acquire some empathy for them and gain a better understanding of the impact of their offence. Victims may hear from offenders explanations as to how the offence came to pass; sometimes, such explanations alleviate their fears. For example, a victim may feel that his house was a target for burglary and then discover that it was quite accidentally chosen, perhaps even due to a thief unintentionally getting off the subway one stop too early.

Restorative justice processes owe their twentieth-century renaissance to the Mennonite Anabaptist tradition, which has sought alternatives to violence. Restorative justice meetings were introduced in 1974 in Elmira, Ontario as a response to juvenile petty crime in an effort to reconcile offending youth with property owners who had been their victims.[19] Proceedings were intended to facilitate repair, understanding, and reconciliation and to avoid court proceedings and prison terms for young offenders. Early practitioners included social workers, youth workers, peace activists, Christian clergy, and a wide variety of volunteers. Successes achieved by the restorative justice movement and the attraction of its ideas in the wake of conspicuous failures in traditional punishment have led to its spread to adult populations in many countries of the world. When mediations became common as alternatives or supplements to court processes in contexts such as divorce, many lawyers entered the restorative justice field. Truth commission processes in South Africa and elsewhere typically claim ties to restorative justice ideals—though the need to integrate legal processes at many points means that such claims are open to dispute.

Recognition for Victims

There is an important sense in which victims of wrongdoing have been used by perpetrators. Perpetrators have not respected their victims as persons and full moral agents but have, instead, exploited them for their own purposes. Con artists and fraudsters have, without right, taken over the property of other persons, treating it as something they can use for their own ends. Assailants have expressed their rage on other persons used as targets or punching bags and not recognized them as moral agents. Rapists have used victims to assert their power by humiliating them and to satisfy sexual lusts and fantasies. Murderers have presumed the right to stamp out the life of others in a relentless pursuit of their own goals. The damage wrought by these and other wrongful acts has physical, mental, and moral dimensions. So far as the moral dimension is concerned, the issue is the profound insult implied by the offence—the humiliation of victims. Needless to say, the real moral status of victims is not diminished by the facts of their victimhood. What is damaged is, rather, their perceived or felt moral status—in short, their sense of human dignity.

In many contexts, what victims need is acknowledgement—a recognition from others that they have been wrongfully harmed. To acknowledge the victimhood of another is to express to that person, in word or deed, awareness that he is injured, likely damaged, and still suffering, through no or little fault of his own. A person who has been grievously injured in a rape or other physical attack, or seriously affected by financial fraud or other misdoing, needs from others a recognition that in this assault she was not treated as she should have been and did not receive the treatment she deserved. Assistance may be needed; much of that assistance will be material and some of it may be supplied by the state. And such matters are of great significance. But equally so are the attitudes of society, family, and friends relating to sympathy, empathy, and recognition of human dignity.

Acknowledgement means indicating that one does know that the other is a victim, that this person has been harmed and has suffered as a result of things that have happened, events over which he or she has had little or no control.[20] In the aftermath of many wrongs, there are obvious physical effects. Typically, there will also be psychological effects including fear and a sense of vulnerability, as well as memories of brutal experience. In addition to these effects, victims may feel demeaned—even shamed—by brutality that has come to them through no fault of their own. Obviously, the effects of wrongdoing range in degrees of seriousness. Since others will not know what it is like to suffer as these people have, there will always remain some sense in which the experiences of victims will not be fully understood by others. Despite this inescapable metaphysical gap between their experience and ours, we should do our best to respond.

Although no one can know exactly what it is like to suffer as another, we can avoid the pitfalls of denying and silencing victims. We can listen to those who want to tell us what they have gone through. Yael Danieli is one of several scholars who has emphasized the baneful effects of people's tendency to avoid accounts of victimization.[21] Such avoidance in effect inflicts "the second wound of silence."[22] There are problems about acknowledging victims, and some requirements of compensation proceedings may even conflict with that acknowledgement. For example, proceedings needed to investigate entitlement may be humiliating, degrading, and lengthy. If a victim has to fight for compensation, the struggle may absorb time and energy that could be used for other aspects of recovery. Moral and emotional breaches resulting in victimhood should be addressed, and doing this may be more difficult than supplying material resources. Even if something like full compensation could be achieved, matters of recovery are not purely material. The central aspect is symbolic. Victims need vindication. Vindication means victory in a moral challenge that is achieved when it is recognized and articulated that persons harmed did not deserve the treatment they received and should have been treated better.

In seeking a sympathetic and sound response to victims, we can search within ourselves to guard against any temptations of blaming them in a quest to preserve our own illusions of safety and control. We can try to understand and empathize with victims without implying that they are lacking in agency and capacity. We can do our best to combine encouragement with our awareness of victim status, and our awareness of that status with sensitivity to prospects for hopeful recovery or improvement. We can support restitution and compensation within reasonable limits, hoping to provide a means toward a restored situation.

Public Acknowledgement: Recognition and Remembering

Though in an ultimate sense it is as individuals that wronged persons feel pain and suffering, there are many contexts in which groups of people are victimized. The most obvious examples involve group conflict: bitter competition, ethnic struggles, wars, oppression, and terrorism. In the aftermath of such things, victims and victim groups may be acknowledged and vindicated by the establishment of memorials, statues, museums, and the like. Examples abound.

A particularly powerful memorial is that of the Oklahoma City bombings. Timothy McVeigh believed that the US government was tyrannical and hoped to inspire revolt against it. He was profoundly influenced by what he regarded as a US government attack on a cult at Waco, Texas. Working with co-conspirators, McVeigh detonated a truck bomb in Oklahoma City in 1995. As a result, 168 people were killed and over 600 injured.[23] To commemorate the victims and survivors, a National Memorial and Museum has been developed "to remember those who were killed, those who survived, and those changed forever. May all who leave here know the impact of violence. May this memorial offer comfort, strength, peace, hope, and serenity."[24] Comprised of a museum, plaza, orchard, reflecting pool, garden, record-keeping centre, and field of empty chairs, the memorial is located where the federal building once stood. There are 168 empty chairs representing those killed; of these, 19 are smaller chairs, representing the children killed.

The 9/11 Memorial in New York occupies eight acres of land in lower Manhattan. It was constructed as a memorial to those who died on 9/11 and in an earlier attack on the World Trade Center (26 February 1993). The names of all the victims are inscribed in bronze on walls surrounding twin memorial pools, marking the towers destroyed in the attacks. An attached museum provides much information through tours, teaching guides, and lesson plans. It is estimated that more than seven million persons have visited the site since its opening in September 2011.

Both campaigns and memorials commemorate the Montreal Massacre of 6 December 1989 when Marc Lépine went to the École Polytechnique in that city and shot 28 people, killing 14 women engineering students and injuring 10 other people including four men. Lépine thought the women had stolen from him an opportunity to study at the institute and raged against them as feminists. At the end of the rampage, he killed himself, having proclaimed in a suicide note that feminists had ruined his life. Much has been done to remember these murders: a National Day of Remembrance held annually in Canada; a White Ribbon Campaign in which men wear white ribbons to mark their opposition to violence against women; and an activist campaign, Action on Violence Against Women. In addition, plays, movies, songs, and annual ceremonies have been created to commemorate the day and remember the victims. Several women whose daughters were killed have been active in campaigns for gun control that have had a considerable impact within the province of Quebec.[25]

Obviously, these are only a few of the many ceremonies and memorials designed to honour victims and survivors. Such memorial sites and observations express a determination, expressed in environments of beauty and hope, that these persons will not be forgotten. Victims killed obviously cannot themselves benefit from such commemorations (unless one posits their surviving in an afterlife to consider the structures). The acknowledgement is for surviving victims, their family members and friends. But public acknowledgement is not only for them. It marks memory and public values, a record of names, sorrow, resolve, and hope. Those killed and injured were lost not only to their families and friends, but to the broader society in which they lived. In Montreal, Oklahoma City, and New York, commemorative sites and actions are enduring expressions of values that mark a new turn.

Apologies

Acknowledgement that victims have been wronged by treatment they did not deserve may be expressed by various agents, and in various ways, and may be public or private. Especially important is the apology, an acknowledgement by the perpetrator.

A perpetrator who has physically or psychologically abused a victim has expressed to that victim a message of profound disrespect, saying in effect that the victim's needs count for nothing as compared to the needs and desires of the perpetrator himself. The perpetrator has said, "You are nothing, you don't count; I am everything, I count; as the one who counts, I can bend you to my will." Insofar as it is the perpetrator who has conveyed this message of profound disrespect, it is he who is best positioned to take it back. If a perpetrator comes to understand that his acts were wrong and seriously damaging to the victim, he may feel remorse as a result, and if that happens, he may express that remorse to the victim in a sincere effort to (somehow) make amends. If the victim can grasp and recognize that remorse, she can understand it as amounting to an acknowledgement of her dignity and the fact that she did not deserve to be treated as she was. In expressing his remorse, the perpetrator has withdrawn the insult, responding to the victim as a person and cancelling his original message. For the victim who felt the threat to her moral agency and status, such an expression of remorse should offer reassurance and a sense of vindication. She never deserved this insult, and the one who insulted her has, himself, communicated the redemptive message.

In harming the victim, the perpetrator expressed a message of insult and an affront to dignity. In the case of a perpetrator convicted after due legal process, legal conviction and sentencing provide public acknowledgement of his violation of public norms. Legal proceedings and a judicial statement establish that what was done was criminally wrong and immoral, resulting in undeserved harm inflicted on the victim. It is as though society is declaring to victims: "your status as a human being deserving decent treatment was challenged when this wrong was committed; that challenge has been defeated; the perpetrator committed a wrong; you did not deserve this treatment; it should not have been challenged." Though conviction and punishment may be understood as satisfying the retributive desires of (some) victims, these public phenomena are more plausibly interpreted as expressions of vindication.

There are various contexts in which apologies may be offered: purely informal, as aspects of mediation or conflict resolution, in therapeutic sessions, in public speeches, or in courts of law. A perpetrator who offers an apology to the victim thereby expresses his own recognition that what he did was wrong, that he should not have done so, and the victim deserved better. He commits himself to not engaging in such acts again and to making practical amends to the victim.

A victim who is offered such an apology finds herself in a position of power with regard to its acceptance. She may accept the apology, reject it, or withhold judgement, adopting a kind of "wait and see" attitude. Her power at this point contrasts with her position of vulnerability and subordination when the wrong was inflicted on her.[26] When a perpetrator apologizes to his victim, roles are reversed due to this shift in power. It is at this point the victim who has the power to decide the direction of the relationship. It is for her to decide whether or not to accept the apology. In the case of apologies that give every sign of sincerity and are accompanied by efforts to make amends, observers may feel that victims should accept the apology, forgive the perpetrator, and move on. They may even believe that the victim has an obligation to accept the apology and to forgive. In the case of serious wrongs, there is no obligation to forgive.[27] Nevertheless, a victim may decide to forgive.

NOTES

1   R.A. Duff, *Punishment, Communication and Community* (Oxford: Oxford UP, 2001).

2   See Chapter 9 in this book.

3   Andrew Oldenquist, "An Explanation of Retribution," *Journal of Philosophy* 85 (1988): 464–78.

4   Oldenquist, 478.

5   See also Govier, *Forgiveness and Revenge*.

6   Feelings should be cognitively understood for this line of reasoning to make sense, even *prima facie*. This point is argued by Christopher Crochetti, "Emotions, Retribution, and Punishment," *Journal of Applied Philosophy* 26.2 (2009): 160–73.

7   Christopher Bennett, "The Varieties of Retributive Experience," *Philosophical Quarterly* 52 (2002): 145–63. I am quoting from the title of this article, obviously.

8   Here we find a similarity to the notion of full restitution. It is equally implausible.

9   Trudy Govier and Wilhelm Verwoerd, "The Problems and Pitfalls of Apologies," *Journal of Social Philosophy* 33.1 (2002): 67–82.

10   Lenny Bernstein, "Boston Marathon Fund Releases Compensation Formula for Bombing Victims," *Washington Post* 15 May 2013 <http://www.washingtonpost.com/national/health-science/boston-marathon-fund-releases-compensation-formula-for-bombing-victims/2013/05/15/187cb4c0-bcd7-11e2-9b09-1638acc3942e_story.html> last accessed 26 June 2014.

11   See Mane Hajdin, "Criminals as Gamblers: A Modified Theory of Pure Restitution," *Dialogue* 26.1 (Spring 1987): 77–86.

12   In this regard, there is some similarity with theorists of restorative justice.

13   Joseph Ellin, "Restitutionism Defended," *Journal of Value Inquiry* 34.2/3 (September 2000): 299–317. See also Randy Barnett, "Pursuing Justice in a Free Society," *Criminal Justice Ethics* 5.1 (Summer/Fall 1985): 30–53.

14   Ellin 185.

15   Perhaps Ellin makes the sort of mistake feminists used to point to—that of carelessly assuming that people will be able to work without other tasks because they will all have domestic partners taking on such duties.

16   Strictly speaking, there is a distinction between restitution and compensation. The former is provided by the perpetrator as something owed back to the victim in return for something taken away. The latter is provided by a third party, typically an institution or government. The two notions reveal a similar difficulty if we think of *full restitution* or *full compensation*.

17   Bernstein.

18   See Arthur Ripstein, "The Philosophy of Tort Law," *The Oxford Handbook of Jurisprudence and Legal Philosophy*, ed. Jules Coleman and Scott Shapiro (Oxford: Oxford UP, 2001) Chapter 17.

19   The young offenders had vandalized 22 properties. They met with victims. One of many places where this case is described is Marc Forget, "The Restorative Approach," Restorative Justice Online, Simon Fraser University Centre for Restorative Justice, 21 Aug. 2003 <http://www.sfu.ca/cfrj/fulltext/forget2.pdf> last accessed 7 July 2014.

20   Govier, *Taking Wrongs Seriously*. See also Trudy Govier, "A Dialectic of Acknowledgement," *Reconciliation(s): Transitional Justice in Postconflict Societies*, ed. Joanna Quinn (Kingston and Montreal: McGill-Queen's UP, 2009) 36–50.

21   Yael Danieli, editor, *International Handbook of Multigenerational Legacies of Trauma* (New York: Plenum Press, 1998).

22   See Chapter 1 in this book.

23   McVeigh was convicted on 11 counts and executed 11 June 2001. Ten people—members of victims' families and survivors of the Oklahoma bombing—were permitted to watch his execution, apparently on the supposition that seeing him die would provide needed satisfaction. This matter is further discussed in Chapter 10 of this book.

24   Jim Yardley, "Uneasily, Oklahoma City Welcomes Tourists," *New York Times* 11 June 2001 <http://www.nytimes.com/2001/06/11/us/uneasily-oklahoma-city-welcomes-tourists.html> last accessed 26 June 2014.

25   See Gun Control News, "20 Years After the Montreal Massacre," 20 Dec. 2009 <http://www.guncontrol.ca> last accessed 7 July 2014.

26   Govier and Verwoerd, "The Promise and Pitfalls of Apology." See also Nicholas Tavuchis, *Mea Culpa: A Sociology of Apology and Reconciliation* (Redford City, CA: Stanford UP, 1991) and Nick Smith, *I Was Wrong: The Meaning of Apologies* (Cambridge, UK: Cambridge UP, 2008).

27   The point here is not that the victim is infallibly correct about the emotions and sincerity of the perpetrator, but that it is up to him or her to accept the apology or not. A victim might wrongly refuse to accept an apology, even though that apology was quite sincere, appropriate, and accompanied by significant and appropriate practical amends.

CHAPTER 9

CARE AND FORGIVENESS

What is involved in forgiveness?[1] A person who forgives overcomes emotions of resentment and grievance, revising her attitudes toward the one who has wronged her. She does not forget what was done to her, but sets it in the past and does not allow it to define the future. A victim who forgives comes to see the individual wrongdoer as a person of positive potential and moral worth, capable of decent action and full membership in the moral community. To be sure, the wrongdoer harmed her, implying insult and humiliation; he did wrong. But not withstanding this situation, the forgiving victim does not consider the perpetrator as a wrong-doer only. She does not regard his wrongful actions as exhaustively characterizing him as a person. This attitudinal stance involves significant reframing. Despite his offence, she is able to understand the offender as an agent whose personhood and agency are valuable and to be valued; moral values of respect and equality enter here. To forgive an offender is to communicate hope for that person and to judge that as an equal member of the moral community, he may be reintegrated in that community.

If, by forgiving, victims are enabled to have a more healthy mental state and move forward in life without dwelling on grievances or harbouring hatred, then forgiveness benefits them as well as perpetrators and society at large. Indeed, that claim is frequently made.[2] The idea here is that victims who forgive replace negative, bitter, and backward looking emotions with more positive ones. They do not cultivate a sense of grievance; they cease to dwell on wrongs committed against them. Coming to see the perpetrator in a positive light, as a person not reducible simply to his offence and capable of reintegration into a moral community, they will overcome their own sentiments of resentment and vindictiveness to move forward with their own lives. One can argue for the beneficial consequences of forgiveness from three perspectives—those of perpetrators, communities, and victims themselves. Regarding victims, further questions arise.

Clearly, the topic of forgiveness begins with a victim focus, but this focus easily shifts: the person to be forgiven is a perpetrator. Victim forgiveness centrally involves a shift in attitudes to perpetrators, and in the end, considering forgiveness will require thinking about perpetrators.

SOUTH AFRICA

In applied ethics and elsewhere, considerable attention has been paid to the topic of forgiveness. An important motivator was the case of Nelson Mandela and the work of the Truth and Reconciliation Commission (TRC) in South Africa. Nelson Mandela spent 27 years in prison at the hands of South Africa's apartheid government. Eventually, after years of international disrepute and considerable turbulence in the country, the government negotiated with him and he was released in 1990. It was Mandela's attitude to his former captors, their agents, and, indeed, the white population of South Africa that established his moral leadership and inspired millions around the world. On his release, Mandela indicated no bitterness or sense of grievance about the many wrongs done to him or the suffering he had undergone. He sought to collaborate with his former enemies, to embrace them in collegiality and friendship, and to work together to move forward in building South Africa as a multiracial country—a "rainbow nation." He did not advocate any form of revenge, but rather sought reconciliation as a basis for moving forward after the bitter struggle over apartheid. In his forgiveness, Mandela was not responding to apologies or other expressions of remorse offered by leaders of the National Party (supporters of Apartheid) or others who might represent white South Africans. That is to say, his forgiveness was not bilateral; it was not a matter where a perpetrator expresses remorse and forgiveness is offered by a victim in response. But neither was Mandela's forgiveness entirely a one-sided matter; he was reaching out to the white population of South Africa, expressing an invitation to them to acknowledge the many wrongs committed against non-whites and commit to moving forward in a new moral framework.[3] Under the leadership of Archbishop Desmond Tutu, the TRC placed great emphasis on forgiveness as a route to the establishment of decent relationships between victims and perpetrators.

Initiatives in South Africa attracted world attention, and the phenomenon of forgiveness in politics fascinated many commentators and academics. Prior to Mandela's release from jail, many analysts had predicted that apartheid would be brought to an end only with a civil war. In fact both the governing National Party and the liberation African National Congress had estimated that some one million deaths would result from such violence. The negotiated settlement, followed by four years of Mandela's leadership and the work of the TRC, were amazingly and enormously successful in averting large-scale violence. The TRC understood itself as victim-friendly—as attending to the experiences, voices, and needs of victims. Indeed, some 20,000 testimonies from victims were heard, and their accounts were taken seriously with many incorporated into TRC's Final Report.

The South African interest in forgiveness at this stage of the nation's history is hardly surprising. Forgiving victims are open to peaceful co-existence and reconciliation, all to the benefit of perpetrators who may be better included in society and to the safety and security of that society itself. For the most part, it is victims who will forgive or not forgive: obviously, forgiveness concerns victims and begins with them. If victims can forgive perpetrators, they will overcome resentment, grievance, and anger to seek cooperative relationships. When forgiveness is explored, the subject is the attitudes, beliefs, and actions of victims and in particular their attitudes toward perpetrators. Those who forgive overcome their resentment and moral anger towards persons who have wronged them, coming to see those persons as human beings and not simply wrongdoers.

Some critics queried whether an agency such as the TRC should have pushed as hard as it did to encourage victims to forgive. Others pointed out that victims often did not receive the compensation they needed, even in cases where their participation in TRC processes should have led to it. It was also argued in some circles that there was, in the end, more benefit from commission proceedings to perpetrators than to victims, due to the amnesties that were often the outcome. In assessments of the work of the TRC, the relationship between individual suffering and grievances (micro level) and political institutions and processes (macro level) was somewhat unclear. Whether macro or micro, forgiving is something in which victims may engage. But the focus of their attitudes and actions, after all, is perpetrators. A victim who forgives comes to relinquish anger and resentment and shifts toward a more generous attitude toward the offender. In the aftermath of intense political conflicts, such attitudinal shifts are conducive to peace and cooperation. Still, many questions arise.

In some contexts—and South Africa was certainly one of them—forgiveness may seem the only alternative to a generalized quest for revenge. Discussions of forgiveness tend to presume that it has a simple opposite: revenge. And indeed, in many cases, especially including political ones, what stands out about victims who forgive is what they do *not* do. They do not seek revenge or take punitive action against perpetrators. Their reflective generosity offers enormous benefits in dramatically reducing the likelihood of violence. The impression of either/or is misleading, however. There is no exhaustive dichotomy between revenge and forgiveness: intermediate possibilities exist. A victimized person or group may fail to forgive and yet not seek revenge or even punishment for an offender. A person who fails to forgive need not be cultivating attitudes of grievance and hatred or launching a campaign for revenge. A victim might, for instance, decide to avoid contact with the offender and leave to others the question of what happens to that person, focussing instead on her own needs and her own recovery. A central problem of theory is that of the false dichotomy between forgiveness and vindictiveness. This dichotomy underlies the assumption that those victims who do not forgive will be angry and resentful, full of hatred for those who have wronged them, and preoccupied with a quest for revenge. The dichotomy is not a true one, because there does exist the intermediate possibility of non-angry non-forgiveness.

Does appropriate forgiveness require the repentance of the perpetrator? What about forgiving unrepentant agents? How firmly should we draw the distinction between a perpetrating agent and his actions? What is the relation between forgiving someone and reconciling with that person? Are some agents unforgivable? If so, which ones and why? We can see from these many important questions how the topic of forgiveness leads us away from the needs of victims themselves.[4]

CARE FOR THE VICTIM

In a recent article, Nancy Stanlick maintains that many accounts of forgiveness fail to take seriously the grave harms that many victims have suffered; she contends that the claim that victims benefit from forgiveness is problematic in some ways.[5] Victims will frequently be concerned with issues of justice, punishment, and moral message regarding the perpetrator. These issues are of great importance. But there are aspects of healing and recovery that concern victims as individuals or with regard to relationships that do not immediately involve the perpetrator. A victim's capacities to function in her own life may have relatively little to do with what happens to the perpetrator. A crucial practical consideration is that of care. In the case of serious wrongs, the victim is an injured person who needs care and the means to go forward. Forgiveness of the perpetrator may be helpful, given the freeing of attention for one's own recovery, the ending of anger, and the absence of vindictive motives and schemes. It may contribute greatly to a victim's peace of mind and constructive attitudes to friends and community. To be sure, forgiveness can be a kind of release for victims and, as a release, highly valuable. But it rarely suffices for healing and restoration. The victim is one person and the perpetrator another. Putting him down will not bring her up, as assumed in some retributive accounts. But neither will bringing him up bring her up, as sometimes presumed by advocates of forgiveness.

Despite good intentions on the part of practitioners and theorists, there is a risk that concentrating on issues of forgiveness will divert us from other matters crucial to the well-being of victims. Stanlick maintains that what is most important for victims of serious wrongdoing is their care and recovery. She contends that it is not forgiveness, even though forgiveness is psychologically and ethically important and of great interest in its own right. There is a risk that emphasizing forgiveness may be just one more thing that supports a shift in attention from victims to perpetrators. For victims of wrongdoing, forgiveness is not the first need or even in some cases a high priority. Forgiving a perpetrator will not by itself provide a fresh start in life for a victim recovering from the serious harm done to her. A victim needs to heal, address the harms that have come to her, regain trust, and build a secure sense of her own agency and capacity for maintaining relationships and moving forward.[6]

A Horrendous Case

An example powerfully illustrating this point is that of Rumana Monzur, a Bangladeshi woman who came to Canada to complete a master's degree in political science at the University of British Columbia. Monzur had completed a year of her studies when she returned to Bangladesh for a visit to her family, including her four-year-old daughter, husband, and parents. Apparently jealous of her academic success, her husband claimed that she had had an affair in Canada. On 5 July 2011, in the presence of their daughter, he attacked her viciously. He gouged out her eyes, bit off part of her nose, and chewed her lips and cheeks, resulting in horrific injuries. Monzur, her daughter, and her parents returned to Canada where her case was widely publicized, and its appalling details aroused outraged sympathy. Considerable funds were raised for her support, and doctors did their best to repair her debilitating and disfiguring injuries. They were unable to restore her sight.[7]

After a period of despair, Monzur began to rally her energy and resume her work. She learned to read Braille and employ technology that could assist her studies. She regained confidence and had the support of many friends whose sympathy, financial assistance, and considerable practical assistance enabled her to adapt to the considerable harm done to her. University friends read course texts to her and helped transcribe her words into her thesis on the effects of climate change on Bangladesh. She and her family were granted permanent resident status in Canada. On 10 July 2013, Rumana Monzur successfully defended her thesis at UBC. Her smiling face appeared in reports in Canadian national newspapers that emphasized her amazing achievement and partial recovery. Described as "graceful," "triumphant," "incredible," and "inspiring," she was shown on television walking with a cane, supported by a university official, to receive her degree. Interviewed, Monzur said that she tried not to think about the attack and preferred to consider herself a survivor and not a victim. Of course she missed her vision. She could remember sights of oceans and other scenery but said she missed most of all seeing her daughter and her parents. She said, "I didn't let those negative emotions get ahold of my thoughts; I thought this is how I am going to do it. I have to do it now."[8]

The point of this moving story is that with the help of many others, Monzur did recover her spirits, her agency, and some physical well-being. Crucial elements in this story are those of care, sympathy, support, and hopeful energy. Monzur's major achievements showed her agency, capacity, and power. In all of this, attitudes to the perpetrator do not seem central. Does she forgive her former husband? We do not know; it seems unlikely, but so far as her future life is concerned, the matter does not appear to be highly significant. She has stated that she does not let negative emotions prevail. But surely those emotions did not all concern her former husband; they would include fear and anxiety about what she would do in life and how she could cope, use her talents, build a life either in Canada or in Bangladesh, and bring up her daughter. Not only did Monzur complete her degree and gain admission to a high-status Canadian law school, she regained her agency and restored her capacity to lead a good life.[9]

Monzur's husband, Hasan Sayeed Sumon, did not live in Canada. The issue of his treatment did not arise for Canadians, and he and his circumstances were given little attention in the Canadian media. In conjunction with the appalling nature of his violence and the gross injuries he inflicted, the circumstances of his absence from the Canadian scene made it possible to concentrate entirely on the care of his victim. With her acute needs and with her family, Monzur was present in Canada and in focus as the victim of these terrible attacks. For the most part, Canadian news has concerned her needs, recovery, accomplishments, and plans. If we ask what happened to Hasan Sayeed Sumon, many Canadians would be likely to respond, "who cares?" And such a harsh response would not be entirely inappropriate. We are likely to react immediately in such a horrifying case to insist that it is the life of the victim and the welfare of the victim that should be of concern. In Bangladesh, Sumon was charged with attempted murder and incarcerated while awaiting trial; he was later found dead in the jail washroom. Initially, cardiac arrest was thought to be the cause of his death, given that there were no visible injuries. Later, marks on his neck and a plastic bag within the room where he was found supported the conclusion that he had been murdered.[10]

This case certainly raises questions about security and treatment of persons detained in Bangladeshi jails, attitudes to gender and violence in Bangladesh, the potential role of the Monzur/Sumon case in setting precedents in that country, and related legal and cultural matters. Monzur was apparently shocked by Sumon's death and disappointed that he did not live to undergo a trial. She had hoped that such trial would expose issues of domestic violence and bring public discussion of gender issues in her home country. In fact, a legal response to his case would have been compatible with her forgiving him. A victim may overcome resentment and grievance against an offender even while believing that his trial and subsequent punishment are good and desirable things.

Questions about perpetrators are not the essence of the matter so far as seriously harmed victims are concerned. Insofar as the well-being of victims is our central concern, our priority should be their emotional and practical needs. We should do our best to support them and assist them, as Monzur's friends and associates did for her. The Monzur/Sumon case does not show that issues of forgiveness are unimportant, even though questions about forgiveness are unlikely to strike us as prominent. Such questions can be raised, even though Sumon is dead.

People have attitudes with regard to the dead, and those attitudes may have significant effects on their actions and relationships. Even though her ex-husband is dead, Monzur's attitudes toward him will be significant in the conduct of her life. They will affect her memories of their life together, the terrible attack, and how she and her parents talk about him and about the marriage. They will also affect what she tells her daughter about her father, what happened to him, and how she became blind. Vindictive attitudes will have different effects from forgiving attitudes. Even in this terrible case, it can be argued that forgiving attitudes should be preferred. But these are not the only alternatives, given other possibilities such as avoidance, silence, or downplaying the terrible events. A person can decide whether or not it is appropriate to revise attitudes toward a wrongdoer and may for various reasons decide to amend them. Indeed, one can ask whether Monzur could forgive Sumon, or should forgive him, and the question makes sense. One can argue that forgiveness would be desirable, if it is possible.

DO VICTIMS EVER HAVE AN OBLIGATION TO FORGIVE?

Common wisdom has it that, whatever benefits forgiveness may bring for perpetrators and communities, there is no moral obligation for victims to forgive. Victims should not be pressed or directed to forgive, even in the interests of the worthy goals of peace and reconciliation. On this view, it is up to victims to judge and define their own attitudes and responses. Against this common wisdom, Espen Gamlund has recently argued that in some circumstances there is an obligation to forgive a repentant wrongdoer. In restricting his case to the repentant wrongdoer, Gamlund makes it clear that he is considering bilateral forgiveness and that only. He is not addressing unilateral forgiveness, cases of forgiveness where the wrongdoer fails to be repentant by denying that what he did was wrong, denying that he did it at all, continuing to do it, or moving away without communicating any moral attitude regarding his offence. In other words, Gamlund is not considering unconditional forgiveness. Nor is he considering invitational forgiveness, forgiveness offered in the hopeful expectation that a perpetrator might respond by accepting and acknowledging his wrongdoing. What Gamlund claims is that in many circumstances, victims have a duty to forgive a *repentant* wrongdoer. He is limiting his argument to cases in which a wrongdoer indicates (through apology or other appropriate gestures) his remorse and repentance. Knowing of the offender's repentance, the victim may respond by offering forgiveness. The perpetrator repents; the victim forgives, in response; hence the situation is bilateral. Gamlund maintains that victims have a duty to forgive in response to repentance, other things being equal, that is to say, unless other considerations outweigh what he refers to as the norm of forgiveness.[11]

Gamlund argues that (other things being equal) a victim has an obligation to forgive a repentant offender because that offender has given a victim *good reason* to revise her judgements about him. In communicating his repentance to the victim through an apology, the offender has in effect renounced his wrongful deed. He has dissociated himself from it and no longer wishes to communicate that what he did was permissible or right. Instead, he is indicating that he will not do such a thing again. In other words, if he could, he would undo the wrong. Gamlund does not argue that such an obligation to forgive would be absolute; his "other things being equal" clause should be noted. Considerations could weigh against the supposed obligation. Gamlund does not argue that forgiveness is obligatory for a victim who would find it very difficult or even impossible. Nor does he address the issue of sincerity in those cases in which repentance is indicated. Further considerations concern (1) the blameworthiness of the agent, (2) the gravity of the harm, and (3) the extent to which the perpetrator is able and willing to compensate the victim for the harm done to her. Considering these conditions, we can see that Gamlund would not argue for a victim's obligation to forgive in the aftermath of serious wrongdoing as in the Monzur case.

In that case, the harm was grave, extreme, and (most obviously concerning her blindness) unrecoverable. It seems highly unlikely that her husband would be lacking in blame for such an attack, and it would be impossible for him or anyone else to compensate for the serious harms she suffered at his hands. As a dead man, her former husband cannot compensate her; had he lived, he would in all likelihood have been confined in jail without economic resources available for compensation. The norm of forgiveness that Gamlund puts forward does not apply in this case; even supposing that there are some victims who have an obligation to forgive, Monzur would not be one of them.

Gamlund's account fits less severe and more straightforward cases, like that of a young man who has written graffiti on his neighbour's freshly painted house. Caught after the act and confronted by his hurt and angry neighbour, the young offender comes to understand that what he did was wrong. He apologizes, offers to repaint the house, and does a good job of that. Responding to these initiatives, the neighbour forgives him, with his compensation being an important factor in the case. There is a significant—in this case almost literal—sense in which the original wrong has been wiped out. (At least, its physical manifestation has been wiped out.) There have been remorse, apology, restitution, and repair. Provided that he judges the young offender to be sincerely remorseful and committed not to do such a thing again, the victim of this minor wrong has good reason to forgive, and on Gamlund's account, he has a moral obligation to do so because the wrongdoer has renounced his deed and the repair has been accomplished.

As applied to wrongs that do not bring lasting physical or psychic damage to the victim, Gamlund's account has some plausibility. It is inappropriate for victims of minor wrongs to retain indefinitely resentful attitudes and a sense of grievance against persons who have offended and later repented to indicate their disavowal of what they did. But on Gamlund's account, there will be no obligation to forgive in cases where the harm is grave, bringing irreversible damage or injury, and where it is impossible to compensate. Wrongs done to victims of beatings and abuse, especially the abuse of children, fall in this latter category. The implication of non-forgiveness need not be ongoing hatred, resentment, or vindictiveness. Rather, a victim may choose to concentrate on his or her own needs and capacities, seeking to restore agency and power and getting on with life. Victims who, in this sense, fail to forgive do not for that reason constitute a threat to peace within their communities or even a threat against the life and security of perpetrators. They simply have a different focus, a focus slanted toward their own recovery. In cases of serious wrongs, such a focus cannot reasonably be criticized.

IS IT ONLY VICTIMS WHO CAN FORGIVE?

It is often claimed that only victims have the standing to forgive. In other words, there is a victim's prerogative such that anyone who is not the victim of an offence cannot properly forgive the offender for that offence. This view of the standing to forgive is often simply assumed as obvious; however, there do exist supporting arguments for it. One is that only the victim knows what he feels and has the capacity to revise his emotions and attitudes, so if forgiveness involves revising those emotions and attitudes, only the victim is in a position to do it. Another is that for someone other than the victim to forgive would be disrespectful to the victim or disloyal to him and to his memory.

Interestingly, several analysts have recently questioned the victim's prerogative or "standing" to forgive.[12] In reflecting on the issue of standing, one approach is to consider which victim is referred to. The most common presumption is that forgiveness is the prerogative of the primary victim (the woman attacked, the man whose house was defaced, the owner of the car with broken windows...). Yet there are other victims to be considered: secondary victims and tertiary victims. On the view that victims have the prerogative to forgive, it would not only be primary victims who have this right; secondary and tertiary victims would also have a prerogative to forgive harms brought to them as a result of harming of the primary victim. Recognizing the plurality of victims, we are led to broaden the standing to forgive so as to shift away from the primary victim. When there are many victims, assuming the victim's prerogative, there will be many who are entitled to forgive. Applying this broadened view literally, in addition to the primary victim, secondary victims would have the right to forgive a perpetrator for harms done to them and tertiary victims for the wrongs done to them. This broadening does not require a departure from the idea that it is victims uniquely who are entitled to forgive. In fact, it develops from that presumption; extensions are due to extensions from the primary victim to other victims of the same act.

The results of this broadened view are, however, somewhat awkward. This account implies that each victim would have the standing to forgive the perpetrator for what was done to him. It is people, not acts, who are forgiven. In its most straightforward sense, the broadened view has different victims forgiving or failing to forgive the same perpetrator for different harms ensuing from the same act. A man who was the primary victim of a beating could, in principle, forgive his attacker for the assault. A secondary victim (the victim's mother) could refuse to forgive the attacker for the harm he brought to her as a result of what he did to her son; he harmed her by depriving her of the companionship and support of her son and brought anxiety and expense to her in the aftermath of the assault on him. The tertiary victim (the neighbourhood community) could refuse to forgive the attacker for the harms imposed on it as a result of the attack on this man; the attack had the result of undermining a sense of physical security and increasing the costs of law enforcement. Clearly, then, these different victims could differ in their responses. Though somewhat awkward and seemingly pedantic in its details, this broadened account is not contradictory and can claim a degree of realism. After all, different harms do come to different people as a result of the same act by the same agent. Different victims may respond differently to that agent, given their own values and psychological make-up and the harms his action has inflicted on them. For one and the same act, an offender may be both forgiven and not forgiven, relative to the responses of these different victims.

Further difficulties and anomalies arise, however, when a victim prerogative account is broadened in this way. Consider that a son is severely beaten and his mother, affected by the beating, is a secondary victim. Now reflect on what a mother is likely to feel: in the aftermath of the beating, she will feel anxiety and concern, sympathy and compassion. Grief and moral indignation she will feel on his behalf; her concern will be for him. Should the issue of forgiveness arise for her, it will not primarily concern the harm done to her as a secondary victim. Rather, it will and should concern what was done to her son, the suffering and harms imposed on him. To put the matter simply, she will be angry with the wrongdoer because of what he did to her son. "The parent resents the wrongdoer for the child's suffering, not for her own," says Glen Pettigrove, discussing this sort of case.[13]

Forgiveness concerns attitudes and actions towards offenders. We live and function in moral communities. Within those communities, our attitudes and actions arise concerning many others and affect many others. Victims have the standing to forgive, but it is not only as victims that we may have that standing. To be sure, people may be indirectly harmed as secondary and tertiary victims, and for that reason, there is truth in the broadened account extending standing to those victims. But that is not the core of the matter, which is how some persons may feel moral anger about the suffering of others. Pettigrove offers an especially thorough and convincing treatment of the issue of standing. He notes that we are often compassionate and sympathetic observers, moved by humanitarian responses to the suffering of others. He maintains that we can have a standing to forgive as a result of those feelings. For a wide variety of reasons, we may be sensitive to the suffering of others when we are not victims ourselves.

Pettigrove cites an example from a film in which the anti-slavery activist, William Wilberforce, is repelled when a friend offers him his slave to repay a gambling debt. If Wilberforce considered whether to forgive this man, the wrongs to be forgiven would be those connected with the man's attitudes toward enslaved persons and ownership and treatment of them. They would not be restricted to the moral failure implied by his offering his slave as a payment. The issue between Wilberforce and this man is that of slavery and attitudes to those persons profoundly harmed by it, namely, slaves. It is not any harms incurred on Wilberforce himself. Were Wilberforce to say that he would "never forgive" the gambling partner and the target of his outrage, he would focus on the treatment of enslaved persons. To insist that the question of forgiveness cannot arise in the case because Wilberforce himself was in no sense a victim of slavery would be incorrect. Wilberforce was not seriously harmed by the gambler's offer, whether as a victim of slavery or as a person whose sentiments were outraged. The issue here is not whether Wilberforce himself should qualify as a primary, secondary, or tertiary victim of an offence. Rather, it is whether the slave-owner should be forgiven his attitude to enslaved people, whom he regards as things to be owned and given away.

As illustrated by this case, we are often in the role of observers or third parties when we speak of ourselves as forgiving, or being unable to forgive, others. The Wilberforce case is constructed from history; other examples of third-person forgiveness may arise in everyday life. For example, a man might consider whether to forgive, or fail to forgive, a colleague who betrayed and mistreated her husband but later felt remorse and tried to repair some of the damage. To forgive this woman would mean to overcome his indignation and anger at what she had done to her husband, to regard her as a moral agent capable of doing better and resolved to do better, and as a person worthy of reacceptance. Her colleague can forgive her without himself being in any sense a victim of her wrongdoing. He is, to be sure, affected by that wrongdoing, but the point is that he was not harmed by it or has anything to forgive regarding harm done to himself. It is more that he is angry at the moral offence against her husband. What is at stake is this man's attitude to his colleague and how "forgiving" he wants that attitude to be. It is his conception of what sort of person she is and how he should regard her, given what she did to her husband. The colleague is a third party in this sort of case; he is not a primary, secondary, or tertiary victim.

Observers too can feel solidarity with victims and, in accordance with their responses in varying circumstances, form and revise their attitudes to offenders.

Pettigrove argues that the issue of third-party forgiveness arises when we feel solidarity with victims and in such cases, third-party forgiveness can be legitimate. He notes that such forgiveness has a different meaning from forgiveness by a victim, and there may be different motives for it. There are different moral constraints as to when it should be offered, and these constraints warrant consideration.[14]

Of particular relevance to the issue of forgiveness is the fact that observers, even those remote from events, may feel rage and moral indignation at what is done to persons with whom they identify. These persons need not be friends or family members; we are capable of feeling rage and indignation about injuries to others with whom we identify as fellow human beings. In a recent account of unreasonable resentments, Alice MacLachlan maintains that in the aftermath of serious wrongdoing, bystanders may feel many emotions: grief, sorrow, rage, shock, horror, sympathy, and hopelessness among them. These bystanders have strong emotional responses even though they are not primary, secondary, or tertiary victims.[15] Much of that anger will be directed to perpetrators. How we respond to and amend our own anger raises questions of justice, care, and in appropriate circumstances, forgiveness. There are many varieties of moral anger, some reasonable and some unreasonable; it is not only as victims that we may feel significant moral anger. If we tie forgiveness to the idea of overcoming resentment of a perpetrator for committing a wrong, we can see, through the broadening of a conception of resentment, a need for further broadening of standing to forgive.

In solidarity with victims, we may feel moral anger and think of ourselves as forgiving or (more commonly) being unable to forgive those who have wronged them. Ordinary language uses (e.g., "It was a struggle, but finally I forgave Mary for what she did to Charles"; "I could never forgive a person who abused a child in that way") do support the notion of third parties (non-victims) retaining their attitudes of moral anger or forgiving.

A further difficulty for the orthodox view that only victims have the standing to forgive arises with regard to self-forgiveness. The orthodox view that only direct victims have the standing to forgive has unwelcome implications in this context. In short, it rules out self-forgiveness. If only victims are entitled to forgive, then on the presumption that perpetrators are not victims of themselves, they are not entitled to forgive themselves. A perpetrator who forgives herself for what she has done does not forgive herself *as a victim* but *as a perpetrator* understanding herself to be guilty. If only victims can forgive, self-forgiveness should be impossible. Yet the notion of "forgiving oneself" does have popular currency and has struck both the therapeutic and philosophical communities as coherent, viable, and important. Suppose that a woman forgives herself for what she comes to understand as wrongdoing, say in a case where she harshly punished a child in the name of discipline. She would not forgive herself as a victim; she would forgive herself as the agent of what she later came to understand to be a wrongful act that harmed her child. If the notion of self-forgiveness is accepted, that provides further reason to re-examine the claim that only victims have the standing to forgive.[16]

TWO SIMPLIFYING DICHOTOMIES

As noted, pressure for victims to forgive may be grounded in a false dichotomy between forgiveness and revenge. A major reason for thinking that forgiveness is good is that revenge, presumed to be its only alternative, is bad. The revenge/forgiveness dichotomy remains tempting and misleading. It is too easy to make the assumption that victims who do not forgive will be hateful and vindictive, seeking revenge and perpetuating dangerous cycles of violence. But this assumption is hasty and incorrect. Victims may have other attitudes, after all: some may be relatively indifferent to perpetrators while seeking to recover with the care and sympathy of other people.

The revenge/forgiveness dichotomy is not the only one threatening a nuanced understanding of forgiveness. The language of victims and perpetrators is another. It is as one who has wrongfully harmed another that a person (the perpetrator) would be considered for forgiveness; it is as one who is wrongfully harmed (the victim) or as one standing in solidarity with victims, that a person would forgive. Thus, the language of forgiveness presumes two roles: that of the victim, who is passive and is harmed by the action of another, and that of the perpetrator, who is active and responsible for wrongfully harming another. The presumption of victim/perpetrator roles is a central conception of forgiveness. It would be incorrect to insist that this presumption is incorrect: clearly there are victims and there are perpetrators. Yet thinking goes astray if we fail to attend to cases in which victim and perpetrator roles are combined. Combined and overlapping roles are found in a number of important situations.

Most simply and obviously, persons who are victims in one act can be perpetrators in another; those who are perpetrators in one act can be victims in another. A person's victimhood can be an important factor in leading to his or her perpetration. Examples are all too easy to find: consider cases where a person has suffered childhood sexual abuse, turns to drugs for comfort, and then become engaged in theft and assault when engaged in the drug trade. A tragic political example is that of Winnie Mandela.[17] For several decades a victim of oppression and isolation under South Africa's apartheid government, Winnie Mandela struggled to bring up her children alone when her husband was in prison. She later became a leader in the anti-apartheid struggle. Eventually, she was complicit in serious black-on-black violence against youth deemed insufficiently loyal to the branch of the anti-apartheid movement with which she identified. Winnie Mandela appeared before the TRC as a perpetrator charged with murder. The victim had become a perpetrator. It is no exaggeration to say that what was done to her as a victim contributed to her later serious wrongdoing and perpetrator role.

In other cases, a person's role as a perpetrator can lead to his victimization. Clear cases of this sequence appear when people are convicted of crimes, then jailed and raped and abused in prison. Many perpetrators of the 1994 Rwandan genocide were jailed in appalling prison conditions, awaiting trial for years due to inadequate facilities in the aftermath of the genocide. They had been perpetrators but later became victims of mistreatment, disease, and delayed legal proceedings.

The victim/perpetrator split falls apart even more clearly in cases where a person appears to be both victim and perpetrator in the same act. Important and moving examples here are those of child soldiers who, under coercion, may commit horrifying acts of violence. Such persons are sometimes referred to as complex political victims, sometimes as complex political perpetrators.[18] One might seek to diminish the challenge of these examples by arguing that child soldiers bear no responsibility for their acts and thus have no status as perpetrators, being victims only. But the force of such arguments will diminish with evidence that child soldiers can and do make some choices about their actions.

A coalescence of victim/perpetrator roles is a feature of other cases. One could be a victim of her own actions, in a case of self-damage. A person might, for instance, be described as a victim of his own ambition, in a case where a persistent struggle for career success alienates family members and friends. Suppose that such a description is literal and accurate. This person would be a victim in the sense of having been passively harmed by something (that is, his ambition) that was overblown and dangerous in the sense that it was apt to be injurious to family relationships. He would be a perpetrator in the sense that it was *his* ambition, decisions, and actions that brought damage to family members and to himself. We do speak of people as being victims of themselves, meaning that they have acted on the basis of some aspect of their character so as to damage themselves. The victim/perpetrator language has to be stretched to fit such a case; indeed, one can mount a logical resistance to this sort of example by questioning agency and passivity.

In cases of "victim becomes perpetrator" and "perpetrator becomes victim," it is possible to preserve the classic victim/perpetrator split by specifying different acts and time frames. Consider again the victim who becomes a perpetrator. Winnie Mandela was a victim of banishment and other wrongs during the 1960s and 1970s; she became a perpetrator of murder and abuse later, during the 1980s. From a logical point of view, there is no messy blurring of roles in this particular case: the acts and times are different. We can appeal to those differences to keep the roles distinct. But strict logic will mislead us here if it leads us to ignore causal relationships between what happened at the earlier times and the attitudes and actions of later times.

These various examples illustrate some of the many cases in which the roles of (passive) victim and (active) perpetrator are blurred or shared. To the extent that these roles are mixed and non-dichotomous, the language of forgiveness may be misleading.[19] Two challenges of special interest are those of mutuality and of self-damage.

Blame, Regret, and Self-Forgiveness

Insofar as she is a victim, a person is not accountable for those actions of which she is a victim. She may, nonetheless, have contributed to the context in which those actions occurred. Though the binary logic of forgiveness does not encourage reflection on such matters, victims may be aware of them and may even go so far as to blame themselves for what happened. Strictly speaking, such blame is inappropriate. If a woman walking alone in a forest is beaten and raped, it is her rapist, not herself, who is to blame for that attack. Injuries from the attack are imposed by him, are his doing, and are not her fault. Taking that walk is something she did, and taking a walk is not a wrongful act. At worst it would have been imprudent, not immoral. The victim of the attack is not to blame for it because the notion of blame does not apply when there is no wrongdoing. Nonetheless, a victim such as this one might blame herself and be encouraged in that attitude by others who think she was unwise.[20]

Blaming herself, a victim in such circumstances might deliberate about whether to forgive herself. This would be (in her mind) forgiving herself for a wrong she did to herself. If a victim acted wrongly and thus set the context for an attack or other wrongdoing, she could correctly come to understand that fact and forgive herself for what she did wrong in the sense of being imprudent. But on the presumption that she did nothing morally wrong, the notion of self-forgiveness does not fit and should not be made to fit. A victim such as this woman need not forgive herself for any wrongdoing in the case, since there is none. What should be at issue here is regret, not blame. Where the context-setting act is normal and innocuous, victims have not wronged themselves or others. It is the attacker who

177

has acted wrongly, and it is he who will need forgiveness—whether from himself, his victim, or community members. When she went for a walk, the woman set the context for her rape, but she is not guilty of that rape or of other wrongdoing in the case. At worst, she is "guilty" of imprudence. She may come to regret what she did, perhaps regard it as unwise; she may regret it deeply and try to get over those feelings. When she tries to "forgive herself," she is indeed trying to amend her feelings about what she did and thinking of what she did as in some sense "wrong." She may be resolving to protect herself by changing her behaviour. All of this may be desirable, commendable, and useful for her mental health. Overcoming negative attitudes, considering one's own habits and capacities, and resolving to act differently in the future have significant similarities with self-forgiveness. But with wrongdoing and appropriate blame missing from the story, these are not standard cases of self-forgiveness and should not be understood as such.

It is primarily for perpetrators that the issue of self-forgiveness arises and can be understood as parallel to the forgiveness of others. An offender may forgive himself in the sense of understanding that he has done wrong, seeing himself as capable of better, understanding that wrong as committed in the past by his past self, and resolving to do better, understanding himself to be capable of making the needed change. He may forgive himself for something he did to another, and such forgiveness can be essential for his moral transformation.[21] There is an emotional shift towards an offender and an offence; the offence is set in the past. And there is a moral shift toward the offender, seeing him or her in a different perspective as a person resolved to change and do better. In this case, the offender is himself the person who forgives.[22]

Mutuality

Mutual forgiveness is called for in many cases where each of two parties (persons or groups) has wronged the other. In their relationships, both have suffered wrong, both have done wrong. What is needed to restore their relationship is acknowledgement by each and forgiveness by each. An individual or group may insist on victim status to avoid any implication of responsibility for wrongdoing. Rhetorically, the cry "but we were the victims" may be used in attempts to justify or exonerate. But it should not do so—either for groups or for individuals. The bitter truth is that those victimized in conflicts have often themselves perpetrated misdeeds, and the fact of their victimization in certain contexts does not disprove that perpetration. It is exonerating—hence tempting, yet so often mistaken—to think of oneself or one's group purely as the wronged party, failing to recognize the significance of one's own actions. The dichotomized framework of victim and perpetrator, underlying the concept of forgiveness, may serve to encourage that mistake.

Consider, as an example, a relationship in which the wife alienates their children from her husband, while the husband hides parts of his income from his wife. The deceived wife may see herself as a victim of the husband's deception and with regard to it, she is indeed a victim—she will see him as having wronged her. As a victim, she was harmed by what he did; as a victim, she may anticipate acknowledgement and apology. In this frame of reference, she is the person who is entitled to forgive and can choose whether to forgive or not. But even if he were to express remorse and she were to forgive, her forgiveness would not suffice to bridge the ruptures in their relationship. It would apply only to one important problem, leaving untouched matters of their relationships with the children. The implication of her forgiving him would be that he was the wrongdoer and she the person wronged, and so far as his deception about income is concerned, this implication is acceptable. But his deception is not the only relevant matter.

If we think of this woman as the innocent recipient of harm imposed by her husband, we have what the language of forgiveness requires: a victim and a perpetrator. Within this frame of reference, the question of forgiveness arises for her; it is the question of whether, as the victim, she should forgive the perpetrator. To focus on his action and the harm it brought to her may be tempting for the wife, of course. As the innocent victim of his damaging action, she will be in a role of moral superiority and the person who is in a position to forgive. But the classic conception of forgiveness is apt to mislead us at this point. Its focus on the victim and the perpetrator is harmful because the husband's deception needs to be considered in context. A significant aspect of that context is his wife's undermining of his relationship with their children and his suspicions relating to that. Perhaps, sensing his deteriorating relationship with the children and suspecting her role in encouraging their alienation from him, the husband suspects that she wants to end their marriage and is deceiving her and reserving some part of his income to protect himself if that happens. At this point, their problems are intertwined. For this couple to work them out, both will have to acknowledge, both will need forgiveness, and both will have to forgive. In short, mutual forgiveness is called for. If the husband and wife forgive each other, they will overcome their anger and resentment against each other and come again to regard each other as partners in a relationship built on respect and cooperation rather than animosity and suspicion. It will be incorrect and unhelpful from the standpoint of their relationship overall for the wife to insist that she is the deserving victim and her husband the guilty perpetrator who needs to repent. The same may be said, of course, if the husband alone insists on taking the role of the righteous and deserving victim.

To judge whether wrongdoing on one side is greater or lesser than on the other will be difficult and unlikely to be useful. Nor should the husband and wife or anyone else arrive at a facile conclusion that these wrongs are morally equivalent or can in some way cancel each other out. Harms done by one wrongful act do not disappear because some other harmful act has been done.

This case brings us back to the issue of blaming the victim. If we say that mutual forgiveness is needed because the wife's interactions with her children are part of the situation in which her husband has deceived her, are we then blaming her for what he did? Are we saying that it was her fault that he deceived her? Are we excusing him for what he did, on the grounds that she, not he, was to blame? Are we saying that she, though a victim, is nevertheless to blame for her own victimization? The answer to all these questions should be negative. Her role in setting the context does not excuse his actions within that context, although it might help to explain them. To fully excuse the husband's actions, we would have to say that he had no choice in the matter. That would be incorrect. Even given the situation, this man decided what to do and is responsible for his own actions. After all, he could have raised with her his difficulties with the children before setting about to deceive her about his income. Of his deception, she is the victim. Is she to blame for what he did? No. He had a choice and made a choice, and of the deception, he is the agent and the wrongdoer. What she did was to significantly affect the situation of that choice, but not to determine it. What the wife is to blame for is something else: her interactions with their children insofar as they were intended to alienate the children from their father.

Insofar as a person is a victim, she is not to blame for what was done to her. But a person who is the victim of one action is not in every context a victim. Many persons, such as this wife, are victims of an action that occurs in a context where they are blameworthy for something else.

Similar considerations apply in complex political cases. Reflecting on 9/11, most commentators thought of the United States as a collectivity and the injured or killed individuals as victims. These people were passive in the attack, they were not agents of it and were in this sense innocent, and they were harmed by externally imposed forces. The perpetrators were the 19 hijackers and, in their role as funders and planners, the leaders of Al Qaeda, including most significantly Osama bin Laden. The stated and inferred motives of the terrorists referred to factors such as global economic inequality, the humiliation of Muslims, the colonial history of Middle Eastern countries, the presence of US troops in the sacred (for Muslims) country of Saudi Arabia, and even the Crusades. Emphasizing the significance of these motivational factors, some commentators wrote in the vein of "chickens coming home to roost," arguing that geopolitical inequities in which the United States and its policies played a central role meant that the United States got what it deserved. These analysts, mostly on the political left, were highly unpopular in the immediate aftermath of the attacks. They were castigated and ridiculed for "excusing" the terrorists and "blaming" the victim.[23] Details and nuances regarding 9/11 are complex and contested, to say the least. But themes in this macro case are significantly similar to those that emerge in the micro case of the husband and wife, discussed above. An agent may bear some responsibility for the situation in which an action occurs while being at the same time a victim of wrongful action in that situation. The fact that a victimized agent has acted so as to set the context for an action does not make that agent responsible or blameworthy for the action itself.

Yes, the United States set much of the context for the attacks. No, it did not carry out the attacks of which it was a victim, nor was it blameworthy for them. The affluence, technology, and power of the United States were resented by many in formerly colonized areas.[24] Its actions as a global superpower, influential in an area of the world emerging from colonization, functioned to establish the context of 9/11. But it was the hijackers and their supporters who organized and orchestrated the attacks. It was they who were the perpetrators, and they who bear responsibility for their own choices and actions. The United States as a victim had played a role in creating the context for terrorist acts. To say that is not to blame the United States for the attacks or to identify it as a perpetrator in the case. The bitter debates between left and right about 9/11 were based on a misunderstanding. Both sides had stories that were in important respects correct.

Story number one: the United States and its citizens were victims and the terrorists were perpetrators. Story number two: the global system is characterized by profound inequalities between nations and peoples who are victims of extreme deprivation, and powerful economic forces in Western nations bear some responsibility for that deprivation. Both stories are incomplete: more accurate narratives would combine accounts of action and passivity on both sides. US policies and actions stimulated resentment and a sense of humiliation among many people; these policies and actions surely merit examination in the aftermath of the attacks. However, emphasizing innocent and outraged victimhood does not encourage reflection on the context and its implications. To say the least, subsequent developments indicate that such reflection would have been profoundly important.

CONCLUDING COMMENTS

The importance of forgiveness, both in personal life and in political affairs, indicates that it should be a central issue for victims. But despite its importance, a focus on forgiveness can be misleading so far as victims are concerned. Should victims forgive perpetrators? This is primarily for victims to decide. But obviously the question concerns perpetrators at least as much as victims themselves. For victims of serious wrongdoing, it is not forgiveness but rather care and recovery that matter most. It is misleading to concentrate so much on forgiveness that we forget the need for victims' care and healing.

Reflections on forgiveness are easily distorted by dichotomous thinking. First, there is the false dichotomy between forgiveness and revenge. A failure to note the possibility of intermediates such as non-angry non-forgiveness may support pressure for victims to forgive and too-eager judgements in favour of forgiveness. The main problem here is that the forgiveness/revenge dichotomy is not exhaustive; there are intermediate possibilities it does not consider. Second, there is the false dichotomy of victim and perpetrator; here, the main problem is that of non-exclusiveness. The dichotomy assumes that one is either a victim or a perpetrator and never both. Yet one and the same person may occupy both the role of victim and that of perpetrator. The paradigm of forgiveness has a victim who has suffered wrong forgiving a distinct person, the perpetrator who has imposed it. That paradigm can be misleading for more complex cases in which victim/perpetrator roles are not mutually exclusive.

It is not only as victims that we may have standing to forgive. Third parties in solidarity with victims have that standing also. Repentant perpetrators who have resolved to reform may appropriately forgive themselves in some circumstances. The notion of self-forgiveness by perpetrators does make sense and has a real role to play in moral transformation. Victims may blame themselves and may think of forgiving themselves. But where they have not acted wrongly, it is regret, not blame, that fits their role in setting the context of wrongdoing. To be sure, victims of serious wrongdoing are likely to feel deep emotions about what has been done to them. They may seek to recover from their feelings so as to be able to move ahead; they may wish to amend negative attitudes and change their actions in efforts to better protect themselves in the future. Forgiveness can play a very useful role here. Victims may also feel a need for reflection, change, and self-forgiveness. In strict logic, there should be no call for self-forgiveness where victims have not done wrong. It is regret, not blame, that fits these circumstances.

NOTES

1   Govier, *Forgiveness and Revenge*. See also Trudy Govier and Wilhelm Verwoerd, "Forgiveness: The Victim's Prerogative," *South African Journal of Philosophy* 21.2 (2002): 97–111.

2   See Margaret Holmgren in "Forgiveness and the Intrinsic Value of Persons," *American Philosophical Quarterly* 30 (1993): 341–51 and "Self-Forgiveness and Responsible Moral Agency," *Journal of Value Inquiry* 32.1 (1998): 75–91.

3   Govier, *Forgiveness and Revenge*. See also, Trudy Govier and Colin Hirano, "A Conception of Invitational Forgiveness," *Journal of Social Philosophy* 39.3 (2008): 429–44.

4   The issue of forgiveness does of course concern victims in contrast to many other issues about wrongdoing, which concern perpetrators. The problem arises if our focus shifts primarily to perpetrators and we fail to attend sufficiently to victims as persons requiring sympathy and assistance.

5   Nancy Stanlick, "Reconciling with Harm: An Alternative to Forgiveness and Revenge," *Florida Philosophical Review* 43 (2010): 88–111.

6   Stanlick cites me among others as being too hasty to assert benefits for victims and not attending sufficiently to needs for care.

7   "UBC Student Blinded in Bangladesh Attack Earns Master's Degree," *Globe and Mail* 11 July 2013; "BC Student Blinded in Bangladesh Attack Earns Master's Degree, Prepares for Law School," *National Post* 11 July 2013.

8   The quotation is taken from "Rumana Prevails," *Daily Star* 12 July 2013 <http://archive.thedailystar.net/beta2/news/rumana-prevails/> last accessed 26 June 2014.

9   Stanlick calls this "reconciling with harm" and sees it as an alternative both to forgiveness and to revenge.

10   Canadian Press, "Man Accused of Blinding UBC Student Dies in Prison: Reports," Huffington Press Canada, 4 Feb. 2012 <http://www.huffingtonpost.ca/news/ubc-blinding/> last accessed 7 July 2014.

11   Espen Gamlund, "The Duty to Forgive Repentant Wrongdoers," *International Journal of Philosophical Studies* 18.5 (2010): 651–71.

12   Glen Pettigrove, "The Standing to Forgive," *Monist* 92.4 (2009): 583–603; Alice MacLachlan, "Unreasonable Resentments," *Journal of Social Philosophy* 41.4 (2010): 422–41; and Kevin Zarogoza, "Forgiveness and Standing," *Philosophy and Phenomenological Research* 84.3 (2012): 604–21.

13   Pettigrove, 589.

14   Govier and Verwoerd, "Forgiveness: The Victim's Prerogative."

15   Alice MacLachlan, "Moral Powers and Forgivable Evils," *Evil, Political Violence, and Forgiveness: Essays in Honor of Claudia Card*, ed. Andrea Veltman and Kathryn Norlock (Lanham, MD: Lexington Books, 2009) 135–58.

16   The importance of self-forgiveness has been emphasized by a number of recent authors. See note 22.

17   Anne Borer describes the case of Winnie Mandela in "A Taxonomy of Victims and Perpetrators: Human Rights and Reconciliation in South Africa," *Human Rights Quarterly* 25.4 (2003): 1088–1116.

18   E.K. Baines and O. Boniface, "Complicating Victims and Perpetrators in Uganda: On Dominic Ongwen," *Justice and Reconciliation: Field Note* 7 (2008): 1–19. See also E.K. Baines, "Complex Political Perpetrators: Reflections on Dominic Ongwen," *Journal of Modern African Studies* 47 (2009): 163–91.

19   Challenges in this area are many and certainly not all of them can be discussed here.

20   The example recalls the case of Susan Brison, described in Chapter 1 of this book.

21   Interestingly, it may be argued that for a perpetrator to accept the forgiveness of another, he must forgive himself.

22   Self-forgiveness by perpetrators is significant in cases where victims are unable or unwilling to forgive. See Byron Williston, "The Importance of Self-Forgiveness," *American Philosophical Quarterly* 49.1 (2012): 67–80.

23   For a treatment of this debate, see Christopher Hitchens, "Stranger in a Strange Land: The Dismay of an Honest and Honorable Man of the Left," *Atlantic Monthly* (Dec. 2001): 32–34; and Glenn Bohn and Kim Bolan, "Thobani Accused of Hate Crime against Americans," *Vancouver Sun* 10 Oct. 2001 <http://globalresearch.ca/articles/BOL110A.html> last accessed 7 July 2014.

24   Orhan Pamuk, "The Anger of the Damned," *New York Review of Books* 48.16 (15 Nov. 2001) <http://www.nybooks.com/articles/archives/2001/nov/15/the-anger-of-the-damned/> last accessed on 14 Sept. 2013. Pamuk argued that a pervasive sense of inferiority and *humiliation* led to support for terrorism. He had witnessed people on the streets of Istanbul in the immediate wake of the 9/11 bombings expressing their anger and resentment of the extreme gap between rich and poor and the powerful role of the United States in the global economic system.

CHAPTER 10

CLOSURE?

Given the likelihood that profound damage resulting from serious wrongs will have lasting effects, there is an understandable desire for an ending. Somehow, at some point, the harms and the horrors should be "over" and people should be able to move on with their lives. There should be finality. The notion of "closure" is used to apply to that goal which, though ill-defined, is presumed to be desirable and achievable. The idea of closure is applied both to primary and secondary victims. In the case of murder, the application is for obvious reasons exclusively to secondary victims—primarily members of the murder victims' families. Much has been said in support of closure, with the most prominent considerations concerning the recovery and well-being of victims of serious wrongs. A popular presumption is that with closure victims can convey a sense of the ending of a tragedy so as to move forward in their lives. Despite this notion being ambiguous and unclear and despite the absence of any general method by which closure could be achieved, appeals to closure are prominent.

ARGUMENTS BASED ON CLOSURE

The notion of closure may play an important role in arguments in favour of forgiveness, apology, acknowledgement, and reparations. It is presumed in such arguments that closure is desirable and achievable by victims and that other people—counsellors, perpetrators, arbitrators, mediators, lawyers, judges—can help them achieve it. The same presumptions about victims' closure guide many arguments about perpetrators. If closure is an important goal for victims—indeed, a goal crucial for their recovery and agency—there are implications about what is done with regard to perpetrators. Arguments based on these assumptions have gained prominence in legal circles, particularly in the wake of the victims' rights movements that began in the 1970s and stemmed from feminism, civil rights, crime victims' rights, and restorative justice movements. A major concern of these movements was the sense of powerlessness experienced by many victims in the legal process. Victims typically had only a small role in legal proceedings and no role in decisions about the sentencing of a convicted accused. Often they were in the role of witnesses and in that role cross-examined harshly. Many complained that they were uninformed about the details of legal proceedings, which in turn could be delayed over many years in ways antithetical to the achievement of closure. Understandably, victims pressed for greater involvement and more respectful treatment. Over the past several decades, victims' concerns have been energetically pursued by many civil society groups.

Victim impact statements have been incorporated in many jurisdictions. At the sentencing stage of a trial, the victim reads a statement about the effects of the crime on himself or herself. In cases of murder, family members' statements are about the person killed and the impact of that loss on them. Obviously, these narrative accounts are from the point of view of the victim rather than the defendant; they often inspire great sympathy and empathy from judge and jurors. Victim impact statements serve to give victims a voice and a role in proceedings where they are not witnesses only, liable to intense cross-examination, but provide narratives from the point of those who have suffered undeserved harms.[1] A problematic aspect is that statements from more articulate victims may have a greater effect on proceedings than those from the less articulate. For this reason, some earlier advocates of victim impact statements have come to doubt them.[2]

In the wake of increased attention to the needs of victims, considerations of closure may affect legal proceedings and have an impact on defendants as well as on victims themselves. Many arguments have been based on the assumptions that victims can achieve closure and that legal proceedings should at the least not prevent them from doing so and at the most enable them to do so. In the name of closure, defendants' appeals may be restricted on the grounds that appeals will bring delays and prolong the legal process, even for many years in some cases, and that a prolonged legal process will prevent victims from achieving closure. Parole hearings may be affected. Sometimes, a convicted person is exonerated on the basis of new evidence and arguments that lead to his release.

Closure, Forgiveness, and Acknowledgement

Not all arguments use the notion of closure to defend punishment or execution. Some employ it in defence of forgiveness and acknowledgement. Accounts defending forgiveness are often based on stories of victims finding emotional release from hatred and resentment and achieving a sense of peaceful finality after they meet with the perpetrator and forgive him or her. Especially in cases of repentance, such encounters may lead victims to a sense of humanity, inspiring shifts away from hatred and resentment in the direction of understanding and acceptance. An apology from the perpetrator may be an important aspect of such an encounter. A key idea here is that if a victim can understand what sort of person the perpetrator is and how he came to attack her, and if she feels his genuine remorse, she will use her understanding to struggle against remaining fears and any sense of self-blame. The encounter with the perpetrator may lead to emotional release, a shift away from anger, and a sense of closure. In issuing a sincere moral apology, the perpetrator acknowledges that he was responsible for doing something profoundly wrong and commits himself not to do it again. A victim who finds such an apology credible will be reassured and better able to move past the wrong; there is a sense of finality in the ending of rage and vindictiveness and the beginning of a life freed from preoccupation with wrongdoing and tragedy.[3]

The idea of closure is also sometimes used in arguments supporting reparations. The presumption in this context is that after careful acknowledgement and consideration of costs, a compensatory settlement will bring a healing sense of finality and somehow literally "settle" things.

Shogo Suzuki discusses the failure of the government of Japan to properly acknowledge and apologize to the so-called comfort women who were victims of sexual slavery during World War II.[4] She explains the reluctance of Japan to apologize as due to fear of compensation suits, political backlash within Japan, and the complicating fact that the victims are from various countries other than Japan. As a result of the lack of apology, she argues, victims have failed to obtain full closure. Suzuki describes the efforts of a non-governmental organization, the Women's International Tribunal of Japanese Military Sexual Slavery, to fill the acknowledgement gap. Her main interest is in the feasibility of third-party acknowledgement in a political context when the perpetrating government will not acknowledge its wrongdoings. The Women's International Tribunal held hearings in 2000, listened to the testimonies of victims, offered support and vindication for them, and acknowledged their suffering as a result of misdeeds of the past. For Suzuki, it would appear that acknowledgement is the core notion underlying closure. Her main interest is in the feasibility of third-party acknowledgement in a political context when the perpetrating government will not admit to its wrongdoings. Her hypothesis is that a non-governmental organization could acknowledge the violations of victims and vindicate them, and in so doing provide closure. The account is interesting and plausible in its emphasis on acknowledgement. But so far as closure is concerned, there is a significant slide in Suzuki's work. Initially, the notion of closure seems to be clearly defined in terms of public acknowledgement of what the victims went through in statements, hearings and proceedings, and memorials to the language of healing and the psychological states of victims. But later there is a shift from public acknowledgement to healing. This slippage avoids the need for crucial intermediate steps explaining just how public acts of acknowledgement connect with emotional senses of ending and finality.

Perhaps public acts of acknowledgement could, and do, provide emotional peace and a sense of finality to wrongs committed decades ago. But whether they do, and how, and what shifts would be required for a sense of finality and peace to be achieved remain to be explored. Acknowledgement is important, and apparently closure is too. But no understanding of how acknowledgement contributes to healing is provided by vagueness and ambiguity in the notion of closure.

Closure and the Case for Capital Punishment

Especially dramatic illustrations of effects on defendants may be found in arguments about the death penalty. Most Western jurisdictions no longer practice capital punishment; in those jurisdictions, then, we do not find arguments that justify the capital punishment of offenders on the grounds that it will bring about closure for victims. The case is otherwise in the United States, where such arguments abound and seem to exercise considerable influence.

Three sorts of arguments have been advanced to support capital punishment: these involve, variously, retribution, deterrence, and closure. Widely recognized problems arise for retribution and deterrence arguments. In the case of retribution, the difficulties include the ease of conflating retribution and revenge and the moral implications of killing under state auspices. In the case of deterrence, a key problem is that empirical evidence is lacking. While it may seem intuitive that capital punishment would be a deterrent to murder, sufficient empirical evidence for that relationship is not found.[5] Given increased attention to victims' issues, arguments based on closure are of considerable interest to persons seeking to justify capital punishment. Their line of reasoning is that family victims of a murder should be able to receive closure, that the execution of the convicted murder is a way (perhaps the only way?) for them to achieve closure, and that, accordingly, convicted murderers should be executed. On such accounts, closure for the victim is to be achieved by the death of the perpetrator. The reasoning here seems to be that because death will be the ending of the perpetrator's life, and the ending of further crime and wrongdoing on his part, it will provide for secondary victims the sense that the criminal is *gone* and can do no further wrong to them or others. In other words, the ending of the perpetrator's life is supposed to convey finality to these victims: the story of the crime is "over" and the perpetrator can no longer be a threat. The perpetrator got what he deserved (at this point a retributive theme is conjoined with the closure theme) and justice was has been served.

A corollary of such arguments, one likely to seem bizarre in jurisdictions without capital punishment, is "right to view" legislation. In many US states, such as Oklahoma, legislation establishes for secondary victims a right to view the execution of a person convicted of murdering a family member. In 2000, John Ashcroft, then US Attorney General, consented to televise on closed circuit television the execution of Timothy McVeigh, the Oklahoma bomber.[6] More than 1,000 people were given the opportunity to see his execution.[7] Of these, only some 300 persons did so. Present at the actual event, behind a glass wall, were 10 representatives of US media, 10 relatives of murdered victims, and 5 persons chosen by McVeigh himself. Victims who saw the execution reported their disappointment and frustration, noting McVeigh's piercing stare, close-cropped hair, and impassive face—and the absence of any indications of remorse. Some observers sought indications of suffering, which also seemed absent.[8] In other cases, people expressed their outrage that the executed person died too easily and did not suffer enough, or that he was provided with resources, such as a last meal and pastoral counselling, which were denied to the murder victim, who likely died in cruel and terrifying circumstances.[9]

Sociologist Nancy Berns considers three prominent claims in US arguments about closure and the death penalty.[10]

1. The death of the killer will provide closure for the victims' families.
2. It is right and therapeutic for victims to want perpetrators to suffer.
3. No one can advocate both for victims and for perpetrators, and anyone who advocates for perpetrators (by opposing the death penalty, for example) is indicating disrespect for victims by doing so.

Lack of clarity in the notion of closure makes it difficult to demonstrate the first claim. The second claim should be controversial from a moral point of view, given its support for the desire that other persons should suffer.[11] It is the third claim that merits special attention because of its either/or presumption. That claim falsely presumes that no one could support both respect for the victims and due process for accused perpetrators. It works insidiously against death penalty critics and has a strong potential for inhibiting expression of their views. Few would be comfortable in a position where they were seen to defend accused murderers while having insufficient sympathy for the victims. The assumption that victims' rights and defendants' rights cannot be defended together is logically flawed and injurious to reasonable public policy. It should be possible to defend the victims' right to have knowledge of their own case, public sympathy, and appropriate rehabilitation and compensation without sacrificing the right of defendants to fair legal process and decent treatment if in prison.

It is, in any event, appalling to think that such an unclear notion as closure could be so central in arguments for state execution.

PROBLEMS OF CLARITY

A us judge, Potter Stewart, while acknowledging that it was difficult to define "pornography," stated emphatically, "I know it when I see it." [12] One might feel the same way about closure. Do we know it when we see it? Or feel it? What is closure?

In the summer of 2013, Peggy Arida was at the controls of a demolition machine and launched the first hack at a home on Seymour Avenue in Cleveland, Ohio. The house had belonged to Ariel Castro, who was convicted on many counts of abduction, confinement, and rape of Gina DeJesus and two other young women. Arida is the aunt of Gina DeJesus. In his plea bargain with the state of Ohio, Castro was sentenced to life plus 1,000 years in prison. He agreed to forfeit the house where the women had been held captive and pay for its destruction. [13] It is tempting to find in this gesture a graphic and intuitive illustration of closure. Physical blows wipe out the site of torture and abuse—finality. It is gone.

To be sure, there is a sense of "know it when you see it" in this case, and it is one that illustrates the intuitive appeal of closure. Something terrible has been terminated, brought to an end. If Arida felt a sense of tremendous satisfaction in striking the first blow, one can certainly empathize with her. But is it likely that the destruction of the house would bring closure for the victims who suffered there? Only a small amount of further reflection shows that "seeing it" or "feeling it" is not sufficient to provide understanding of closure for victims in this horrifying case, if by closure we mean an ending to emotional suffering and trauma. The house was the site where these three young women were captured and imprisoned, beat, poorly fed, raped, abused, and often kept chained for years. Smashing it may have been satisfying to all of them; indeed, one of the young women was present to watch it. But it would not and could not wipe out memories, replace lost years, or heal physical wounds. Similar things may be said for the years of sorrow and anxiety experienced by their family members.

What is closure? Here are just a few of many possibilities:

1. A sense of no longer being upset by what has happened.
2. A sense that attention can shift away from this wrong.
3. A sense of being no longer preoccupied with the wrong.

4. A sense of being able to move on, move forward.
5. Healing.
6. A sense of understanding what happened and what was done about it.
7. A sense that "it's over"—the aftermath of the wrong has been brought to a successful conclusion.
8. A sense that one has what is needed to recover from tragedy.

Some of these possibilities, such as healing and moving forward, are themselves hard to define. Some may embody the desires of third parties ("we've got to move on"; "are we never going to stop hearing about this?"; "I've heard enough about these people and their suffering") more than those of the victims themselves. Others (no longer being upset, understanding what happened, it's over) are desirable but, for serious wrongs, likely to be unrealistic.

The notion of closure combines themes of vindication, fact-finding, acknowledgement, legal process, retributive justice, healing, getting over it, and moving on. In contexts of victimhood the term is both vague and ambiguous. If process and policy are going to be amended to facilitate closure, we need at least to know what closure is. Any notion that guides counselling, public policy on appeals, sentencing, and parole, and affects victims' expectations about their own well-being should, minimally, be well-defined. If we do not know what closure is, we will not know how to seek it or whether it has ever been achieved. A guiding theme is that things will be brought to a satisfactory and satisfying ending. But whether that finality is to be legal, rhetorical, or psychological is not clear.

Not surprisingly, this lack of clarity is noted in recent examinations of arguments about closure. Legal scholar Susan Bandes objects to appeals to closure, describing the concept as obscure and ambiguous.[14] She says that the notion has tended to be an umbrella one, awkwardly combining themes of finding answers, catharsis, victims meeting with perpetrators, verdict and sentencing in legal contexts, and unrealistic notions of finality. Bandes points out that appeals to closure are common in US reasoning about capital punishment, particularly with reference to victim impact statements. (She does not support such arguments.) She allows that emotions are important and appeals to them may be legitimate in many contexts. She emphatically opposes any integration of therapeutic ideas into the legal realm and regards appeals to closure as movements toward such integration. Bandes argues persuasively that the trial is in any event a poor venue for the authentic expression of emotion.

The purpose of a trial of an accused person is to determine whether or not that person has committed the crime of which he or she is accused. The point of a sentence is to determine what punishment is appropriate, presuming that the accused person has been found guilty of a crime. A sentence is appropriate depending on the degree of harm of the crime and the blameworthiness of the convicted person. Those considerations are properly based on the law as a general principle, precedents in relevantly similar cases, and specific aspects of the defendant's life history and accountability. They are not properly based on the sentiments and desired goals of primary and secondary victims. Clearly, a person who has murdered a member of a forgiving family does not deserve a shorter sentence than one who has murdered a member of a vindictive family. A person who has murdered a member of a highly articulate and socially respected family does not deserve a longer sentence than one who has murdered a member of a vulnerable and inarticulate family. Important as victims are, and recognizing the need to hear their voices and provide sympathy and care, it is not their feelings and needs that should dictate legal process, convictions, or sentences. Even if the notion of closure were clear, it would not provide an appropriate guide for legal process.

Nancy Berns is another scholar who has argued against appeals to victims' closure.[15] For her, the idea of closure is primarily an emotional one. She argues that a key pitfall in appeals to emotions is that societies tend to have notions of how a person is supposed to feel—rules for emotion, in effect. People who don't feel "in the right way" or cannot express their feelings according to social norms may be discredited. Rhetoric about closure emphasizes the well-being of victims but may perversely work against their interests by giving them unrealistic expectations of finality and ending. Against the idea of finality, and commenting on the McVeigh case, Berns states that when a family member is murdered, the grief of that family cannot be expected to simply end. And clearly, the judicial fate of perpetrators should not depend on the emotive capacities of secondary victims. Furthermore, third parties can also subtly exploit notions of closure when they convey the message that "this should stop" and "we simply do not want to hear about this any more." Often there is a short attention span for tragedy, and compassion fatigue sets in.

Writing about sexual abuse, Berns deemed the notion of closure unrealistic because the effects of childhood abuse are so profound and remain with victims for the rest of their lives.[16] She considers the case of boys abused by Jerry Sandusky, a coach at Pennsylvania State University, to illustrate how public calls for closure may amount to a barely disguised insistence that the story should go away. For the university itself and for family and friends of accused persons and witnesses, such a result might be desirable but would enable escaping from unpleasant truths about sports and coaching heroes. Third parties might seem to be in solidarity with victims when demanding that public attention should cease and we should be done with this, but in fact their motivations often lie elsewhere. Those identified institutionally or by relationship with accused perpetrators may feel the costs of prolonged attention, while others may simply be tired of hearing sordid tales. The closure language may be misleading, so far as identification with victim interests is concerned. Any notion that victims would somehow cease to be damaged if court proceedings ended or newspapers ceased to comment on the matter has little force.

Sexual abuse results in damage to vulnerable children due to the repeated intimate acts of powerful adults. This damage affects a fundamental area of human functioning, one central in adult life. The emotional damage of sexual abuse is unlikely to simply "end," and the result is even more unlikely if it is presumed to result from legal proceedings and them alone. A well-conducted trial in which victims were treated respectfully, followed by a sentence and the incarceration of the offender, could convey to victims a sense of vindication and security and a reassuring awareness that the offender, while in prison, would be kept away from other children. But these things would not wipe out memories and the fears related to them, nor would they be likely to facilitate adult sexual functioning. Court proceedings, testimony, and counselling have stages, and one or another stage could be over, but thinking in terms of closure for the whole matter of sexual abuse is simply unrealistic. Instead of focussing on closure, a mythical notion in this context, Berns quite reasonably argues that people would do better to help young people, prevent further sexual abuse, and face up to difficult cultural truths about vulnerability, sport, and sex.

Another legal scholar, Jody Madeira, acknowledges that the notion of closure is unclear, but nevertheless offers a defence of its use, even in death penalty arguments.[17] Madeira notes as key themes of closure "getting over it," "putting it behind you," "moving forward," catharsis, vindication, and getting an answer to your questions. She acknowledges that most legal scholars assert that pursuing closure for victims' families in capital proceedings amounts to a grievous error. She disagrees with them on that point, noting with approval US Attorney General Ashcroft's consent to televise on closed circuit television the execution of Timothy McVeigh, an authorization given expressly so that people could see it and "effect closure."[18] Madeira acknowledges that what is most likely to assist victims in achieving some sense of ending is simply the factor of time. She maintains that closure should be considered as a process, not a state. She recognizes that "closure" has become a buzz word and popular media term, sometimes creating false expectations in victims. Nevertheless, she argues that, properly understood, closure for victims is a worthy goal and the notion deserves the prominence it has received. Madeira maintains a "communicative theory" of closure, arguing that there are not distinct types (legal, emotional, psychological). Rather, she claims, closure is a cluster concept, the process of achieving "it" will involve both internal and external factors, and it may result from participating in trials. Speaking of murder victims' families, she claims that they will achieve closure through a process that balances grieving and vengeance.

Guiding themes in this defence are those of finality and peace of mind. Narrative plays a key role: victims will impose for themselves an account that gives meaning to what has happened and conveys a sense of the victim's control over events. Narratives are constructed to provide a form so as to make some kind of sense of events. Madeira quotes approvingly a claim that "the condition of narrative is unsurpassable," suggesting that it is not inappropriate for legal processes to be oriented toward the achievement of victims' closure conveyed by narrative as an overriding goal.[19] She claims that a trial, leading to conviction, sentencing, and in some cases execution, even execution witnessed by victims, is conducted properly when it contributes to victims constructing for themselves a satisfying narrative of what has befallen them.

Crucially, Madeira neglects at this point the fundamental fact that criminal trials are to determine questions of the guilt and blameworthiness of the defendant. These are the essential elements of criminal justice proceedings. Respect for victims is highly important, as are acknowledgement and compensation for them. Those goals should be sought and can be achieved. But they do not and should not require flawed judicial processes so far as the trial and sentencing of accused persons are concerned.

Just what closure should be remains unclear in the context of Madeira's defence. Notions of "umbrella," "cluster," and communication are not helpful, and lack of clarity in the notion of closure remains. Legal proceedings are properly about the guilt and blameworthiness of the defendant, not the psychological or emotional condition of the victim. Closure for victims is not an appropriate goal for legal proceedings, which properly concern the guilt and blameworthiness of a defendant. Victims' recovery and well-being are highly important, but not—nor should it be—the only consideration, and certainly not the determining consideration, for legal policy about wrongdoing. Even on the supposition that the notion of closure were to be well-defined, it would provide a poor basis for public policy on matters of law and punishment.

But now let us, contrary to fact, assume the clarity of the closure concept. Let us suppose we have consensus on a definition, one centrally related to victims' well-being. For the sake of argument, let us define closure as some definite desirable condition X, which is well-understood and achievable by surviving primary and secondary victims. Problems still remain. X may be achieved in different ways by different people: by the execution of a perpetrator, by watching that execution, by detailed knowledge of events leading up to the wrong, by therapeutic counselling, by restorative justice proceedings, by forgiveness, by public acknowledgement, by the passage of time, and so on. So let us make a further supposition, again contrary to fact, that for all victimized persons this condition X will be achievable by the same means.

Even on these assumptions, it would remain incorrect to give victim testimony the main logical weight in legal arguments about guilt and punishment. Those issues are properly addressed by considering relevant law and the actions, circumstances, and character of convicted persons, as properly treated under that law. Important as they are, the feelings and needs of victims are not properly a relevant factor here.

OUTSIDE THE LEGAL CONTEXT

If a suspected perpetrator is tried in a court of law, that person is a defendant subject to the power of the state. In that situation, an accused person needs and is entitled to protection by fair process and judgement according to law. The backdrop of state power (on the supposition that it is fairly legitimate and not itself overwhelmed by the power of armed gangs or warlords) makes the situation special, and the vulnerability of the accused person to that power is the basis of a need for special protection. Hence, in legal contexts, the focus on the perpetrator. That focus has understandably frustrated many victims, who feel ignored at best, disrespected and even re-victimized at worst. When we shift outside the legal context, perpetrators and suspected perpetrators are not at the mercy of state power and in the extra-legal situation not especially entitled to protection by due process. In extra-legal contexts, there is every reason to focus on victims and their needs.

Legal contexts are not, of course, the only ones in which questions arise about the treatment of victims. Broader social and ethical contexts are also of enormous importance. To neglect them would be a mistake.

The fact that the notion of closure is too unclear to be used in arguments about legal process is insufficient to show that it cannot be used elsewhere. Perhaps closure, or something like it, is of central importance in moral and social contexts where a sense of ending can be reached by primary and secondary victims who will then be able to get over the harms that have befallen them and be enabled to move forward in life. Perhaps it is just that sense of finality that friends and counsellors should seek to support. We might think that closure in some sense of the term is a worthy goal outside the law, though not a sound guide to proper legal process.

But crucial problems of clarity arise again. The basic facts of individual variability and that we do not know what closure is remain as fundamental challenges. In most cases, it would not be desirable for victims of serious wrongs to forget what happened to them. And it would likely be impossible even if desirable. Memories will fade in vividness and emotions will diminish in intensity, but that does not mean that grief and suffering have ended and are over—only that there have been changes in their quality. Nor can useful clarification be found in considering notions of moving on or going forward. In a truistic sense, people are always "moving on": days, months, and years will pass. People will age; surroundings will change; circumstances will change—and, with these changes, preoccupation with wrongs will diminish. But what sorts of changes and what degree of attention shift constitutes truly moving on in a recovery sense is not easy to specify.

Similar comments can be made with reference to the expression "going forward." Obviously, time will pass and circumstances will change, and the passage of time is likely to contribute to a diminution of suffering and preoccupation with the wrong. But again, what would constitute a recovery is unclear. Moving on is too vague to be a social or personal goal or to clarify what is meant by closure. As residues of tragedy, memories and emotions will persist. Victims of serious wrongs do not simply forget.[20] So far as emotions and attitudes are concerned, only rarely can there literally be an ending. Thus, the expectation of an ending or finality is more likely to be frustrating than useful.

In the light of these considerations, the notion of closure should not guide our assistance to victims. It is unclear, and, so far as it is clear, it is unrealistic. Clearly, difficulties with the closure concept do not show that victims' needs should simply be ignored. Difficulties with closure indicate that the concept is an incorrect framing of our attention to and concern for their needs.[21] Whether through social agencies and institutions or in families or friendships, society has obligations to assist victims, to do their best to provide them with what they need. To argue against misuses of the notion of closure is not to argue against support for victims. It is, rather, to argue that support be more realistically and sensitively directed. Assistance to victims may fall inside or outside legal proceedings, but in whatever context, it should not be sought in the name of closure. Rather, friends, family, social institutions, and victims themselves should try to provide support and assist efforts at recovery and repair to the extent that such efforts are realistically possible—whether in the area of counselling, physical rehabilitation, or both.

What do victims need from those around them? Sympathy, empathy, and patience. Listening, not dismissing, and seeking to understand. Acknowledgement. Psychological support. Flexibility. Material support and practical assistance. Encouragement not to construe themselves as forever in the victim role. Recovery of agency, a sense of purpose and competence. These should be supported and not undermined. Especially crucial is repair in areas of agency, providing for damaged persons to leave the victim role and make and implement central decisions about their own lives.

DISASTER AND ILLNESS

As noted earlier, there can be victims without perpetrators, and the possibility is clearly allowed by ordinary language usage. It is, however, easy to forget when concentrating on wrongdoing. People can be victims of disease and disaster. When we speak of victims of wrongs, perpetrators are implied, but in contexts of illness and disaster, there are no perpetrators unless one shifts to theology and contemplates the possibility of blameworthy acts of God.

In the summer of 2013, much of southern Alberta was seriously affected by floods. News headlines repeatedly referred to victims: "Province fields tough questions from flood victims in Calgary"; "Displaced flood victims feel forgotten"; "Utility scam focuses on flood victims"; "Pre-loaded debit cards for Calgary and Canmore flood victims."[22] These people were regarded as victims because they, through their property, had suffered damage through little or no fault of their own. There was no perpetrator in these circumstances, but there were victims. As in cases of wrongdoing, these people were passive in the damaging acts and harmed by an external force through no choice of their own. As in some cases of wrongdoing, questions could be raised about bearing some degree of responsibility for what befell them; for instance, a person might have chosen to build an expensive home in a potential flood zone or kept a valued grand piano in the basement while living beside a lake. However, in this case, most bore little or no responsibility for unpredictable flood damage to their property.

When we consider aid to victims, the focus is on harmed persons who need understanding, sympathy, and practical assistance. Whether those persons have been harmed as a result of illness, natural disaster, or wrongdoing is not directly relevant when we come to consider these needs. If a woman cannot walk, she will need assistance in many areas of her life, whether her inability results from an illness, a natural disaster, or an attack. The character of the cause will not alter the fact of her inability or its detailed nature—though it is likely to powerfully affect her attitudes and emotional state.

In 2012, the US swimmer Victoria Arlen, 18 years old, won four medals in the Paralympic Competition in London, England. At the age of 11, Arlen had contracted a rare viral disease, transverse myelitis. She was in a coma for nearly two years. She regained consciousness and, eventually, considerable strength in her upper body, although she remained paralyzed from the waist down and unable to walk. With great determination, she caught up with her studies and was able to graduate from high school at the same time as her two brothers. (She is one of triplets.) She resumed competitive swimming in which she had participated as a young girl, adapting her style so that all her power came from her arms. Her stunning success in that endeavour is indicated by her triumphs in 2012.[23] Yet, in August 2013, Victoria Arlen was disqualified as a disabled athlete by the International Paralympic Committee, based on a medical report indicating that there was some (slight) possibility that she might walk again some day. Although she had not been able to walk for seven years, she was barred from competing in the Paralympic Swimming Championships in Montreal. The issue was not whether she had suffered from disease but, rather, whether her resulting disability was permanent.

In this story, Arlen has twice been a victim—first of her rare and serious viral disease that left her partially paralyzed and then of the inflexible judgement of the committee that barred her from competing in the sport she loved. In both contexts, she was harmed by an external force; in one, it was a natural event whereas in the other there were human perpetrators.[24]

Arlen was a victim of her illness. There will be no finality to the harms that resulted from it, given her prolonged inability to walk and despite her successful struggles to catch up with schooling while training as a swimmer and to adapt her life to reach goals compatible with her abilities. It would be inappropriate to speak of finality or anything like closure in this situation. Yet Arlen did not remain a victim. Her case illustrates the ways in which a damaged person may transcend the passivity of victimhood by defining goals and working toward them. The paralympic medals she won in the London 2012 competition showed that her prolonged and determined efforts had brought her success. She had reached—even exceeded—her goals.

Even without those victories, even if she had never progressed to the Olympics at all, there would have been an important sense in which Arlen had moved beyond victimhood. Rather than bemoaning her fate and crying out against cosmic injustice, she set goals for herself and worked toward them. She did not allow the damage that befell her to define her. Yes, she was a victim of a terrible and handicapping disease, but her identity was not that of a victim. The fundamental point of Victoria Arlen's story is that she became an agent in her own life. Clearly, she had a powerful sense that she could do something to improve her life, that she could work to meet challenges and accomplish valued goals. In the summer of 2013, Arlen was again a victim—this time not of disease but of the inflexible decisions of human agents on a committee. Various disability organizations indicated they would help her family to fight the ruling. Hopefully, protests and further deliberations will restore her disability status, allowing her to compete again. If it does not, that will be a new challenge for her to overcome. Her past achievements show that there is every likelihood that she will do just that, either in an athletic context or some other. This case illustrates the importance of agency.

AGENCY

Agency is the capacity to form intentions and cause things to happen on the basis of those intentions. A sense of power results. In the case of long-term difficult goals, that capacity will be known by the agent and likely to provide a significant sense of satisfaction and self-esteem. For modest goals, though, a person may not even notice her capacity and agency.[25] Most people simply assume that they can drink coffee, dress themselves, walk to a local store, purchase a few groceries, take them home, and prepare for themselves a modest meal. These simple activities do require agency: the shopper has formed her intentions and has been able to exert causal power in the world to do what she has decided to do. Equally fundamentally, she has been able to decide to do it. In such a mundane case, we tend to take our agency for granted. That agency will be noticed when it is absent or challenged, as in the case where a person cannot walk due to a disability, is denied admission to the store on the grounds of race, or finds herself unable to cook due to memory problems.

Both capacity and power are required for agency. A person's subjective feeling of power is quite distinct from the objective conditions in which she will seek to implement her plans. Nevertheless, that sense of power may enable her to alter objective conditions. A person who is an agent is not someone with a fixed character who finds herself in a fixed situation. She is one who can seek to amend her character and carefully consider her goals and intentions. She can flexibly adapt her intentions to fit a changing situation. She can strive to alter her situation and expand her options and opportunities. Social and cultural factors are obviously also important as they affect our expectations about what will happen and our responses to what we expect.

"We may regard ourselves as agents, the thinkers of our thoughts and the originators of our actions," said Christine Korsgaard, writing about agency.[26] On her account, to think of oneself as an agent is to think of oneself as a kind of uncaused cause or unmoved mover. It is to consider oneself as initiating thoughts and actions, not as simply being affected by forces outside the self. Though powerfully and movingly expressed, this model requires some supplementation. There are problems about the connection between rationality and morality that are presumed in Korsgaard's account, which stems from Kant.[27] Korsgaard's conditions are not enough to support sound agency; after all, one can think one's own thoughts when those thoughts are deeply irrational and one can originate one's own actions when those actions are profoundly immoral. We will need to supplement the account if we are to identify a sense of agency that can be positively recommended to victims. Korsgaard's inspiring phrases provide necessary conditions of desirable agency, not sufficient conditions. Agency as thinkers of our thoughts and originators of our actions does not guarantee either rationality or morality. After all, even a person strongly identifying herself with the victim role can think her own thoughts and originate her own actions. She might, for example, include in her own thoughts a persistent bemoaning of her fate as someone harmed through no fault of her own. She might act by making no initiative to creatively change her situation and extend her own capacities, managing her life by exploiting the sympathy of others to get an undue share of attention and resources.

Thinking and acting in such ways as these, a victim would be a thinker of her thoughts and originator of her actions, whether or not she considered herself to be such. She would be an agent in her role as a victim and could very well exploit that role to her advantage. But she would not be adapting to the harm she suffered by seeking constructively and creatively to expand her own capacities and activities. Advocating agency for victims, we have something further in mind: that a victim should seek to accept and develop her own abilities and, within reasonable bounds, accept responsibility for her own life. The victim who achieves responsible agency will do her best to resist any role or identity as a victim and develop her own capabilities on the basis of personal creative deliberations about what she can do and could learn to do. She will think of herself as capable of acting on her own behalf and going forward in life without exploiting a victim role to use the resources and talents of others.

In a useful article, Susan Wendell writes about victimization and oppression.[28] Wendell distinguishes four perspectives: those of the oppressor, the victim, the responsible agent, and the observer/philosopher. From the perspective of the oppressor, circumstances are generally fine; if a victim finds herself in a disadvantageous position, it is she herself who is to blame. Victims themselves may come to adopt an oppressor perspective if that oppressor's viewpoint dominates in a culture. Failing to understand the influence of social conditions and assumptions, victims may blame themselves for what has befallen them and feel guilty about it. Victims who have unwittingly taken on an oppressor perspective need to be liberated from it.

From the perspective of the victim, there should be no self-blaming. The victim will understand that what has happened to her is not her fault but is, rather, due to something external—either the actions of a perpetrator or (in the case of disaster or disease) external forces. This is progress, but the problem is that being a victim can so easily become a central aspect of one's identity. It can lead to a "poor me" perspective and, in the case of wrongs, a tendency to blame someone else for one's fate. There is something tempting about the victim identity; it may provide excuses for avoiding choices and allow one to see oneself as blameless. A person who is a victim may not wish to engage in a struggle for his or her rights, and if a victim does not resist his circumstances, he will not provoke resistance from these others. More beneficially, a victim may come to realize that she is one of many harmed and suffering people and gain a sense of solidarity with others in a similar situation.

And yet the victim perspective has pronounced disadvantages. Most significantly, it is too passive and obscures the actual or potential power that victims have to make and implement choices. It does not encourage constructive agency; it tends to be depressing and lack energy and hope.[29]

Far better, Wendell argues, is the perspective of the responsible agent. Wendell notes that resources for this perspective can be found within the victim perspective, when a victim realizes that she did, after all, live through what happened to her and may be able to protect herself from similar harms in the future. Developing responsible agency, a victim may refuse to be powerless and use thought and imagination to develop her capacities. She may attempt to move forward to learn about possibilities; she may make and implement choices, giving herself credit for the good and productive things she has done, developing a sense of purpose, and working toward the goals she has adopted for herself. She may in these ways take responsibility for her own life. With this sense of responsibility, a victim shifting into agency will move beyond blaming the perpetrator. She will realize that she need not grant this person power over her life and that any relationship she has with a perpetrator is merely one among many. In cases where there is a perpetrator, that person is indeed to blame for his wrongdoing in the past. But the perpetrator is not in a position to determine the victim's capacities and actions in moving forward. Even in cases where physical abilities are limited, many victims preserve the power to deliberate and creatively develop their actions and opportunities.

Finally, Wendell explains the perspective of the observer or philosopher, who reflects on harming situations, looking backward and seeking causes.[30] A fundamental difference between the observer perspective and that of the responsible agent is the feature of time orientation. The agent seeking to act constructively is looking forward to determine what she chooses to do and how she might choose to do it. The observer/philosopher is engaged in analysis, looking backward in an effort to understand the nature and causes of what happened. The observer may acknowledge some cases in which a victim has contributed to the context in which she was harmed, allowing herself to be in the wrong place at the wrong time and as a result exposed to damage from disease, disaster, or wrongdoing. An observer account could even reduce the responsibility of some perpetrators due to the recognition of the conditions of their actions; efforts at understanding will be made, though the responsibility of perpetrators is not to be eliminated.

If at all possible, a victim should transcend victimhood to regain the perspective of the responsible agent. He should be responsible in the sense of taking responsibility for actions. As Wendell acknowledges, responsibility is a matter of degree. For some seriously damaged victims, at some stages, that degree may be small. Such victims may have limited choices, a restricted understanding of what would be involved in making those choices, and only a limited likelihood of success. Victims may be harmed so seriously that their responsibility and agency are reduced; only in cases of serious mental impairment would it be impossible to further develop their agency. Where agency is possible, it is fundamental for living a life of energy and hope. Deliberating, making choices, and working to implement those choices could build further capacities. These basic truths apply to those who have been victims of illness, natural disaster, or wrongdoing.

None of this is to deny the importance of relationships and social context. When we participate in life we are in a social world. Our participation is understood by ourselves and others in terms of cultural expectations that affect what we do, what we think ourselves to be doing, and what we can manage to do. For obvious reasons, social attitudes toward victims are highly important for their agency. Expectations of closure may emerge from a kind of social resistance to the very sense of entitlement that deference creates. By deferring, we are led to give victims respect and power in legal and other contexts. Contemporary attitudes of deference toward victims constitute an improvement over past attitudes of silencing and blame. And yet they have their pitfalls. Deferring uncritically and too much, we may extend to victims undue respect (for example, in the uncritical acceptance of testimony) or too much power (for example, when highly articulate and vindictive victims sway judges to impose inappropriately harsh sentences on offenders).

In the nature of the case, victims have been harmed and need repair. In the nature of the case, they have not primarily been the agents or forces bringing harm to themselves. From these features, it is only a short logical step to understand victims as suffering and innocent, in need of our respect and assistance. What is required is to respond to those needs as sensitively and effectively as possible without undermining victims' agency. To extend deference too far is to risk discouraging a sense of responsibility. In its legitimation of passive expectation of sympathy and having the moral upper hand, the victim role poses temptations. Because indulging these temptations can make it comfortable to remain in a victim role, it will prevent the development of responsible agency. A society fascinated with victimhood and suffering and inclined to strong sentiments of solidarity with victims may unwittingly encourage in victims passivity and self-defeating expectations.

Not every disabled person will become a successful athlete like Victoria Arlen or Terry Fox; not every member of a murder victim's family will become an advocate for legal reform; not every flood survivor will become an activist leader. So far as possible, victims should become survivors. Inspiring narratives are valuable and they do indeed inspire, supporting energy and hope. But they should not be promulgated so as to impose unrealistic expectations on injured persons. What is crucial for victims is not to become heroic or saintly survivors but to develop and maintain responsible and creative agency. There is a corollary for those assisting victims: we should encourage, and not undermine, their constructive agency.

In a society that silences victims, they are apt to be silent. In a society that blames victims, they are apt to feel guilty. In a society that defers to victims, they may give in to the temptations of the victim role. Emphasis on agency seems best developed in restorative justice accounts, where victims are regarded as citizens sharing responsibility for actions in the aftermath of suffering and wrongdoing.

NOTES

1   Susan Bandes, "Victims, 'Closure,' and the Sociology of Emotion," *Laws and Contemporary Problems* 72 (2009): 1–26 <http://scholarship.law.duke.edu/lcp/vol72/iss2/2/> last accessed 20 Oct. 2013.

2   Jeffrie Murphy, personal conversation.

3   For a discussion of apology see Govier, *Taking Wrongs Seriously* Chapter Four.

4   Shogo Suzuki, "Overcoming Past Wrongs Committed by States: Can Non-State Actors Facilitate Reconciliation?," *Social and Legal Studies* (2012): 201–13.

5   See Chapter 8 of this book.

6   See Chapter 8 of this book.

7   Jody Lynée Madeira, "Why Rebottle the Genie? Capitalizing on Closure in Death Penalty Proceedings" *Indiana Law Journal* 85.4 (2010): 1478–1525 <http://papers. ssrn.com/sol3/papers.cfm?abstract_id=1347844> last accessed on 16 June 2014. Madeira broadly defends closure arguments in favour of the death penalty, while acknowledging that her position contradicts those of other legal theorists writing about the topic.

8   Peter Grier and Dante Chinni, "For Survivors, Execution Isn't the End," *Christian Science Monitor* 11 June 2001 <http://www.csmonitor.com/2001/0611/p1s2. html> last accessed 26 June 2014. See also Andrew Cohen, "Timothy McVeigh and the Myth of Closure," *The Atlantic* 11 June 2012 <http://www.theatlantic.com/national/ archive/2012/06/timothy-mcveigh-and-the-myth-of-closure/258256/> last accessed 28 Nov. 2013.

9   Michael Lawrence Goodwin, "An Argument Against Allowing the Families of Murder Victims to View Executions," *Journal of Family Law* 36.4 (1997) <http://www. pbs.org/wgbh/pages/frontline/shows/execution/readings/against.htm> last accessed 13 Oct. 2013.

10   Nancy Berns, "'Closure' Harms Sexual Assault Victims," *Closure Blog* 9 Nov. 2001 <http://www.nancyberns.com/%E2%80%9Cclosure%E2%80%9D-harms-sexual-assault-victims.html> last accessed 26 June 2014.

11   Much more needs to be said, but to fully explore this theme would take us too far from the topic at hand.

12   Cited in Cohen.

13   Tim Walker, "Cleveland Kidnapping: Victim Watches and Spectators Applaud as Ariel Castro 'House of Horrors' Torn Down," *The Independent* 7 Aug. 2013 <http:// www.independent.co.uk/news/world/americas/cleveland-kidnapping-victim-watches-and-spectators-applaud-as-ariel-castro-house-of-horrors-torn-down-8750339.html> last accessed 26 June 2014.

14   Susan Bandes, "Victims, 'Closure,' and the Sociology of Emotion," *Law and Contemporary Problems* 72 (2009): 1–26.

15   Nancy Berns, "Contesting the Victim Card: Closure Discourse and Emotion in Death Penalty Rhetoric," *Sociological Quarterly* 50.3 (2009): 383. Berns refers to arguments for capital punishment, based on the need for families of murder victims to achieve closure, as the "new retributivism."

16   Berns, "'Closure' Harms Sexual Assault Victims" and "Contesting the Victim Card."

17   Madeira.

18   Madeira 1501.

19   A narrative that is emotionally satisfying may contain a number of over-simplifications, false statements, and relevant omissions. This highly important point is neglected by Madeira.

20   Despite the prominence of the cliché, "forgive and forget," forgiveness does not entail forgetting. This point is granted by theorists, though the cliché retains its

popularity in common discourse. For further discussion, see Govier, *Forgiveness and Revenge* Chapter Three.

21 The fact that this oft-used concept cannot be clearly defined does not show that all forms of concern for victims' closure amount to a mistake, of course. It indicates, rather, that in some significant contexts, those concerns are misconstrued.

22 *Calgary Herald* 21 July 2013; CBC News, 13 Aug. 2013; CTV News, 13 Aug. 2013; CTV News, 29 June 2013.

23 CBC Sports, 13 Aug. 2012.

24 Kristin Duquette, "I Stand by Victoria Arlen," *Huffington Post* 19 Aug. 2013 <http://www.huffingtonpost.com/kristin-duquette/victoria-arlen-paralympics_b_3758407.html> last accessed 26 June 2014.

25 Ci Jiwei, "Evaluating Agency: A Fundamental Question for Social and Political Philosophy," *Metaphilosophy* 42.3 (2011): 261–81.

26 Korsgaard, quoted in Fritz J. McDonald, "Agency and Responsibility," *Journal of Value Inquiry* 44.2 (2010): 199–207.

27 There are also metaphysical questions about how to make sense of an uncaused cause; these are too substantial to be considered here.

28 Susan Wendell, "Oppression and Victimization: Choice and Responsibility," *Hypatia* 5.3 (1990): 15–46.

29 Wendell notes that the victim perspective may be taken by a person who is not himself or herself a victim, but rather, one who feels outrage and sorrow on the victim's behalf.

30 Wendell's perspective is obviously that of the observer/philosopher, as is my own.

MATTERS OF METAPHYSICS

GOD AND MISFORTUNE

For some, and nearly everyone in days gone by, questions about suffering and moral merit were posed in the context of God and His intentions and capacities. Why did God allow evil, bad things, and misfortune, to occur? If He was all-powerful, all-knowing, and all-good, He was able to know that evil would be present in His world. Given that He was able and should have been willing to prevent it, the presence of evil required an explanation. Why do innocent people suffer? Why are people killed and injured by natural catastrophes? Why do they brutalize and harm each other? From what cause? For what purpose? Where is God? The question "why?" has inspired theories of theodicy, which offer accounts that provide answers and relieve God of responsibility for the suffering of the world.

Why do bad things happen to good people? Why do bad things happen to any people? Why do bad things happen at all? And what sorts of things are bad? In this work I have not treated the problem of evil in a context where an all-powerful God is assumed. Rather, I have been concerned with a modern version of that problem and, in particular, with our attitudes to those persons harmed by "bad things" that happen—in other words, with our attitudes to the victims of disaster, illness, and wrongdoing. It is, however, useful to briefly consider secular concerns in their relation to older questions about human suffering, set in the framework of religious beliefs.

In Western thought, a common beginning was to distinguish natural evils such as earthquakes, tidal waves, volcanoes, and ice storms from moral evils such as torture, murder, genocide, and rape. For natural evils, a standard response was to argue a need for a universe proceeding in a regular predictable way. The prevailing assumption was that a Creator God set up a regular world within which the regular action of physical entities such as the earth, moon, sun, oceans, tides, and winds results sometimes in events such as earthquakes and tsunamis. These we human beings regard as bad because they cause damage to our bodies and property. Within such an account, it may be argued that it would be even worse for human beings if nature were irregular and permitted no understanding and prediction. On this view, natural disasters and misfortunes are compatible with God's having done His best for humankind. In contrast with natural evil, moral evil is typically taken to result from the fact that God created human beings with free will, meaning that we have capacities for moral choice based on reflection and deliberation. Having these capacities, human beings can choose to act wrongly and very often do. The effects on other human creatures can be brutally damaging.

There is a tendency to think of natural evil and moral evil in dichotomous terms. Yet natural evil and moral evil are not mutually exclusive. There are plenty of mixed cases in which bad things happen because of a natural event (a flood, for example), partially caused by human activity (deforestation, for instance), or harm caused by a natural event is compounded by a flawed human response to it, as in the case of Hurricane Katrina.

We may seek explanations in terms of material causes and conditions; we then ask what caused an event X in the sense of what antecedent events and conditions resulted in X happening. Here we seek a cause. We may also seek explanations in terms of reason and purpose; we then ask what was the point of X and seek an answer to the "why?" of purpose. If there is a Creator God who is all-powerful and all-knowing, explanations in terms of cause and those in terms of purpose will ultimately coincide. For anything that happens, the material cause will be antecedent conditions and events in the world. If the Creator God exists, He set these up and could anticipate what would flow from any event. Knowing what would happen and having the power to prevent it, He would in a sense intend it to happen. For any event X—good, bad, or indifferent—the ultimate cause of its happening would be God's creation of the world. The ultimate reason, or purpose, would lie also in God. There is a sense, then, in which material causes and moral reasons coincide, having their common source in the mind of God.

In a secular framework, there is obviously no presumption of a divinely established order: material causes and purposive reasons cannot be expected to coincide.

No supreme Creator entity exists to establish material causes and conditions according to its own purposes and intentions. Natural events will occur regularly and in scientifically explicable ways within the natural order. An earthquake is a paradigm case. In an earthquake, many thousands may be killed, maimed, and suffer serious loss of property and social dislocation—as in Lisbon in 1755, Haiti in 2010, and Japan in 2011. From the point of view of damaged persons, an earthquake counts as a seriously harmful thing, and hence as a bad thing—whether God exists or not. It may even appear as an evil to those who feel comfortable using that term. But let us for the moment keep to the term "badness" and accept that an earthquake in a populated area is a bad thing in the sense that it is bad for human beings and other sentient creatures harmed by it, due to premature death and damage to body and property. In the older theological framework, natural evils such as earthquakes may be deemed naturally occurring bad things—evils. (The Lisbon earthquake of 1755 inspired several eighteenth-century theodicies.) In a secular frame of reference, while the value assessment remains negative; the cause is entirely material.

Also within the category of natural events are illness and disease. Fundamentally, disease is something that happens to human bodies and is naturalistically explicable in terms of events in the physical and biological world. We generally accept that there is a material scientific explanation as to why diseases occur and how they progress. For many diseases, there is no need to look outside the framework of natural events. We generally hold that a naturalistic framework for explaining events and syndromes will apply to many phenomena we do not yet understand. For example, explanations of allergies and fibromyalgia, though not known, are generally presumed to lie in some sequence of natural events exclusive of the actions and omissions of intentional agents. From this point of view, those who suffer from disease are victims of natural phenomena, just as persons harmed by earthquakes and tidal waves are victims of them.

But the omission of human agency here oversimplifies both disease itself and our attitudes toward it. Rightly or wrongly, most of us do think of human actions and omissions as having something to do with the occurrence, progression, and management of disease. If a man who has lung cancer was a heavy smoker for many years, it is likely that his smoking was at least a partial cause of his getting that disease. Human actions and omissions do enter into the matter, then; it is likely that this man bears some responsibility for his illness. As a cancer sufferer, and in some sense a victim, this man is at the same time an agent of his illness. The same may be said of the morbidly obese woman who becomes diabetic, cares for herself badly, and dies at 50 of kidney failure. Mixed cases are many: unfortunate events and careless actions combine in the causal framework. When human responses are part of the causal story, we apply moral language to the actions of agents involved in caring for human bodies. That, obviously, includes sufferers themselves.

A modern parallel to the older category of "moral evil" is human wrongdoing. We human beings wrong each other in numerous ways; we also become victims of such acts as assault, theft, maiming, torture, and killing. In the context of such wrongs, human acts are central. The explanatory framework that predominates here is one of accountability, of responsibility and blame. Moral terms are appropriate for such cases, and we use them when we ask and respond to the cries of "why?" Our explanations refer first and most of all to the motives and intentions of moral agents, those who acted and whom we designate as perpetrators. The agents of harm are human beings acting for motives, acting with knowledge and on the basis of their own intentions; in standard circumstances, they are regarded as accountable for what they have done. The classic scenario is one in which a guilty perpetrator acts on an innocent victim, to whom he brings harm. In an explanatory framework that is moral in nature, perpetrators are blamed for the wrongs they have done to victims. People act, and their actions are conceptualized and evaluated in moral terms.

RESPONSIBILITY?

In his famous essay "Freedom and Resentment,"[1] P.F. Strawson describes two different attitudes or stances that we take towards our fellow human beings. One, he says, is a participant attitude. When we adopt the participant attitude, we see those with whom we interact as fellow human beings who are normal persons with a moral capacity to control their actions and take proper account of others. We do not regard them as needing therapy or treatment in order to control what they do. The other attitude, Strawson says, is an objective one: we have an objective stance to another human being insofar as we regard him or her as morally incapacitated. For example, if I believe that an aging woman is suffering from dementia, I do not hold her accountable when she gives me incorrect information about her family members. I believe that her failing memory, resulting from the condition of her brain at an advanced age, causes her to be forgetful and confused. I do not hold her accountable for her mistakes because there has come to be an important sense in which I accept that she is no longer an agent with full moral capacities. I do not blame her for her errors. To the extent that I regard her in this way, I do not regard her as a participant in moral and social life; I take an objective attitude to her.

Strawson maintains that for us as human beings in a social world, the participant attitude is indispensable. Although aspects of moral capacity and control may be debated, for particular agents and specific acts, and although our views about cases may change on the basis of fresh information and increased understanding, it would simply be impossible for us to adopt an objective attitude to all other human beings in all contexts. We have to interact with others who are our fellow human beings and co-participants in our social world. When we do interact in this way, we regard our fellow human beings as persons who think, have motives and intentions, and act to bring about results. In ways positive or negative, much of what they do affects us, and much of what we do affects them. Regarding actions and omissions, we make moral appraisals and come to feel such emotions and attitudes as resentment, forgiveness, and gratitude. These presume evaluations, many of which are from a moral perspective.

To more fully appreciate Strawson's account, we may consider a wholly materialistic theory within which our attitudes towards human beings (including ourselves) is purely objective. Within such a theory, what we now regard as intentional actions and attitudes, to which reasoning and reflection are necessary and relevant, are understood as results of prior events emerging from antecedent processes in our brains. Let us refer to a theory of this type as Grand Materialism. Concerning Grand Materialism, old philosophical problems clearly arise, most obviously the classic chestnuts: determinism and free will, mind and body. Such problems have been with us for millennia and are not going to disappear any time soon.[2] But nor, Strawson argues, can we lose our participant attitude to ourselves and other human beings. Even if some version of Grand Materialism were true and known to be true, we would remain social creatures, co-participants in a social world. In that world we would interact and do so on the basis of moral (in Strawson's terms, reactive) attitudes.[3] We cannot help being the sorts of social creatures we are and feel emotions and attitudes that fit our nature. We do, and will, hold at least some persons accountable for at least some of the things they do. Even if a well-corroborated version of Grand Materialism were to exist and to entail the falsity of our metaphysical presumptions about moral capacities, its truth would be irrelevant for our social life and human interactions.

Proceeding from a broadly Strawsonian perspective, let us think again about some of the bad things that happen to people. There are cases such as the earthquake, where our explanation of what is bad, what went wrong, has to do solely with events in the natural order; such cases do not elicit from us any reactive attitudes because we are not considering harm due to human intervention or omission. An earthquake imposes itself on the human social world. Our responses to it are certainly within that world and affected by its agents and their practices. But the earthquake itself does not typically result from the intentions of moral agents. Though some religious thinkers may seek to explain earthquakes in terms of the intentional actions of a divine entity, for secular thinkers—and for many liberal religious thinkers—earthquakes are simply natural events. To be sure, they are large and dramatic events; they are often events seriously harmful to human beings and other sentient creatures. Judged from the perspective of affected sentient creatures, earthquakes are bad things. But in the absence of theological beliefs, they are not regarded as resulting from the decisions of actors; they are in no sense intentional actions.

Moving on to the mixed case, we begin to consider the effects of the earth-quake on real people interacting in a social context with a variety of agents, institutions, and practices. In such a context, it is highly likely that some harms will result from human actions or omissions. Moral judgements, responsibility, blame, praise, and reactive attitudes will come into play at these points.

The same may be said concerning diseases. To the extent that we are considering events affecting human bodies, we are in the domain of objective attitudes; to the extent that we are considering human agents and their responses to those events, we are in the domain of participants and reactive attitudes. Illness, disease, and suffering are bad things for human beings, just as damaging earthquakes and tidal waves are bad things. The development of diseases is, for the most part, a sequence of natural events not presuming specific human actions for better or worse. Nevertheless, some aspects of these developments may be wrongs for which intentional agents may be held accountable, as in a case where medical administrative personnel confuse appointment times, resulting in neglect and injury to patients.

Shift now to a case where wrongdoing predominates. If a woman is raped, something bad happens to her, but the rape is not a mere happening. It is an action. There is not just a rape: someone has raped someone else. The rapist is a person and a moral agent, and insofar as he has moral capacity, he is an agent who can deliberate, decide what to do, and guide the motions of his human body. If we ask why a particular man raped a particular woman in some context, much of the explanation has to be in terms of what he resolved to do and did. Why did he rape her? When we ask and seek to respond to these kinds of questions, we are asking about human motives and intentions in the territory of human values.

In such a context, reactive actions are appropriate, and we will hold a rapist accountable for what he did. The point is: he did it. What he did, he did. It didn't just happen. It is misleading to say, as we so often do, that someone "was raped," because the passive tense in this expression omits agency. One person raped another. Why? Why did he rape? Why did he rape her? For what purpose, if there was any purpose? What did he think he was doing? We may ask what made him do it, but without a special context of extreme coercion, such as soldiers being ordered to rape in time of war, what made him do it is not really the appropriate question. He raped her—that is the point, and we are in a context where moral language, agency, responsibility, and blame clearly apply. If we were operating in the context of a theodicy, we would ask why God allows people to rape and to be raped, why God made us the sorts of people we are, and what purpose of God's is served by people living through the harm and suffering that result from rape. The answer would be, broadly, that this is a context of moral evil in which the explanatory framework is, broadly speaking, one of human moral capacity and moral action. But we do not need supernatural commitments to reasonably judge that the rapist, a moral agent, chose to rape this person and is responsible for doing that. Even in a world where the prevailing perspective is a secular one, this question and its answer will retain moral dimensions, for the sorts of reasons offered by Strawson.

A MIXED, AND SECULAR, PERSPECTIVE

People may be harmed by natural events, by illness and disease, by wrongs committed by others and sometimes by their own responses or their own self-neglect, and by various and assorted combinations of these things. Some of those harmed we regard as victims. Damage is done to them, they suffer, and we respond. Or we ourselves are victims. To think of someone as a victim is to think of him or her in two ways: first, the victim is deemed to be harmed; and second, the victim is deemed not to be causally or morally responsible for the harm, which was imposed by some external force or power. In response to victimization, two elements are prominent: compassion in response to harm and fairness in response to innocence.

When we see our fellow human beings suffering, we feel sympathy and empathy, we feel compassion or co-passion, a feeling with them, a kind of human emotional solidarity. Adam Smith and David Hume emphasized human sympathy in their eighteenth-century writings; Hume famously said that the minds of men are mirrors to one another.[4] If I go into a room of cheerful people, I am likely to become cheerful too, but the more sobering corollary is that if I go into a room of depressed people, I am likely to feel depressed. Thus, co-passion, or compassion: we feel a need to respond with attitudes and feelings of sympathy. One regarded as a victim is seen as a person to whom a sympathetic and compassionate response is appropriate.

The other reactive response to victims is based on a sense of fairness. This sense underpins the older problem of evil, and one of the interpretations of the cry "why do these things happen?" is "where is the justice in this case?" Why should this happen, why did such a bad thing happen to such a good person, a person who always behaved well, who was of great value to his community, who did his best for his fellow human beings and deserved nothing but the best? If there is fairness in the world, this person should have done something to deserve his bad fate, but there is nothing we can find to indicate that. He did nothing to deserve this terrible illness, which overcame him at a relatively young age. We feel an impulse to judge the universe: this should not have happened to this man. If he was a victim not of disease but of crime, and we demand again to know why, to understand how it could be that this bad thing happened to this good person, we will demand justice in the situation. Our cry of "why?" will be followed by a felt urge that somehow justice should be done. Who did this thing? Not God, if there is no God. Who is to blame for it? Not God, if there is no God. There was some agent: a human perpetrator, and when this person is caught, questions arise as to how he or she should be punished.

If a perpetrator with normal moral capacities commits wrongs, bringing serious harm and damage to a victim, our sympathy for the victim will be accompanied by a sense that the resulting situation is profoundly unfair. If one person does wrong, why should another person suffer? A sense of injustice is likely to lead to a drive to "make things right," leading to a concern to hold perpetrators accountable. Justice, in the aftermath of wrongdoing, is most often presumed to concern what should be done to, and with, its perpetrators. Barring exceptional circumstances, we regard perpetrators as moral agents responsible for doing what they did, and we blame them for the harm and suffering brought through their actions to victims. Assuming there is no God to arrange for cosmic justice, human justice has to be wrought through human agents and institutions. And thus we shift from considering the wrongful act in which both perpetrator and victim are parties to examine the practical and theoretical issues of law and punishment. We ask how should the perpetrator be punished, presuming that his or her guilt has been legally established?

In pursuing this and related questions, we may shift away from thinking about victims as such. We may be unaware of this shift or we may justify it on the assumption that justice will be brought to victims when perpetrators are found guilty and appropriately punished. Thinking along these lines, we often presume that justice for victims is achieved by imposing punishments on perpetrators, and we attend peripherally to victims by importing such notions as closure and victim impact into criminal procedures.

To the extent that we are dealing purely with the intentional actions of moral agents, our predominant framework will be one of moral evaluation and moral response. There is a tendency here to blame perpetrators and concentrate on the question of what should be done to them. Shifts and omissions are noteworthy here. We have moved from victim to perpetrator, and we too easily forget the logical jump from blaming and punishing the latter to repairing the former. This book attempts to correct for that impulse and focus on victims primarily.

NOTES

1   P.F. Strawson, "Freedom and Resentment," *Proceedings of the British Academy* 48 (1962): 1–25.
2   One is reminded here of what Kant says about metaphysical questions. There are definite limits on what we can sensibly say about them, but we are driven to ask them and will always be so.
3   'Strawson. See also, Michael McKenna and Paul Russell, "Perspectives on P.F. Strawson's 'Freedom and Resentment,'" *Free Will and Reactive Attitudes*, ed. Michael McKenna and Paul Russell (Farnham, UK: Ashgate, 2008) 1–18. Their essay is a helpful introduction to the volume. Also helpful is Ted Honderich, "Freedom and Resentment,"

The Determinism and Freewill Philosophy Website <http:www.ucl.ac.uk/~uctho/dfwlintroindex.htm> last accessed 16 June 2014. Honderich points out that the participant attitude and the objective attitude, as Strawson describes them, are not mutually exclusive. He also adds that one may have such attitudes to oneself. If A acts so as to harm or benefit B, then B, in taking a participant attitude to A, will understand A as a moral agent to whom he might properly respond with anger, resentment, forgiveness, gratitude, or some other reactive attitude. The same holds if B himself acts so as to benefit or harm himself. He may look at himself as an accountable agent and hold himself responsible, or he may look at the benefit or harm resulting from his actions as something that "just happened" and see his own decisions and actions as flowing inevitably from circumstances or as having no role at all. The phenomenon is highly relevant to the topic of self-forgiveness.

4   David Hume, *A Treatise of Human Nature*, ed. L.A. Selby-Bigge (1888; Oxford: Clarendon Press, 1965), 365.

SELECTED
BIBLIOGRAPHY

Aarts, Petra. "Intergenerational Effects in Families of WWII Survivors from the Dutch East Indies." *International Handbook of Multigenerational Legacies of Trauma*. Ed. Yael Danieli. New York: Springer 1998. 175–87.

Adler, Jonathan. "Epistemological Problems of Testimony." *The Stanford Encyclopedia of Philosophy*. Ed. Edward N. Zalta (Spring 2014). <http://plato.stanford.edu/archives/spr2014/entries/testimony-episprob/>. Accessed 13 Aug. 2014.

Anderson, Elizabeth. "Feminist Epistemology and Philosophy of Science." *The Stanford Encyclopedia of Philosophy*. Ed. Edward N. Zalta. Fall 2012. <http://plato.stanford.edu/archives/fall2012/entries/feminism-epistemology/>. Accessed 8 Nov. 2012.

Andrighetto, Luca, and Ishani Banerji. "The Victim Wars: How Competitive Victimhood Stymies Reconciliation Between Conflict Groups." *The Inquisitive Mind* 5.15 (2012). <http://www.in-mind.org>. Accessed 12 Oct. 2013.

Anscombe, Elizabeth. "What Is It to Believe Someone?" *Rationality and Religious Belief*. Ed. C.F. Delaney. Notre Dame, IN: U of Notre Dame P, 1979. 141–51.

Appiah, Anthony. *The Ethics of Identity*. Princeton, NJ: Princeton UP, 2005.

Arias, Arturo, ed. *The Rigoberta Menchú Controversy*. Minneapolis: U of Minnesota P, 2001.

Baines, E.K. "Complex Political Perpetrators: Reflections on Dominic Ongwen." *Journal of Modern African Studies* 47 (2009): 163–91.

Baines, E.K. and O. Boniface. "Complicating Victims and Perpetrators in Uganda: On Dominic Ongwen." *Justice and Reconciliation: Field Note 7* (2008): 1–19.

Bandes, Susan."Victims, 'Closure,' and the Sociology of Emotion." *Law and Contemporary Problems* 72 (2009): 1–26. <http://scholarship.law.duke.edu/lcp/vol72/iss2/2/>. Accessed 20 Oct. 2013.

Barnett, Randy. "Pursuing Justice in a Free Society." *Criminal Justice Ethics* 5.1 (Summer/Fall 1985): 30–53.

Beah, Ishmael. *A Long Way Gone: Memoirs of a Boy Soldier.* Toronto: Douglas and McIntyre, 2007.

———. *Radiance of Tomorrow: A Novel.* New York: Penguin, 2014.

Beckmann, Nadine. "AIDS and the Commodification of Suffering." Talk delivered to the Centre for African Studies, University of Leeds, November 2010.

———. "The Commodification of Misery: Markets for Healing, Markets for Sickness." Paper for the Open University, UK. <http://www.bias-2011-beckmann.pdf.> Accessed 6 Sept. 2013.

Bennett, Christopher. "The Varieties of Retributive Experience." *Philosophical Quarterly* 52 (2002): 145–63.

Berns, Nancy. "Contesting the Victim Card: Closure Discourse and Emotion in Death Penalty Rhetoric." *Sociological Quarterly* 50.3 (2009): 383–406.

Borer, Anne. "A Taxonomy of Victims and Perpetrators: Human Rights and Reconciliation in South Africa." *Human Rights Quarterly* 25.4 (2003): 1088–1116.

Brabeck, Kalina. "*Testimonio*: A Strategy for Collective Resistance, Cultural Survival, and Building Solidarity." *Feminism and Psychology* 31.2 (2003): 252–58.

Braithwaite, R. "Restorative Justice: Assessing Optimistic and Pessimistic Accounts." *Crime and Justice* 25 (1999): 1–127.

Brison, Susan. *Aftermath: Violence and the Remaking of a Self.* Princeton, NJ: Princeton UP, 2003.

Brothers, Doris. *Falling Backwards: An Exploration of Trust and Self-Experience.* New York: W.W. Norton, 1995.

Christie, Nils. "Conflicts as Property." *British Journal of Criminology* 17.1 (1977): 1–15.

———. "The Ideal Victim," *From Crime Policy to Victim Policy.* Ed. E. Fattah. Basingstoke, UK: Macmillan, 1986. 17–30.

———. *A Suitable Amount of Crime.* London: Routledge, 2004.

Coady, C.A.J. *Testimony: A Philosophical Study.* New York: Oxford UP, 1992.

Crochetti, Christopher. "Emotions, Retribution, and Punishment." *Journal of Applied Philosophy* 26.2 (2009): 160–173.

Dallaire, Romeo. *They Fight Like Soldiers, They Die Like Children.* Toronto: Random House, 2010.

Danieli, Yael, ed. *International Handbook of Multigenerational Legacies of Trauma.* New York: Plenum Press, 1998.

Duff, R.A. *Punishment, Communication and Community.* Oxford: Oxford UP, 2001.

Ellin, Joseph. "Restitutionism Defended." *Journal of Value Inquiry* 34.2/3 (September 2000): 299–317.

Enns, Diane. *The Violence of Victimhood*. University Park, PA: Pennsylvania State UP, 2012.

Fackenheim, Emil. *To Mend the World*. New York: Schocken, 1982.

Faulkner, Paul. "On the Rationality of Our Response to Testimony." *Synthese* 131.3 (2002): 353–70.

Frey, David. *A Million Little Pieces*. New York: Anchor, 2004.

Fricker, Elizabeth. "Secondhand Knowledge." *Philosophy and Phenomenological Research* 73.3 (2006): 592–618.

Fricker, Miranda. *Epistemic Injustice and the Ethics of Knowing*. New York: Oxford University Press, 2007.

Gamlund, Espen. "The Duty to Forgive Repentant Wrongdoers." *International Journal of Philosophical Studies* 18.5 (2010): 651–71.

Gilbert, Daniel T., and Patrick S. Malone. "The Correspondence Bias." *Psychological Bulletin* 117.1 (1995): 21–38.

Goodwin, Michael Lawrence. "An Argument Against Allowing the Families of Murder Victims to View Executions." *Journal of Family Law* 36.4 (1997) <http://www.pbs.org/wgbh/pages/frontline/shows/execution/readings/against.htm>. Accessed 13 Oct. 2013.

Govier, Trudy. *A Delicate Balance*. Boulder, CO: Westview Press, 2002.

———. "A Dialectic of Acknowledgement." *Reconciliation(s): Transitional Justice in Postconflict Societies*. Ed. Joanna Quinn. Kingston and Montreal: McGill-Queen's UP, 2009. 36–50.

———. "Duets, Cartoons, and Tragedies: Struggles with the Fallacy of Composition." *Pondering on Problems of Argumentation: Twenty Essays on Theoretical Issues*. Ed. Frans van Eemeren and Bart Garssen. Houten, The Netherlands: Springer 2009. Chapter 7.

———. *Forgiveness and Revenge*. London and New York: Routledge, 2002.

———. "Needing Each Other for Knowledge: Reflections on Trust and Testimony." *Empirical Logic and Public Debate: Essays in Honour of Else M. Barth*. Ed. Erik C.W. Krabbe, Renee Jose Dalitz, and Pier A. Smi. *Poznan Studies in the Philosophy of the Sciences and Humanities* 35. Amsterdam: Rodolphi, 1993. 13–26.

———. *Social Trust and Human Communities*. Kingston and Montreal: McGill-Queen's UP, 1997.

———. *Taking Wrongs Seriously: Acknowledgment, Reconciliation, and the Politics of Sustainable Peace*. Amherst, NY: Humanity Books/Prometheus, 2006.

———. "When Logic Meets Politics: Testimony, Distrust, and Rhetorical Disadvantage." *Informal Logic* 15.2 (1993): 93–104.

———, and Colin Hirano. "A Conception of Invitational Forgiveness." *Journal of Social Philosophy* 39.3 (2008): 429–44.

——, and Wilhelm Verwoerd. "Forgiveness: The Victim's Prerogative." *South African Journal of Philosophy* 21.2 (2002): 97–111.

——, and Wilhelm Verwoerd. "The Problems and Pitfalls of Apologies." *Journal of Social Philosophy* 33.1 (2002): 67–82.

Gunther, Randi. "The Second Wound: Blaming the Innocent Victims of Sexual Abuse." *Psychology Today* (26 Oct. 2012). <http://www.huffingtonpost.com/randi-gunther/sexual-abuse2_2013443.html> Accessed 20 Sept. 2013.

Hajdin, Mane. "Criminals as Gamblers: A Modified Theory of Pure Restitution." *Dialogue* 26.1 (1987): 77–86.

Hardwig, John. "The Role of Trust in Knowledge." *Journal of Philosophy* 88 (1991): 693–708.

Holmgren, Margaret. "Forgiveness and the Intrinsic Value of Persons." *American Philosophical Quarterly* 30 (1993): 341–51.

——. "Self-Forgiveness and Responsible Moral Agency." *Journal of Value Inquiry* 32.1 (1998): 75–91.

Holohan, Carole. *In Plain Sight: Responding to the Ferns, Ryan, Murphy and Cloyne Reports*. Amnesty International <http://www.amnesty.ie/sites/default/fles/INPLAINSIGHT(WEB_VERSION).pdf>. Accessed 14 Nov. 2012.

Honderich, Ted. "Peter Strawson: Freedom and Resentment." The Determinism and Freewill Philosophy Website. <http:www.ucl.ac.uk/~uctho/dfwlintroindex.htm>. Accessed 16 June 2014.

Hume, David. *Enquiry Concerning Human Understanding*. 2nd ed. Ed. Eric Sternborg. Indianapolis: Hackett, 1993.

——. *A Treatise of Human Nature*. Ed. L.A. Selby-Bigge. 1888; Oxford: Clarendon Press, 1965.

Janack, Mariane. "Standpoint Epistemology without the 'Standpoint'? An Examination of Epistemic Privilege and Epistemic Authority." *Hypatia* 12.2 (Spring 1997): 125–39.

Jiwei, Ci. "Evaluating Agency: A Fundamental Question for Social and Political Philosophy." *Metaphilosophy* 42.3 (2011): 261–81.

Jones, Karen. "The Politics of Credibility." *A Mind of One's Own: Feminist Essays on Reason and Objectivity*. Ed. Louise Anthony and Charlotte Witt. Boulder, CO: Westview Press, 2002. 154–76.

Khouri, Norma. *Forbidden Love*. New York: Random House, 2003.

Lerner, Melvin. *The Belief in a Just World: A Fundamental Delusion*. New York: Plenum, 1980.

Lewis, David. "What Experience Teaches." *There's Something about Mary*. Ed. Peter Ludlow, Yulin Nagasawa, and Daniel Stoljar. Boston: MIT Press, 2004. Chapter 5.

Loftus, Elizabeth. "Make-Believe Memories." *American Psychologist* 58 (2003): 864–73.

MacLachlan, Alice. "Moral Powers and Forgivable Evils. *Evil, Political Violence, and Forgiveness: Essays in Honor of Claudia Card*. Ed. Andrea Veltman and Kathryn Norlock. Lanham, MD: Lexington Books, 2009. 135–58.

———. "Unreasonable Resentments." *Journal of Social Philosophy*. 41.4 (2010): 422–41.

Madeira, Jody. "Why Rebottle the Genie? Capitalizing on Closure in Death Penalty Proceedings." *Indiana Law Journal* 85.4 (2010). <http://papers.ssrn.com/sol3/papers.cfm?abstract_1d=1347844>. Accessed on 16 June 2014.

Maran, Meredith. *My Lie: A True Story of False Memory*. New York: Jossey-Bass Wiley, 2010.

McDonald, Fritz J. "Agency and Responsibility." *Journal of Value Inquiry* 44.2 (2010): 199–207.

McKenna, Michael, and Paul Russell. "Perspectives on P.F. Strawson's 'Freedom and Resentment.'" *Free Will and Reactive Attitudes*. Ed. Michael McKenna and Paul Russell. Farnham, UK: Ashgate, 2008. 1–18.

McMahan, Jeff. "Child Soldiers: An Ethical Perspective." *Building Knowledge about Children in Armed Conflict*. Ed. Scott Gates and Simon Reich. Pittsburgh: U of Pittsburgh P, 2013. 27–36.

Medina, Jose. "The Relevance of Credibility Excess in a Proportional View of Epistemic Injustice: Differential Epistemic Authority and the Social Imaginary." *Social Epistemology* 15.1 (2011): 15–35.

Mosby, Ian. "Administering Colonial Science: Nutrition Research and Human Biomedical Experimentation in Aboriginal Communities and Residential Schools, 1942–1952." *Social History* 46.91 (May 2013): 145–72.

Nagel, Thomas. *Mortal Questions*. New York: Cambridge UP, 1979.

Nathan, Debbie. *Sybil Exposed: The Extraordinary Story Behind the Famous Multiple Personality Case*. New York: Free Press, 2011.

Oldenquist, Andrew. "An Explanation of Retribution." *Journal of Philosophy* 85 (1988): 464–78.

Origgi, Gloria. "Epistemic Injustice and Epistemic Trust." *Social Epistemology* 26.2 (2012): 221–35.

Pamuk, Orhan. "The Anger of the Damned." *New York Review of Books* 48.16 (15 Nov. 2001). <http://www.nybooks.com/articles/archives/2001/nov/15/the-anger-of-the-damned/>. Accessed 14 Sept. 2013.

Paul, L.A. "What You Can't Expect When You're Expecting." *Res Philosophica* 2015, forthcoming.

Pettigrove, Glen. "The Standing to Forgive." *Monist* 92.4 (2009): 583–603.

Pinto, R.C. "Govier on Trust." *Informal Logic* 33.2 (Spring 2013): 263–91.

Ripstein, Arthur. "The Philosophy of Tort Law." *The Oxford Handbook of Jurisprudence and Legal Philosophy*. Ed. Jules Coleman and Scott Shapiro. Oxford: Oxford UP, 2001. Chapter 17.

Rosen, David M. *Armies of the Young: Child Soldiers in War and Terrorism.* New Brunswick, NJ: Rutgers UP, 2005.

Rosenblat, Herman A. *The Angel at the Fence.* New York: Berkeley Books, 2009.

Ross, L. "The Intuitive Psychologist and His Shortcomings." *Advances in Experimental Social Psychology.* Ed. L. Berkowitz. New York: Academic Press, 1977. 173–200.

Ross, Lee, and Richard Nisbett. *The Person and the Situation: Perspectives in Social Psychology.* Toronto: McGraw-Hill, 1991.

Seltzer, Margaret. *Love and Consequences.* New York: Riverhead Books, 2008.

Sen, Amartya. *Identity and Violence: The Illusion of Destiny.* New York: Norton, 2007.

Smith, Michelle. *Michelle Remembers.* New York: Pocket Books, 1989.

Smith, Nick. *I Was Wrong: The Meaning of Apologies.* Cambridge, UK: Cambridge UP, 2008.

Stanlick, Nancy. "Reconciling with Harm: An Alternative to Forgiveness and Revenge." *Florida Philosophical Review* 43 (2010): 88–111.

Stoll, David. *Between Two Armies in the Ixil Towns of Guatemalans.* New York: Columbia UP, 1994.

———. *Rigoberta Menchú and the Story of All Poor Guatemalans.* Boulder, CO: Westview Press, 1999

Stolorow, Robert D. "What Is Character and How Does It Change?" *Psychology Today* 12 March 2012.

Strang, Heather. *Repair or Revenge: Victims and Restorative Justice.* Oxford: Oxford UP, 2002.

———. "Victim Evaluations of Face-to-Face Restorative Justice Conferences: A Quasi-Experimental Analysis." *Journal of Social Issues* 62.3 (2006): 281–306.

Strawson, P.F. "Freedom and Resentment." *Proceedings of the British Academy* 48 (1962): 1–25.

Suzuki, Shogo. "Overcoming Past Wrongs Committing by States: Can Non-State Actors Facilitate Reconciliation?" *Social and Legal Studies* (2012): 201–13.

Szablowinski, Zenon. "Between Forgiveness and Unforgiveness." *Heythorp Journal* (May 2001): 471–82.

Tavuchis, Nicholas. *Mea Culpa: A Sociology of Apology and Reconciliation.* Redford City, CA: Stanford UP, 1991.

Thomas, Laurence. *The Americanization of the Holocaust.* Baltimore: Johns Hopkins UP, 1999.

———. "The Morally Obnoxious Comparisons of Evil." Fritz Bauer Institut Papers 2002. <http://www.laurencethomas.com/Evils.pdf>. Accessed 24 June 2014.

———. *Vessels of Evil: American Slavery and the Holocaust.* Philadelphia: Temple UP, 1993.

Vice, Sue. "False Memoir Syndrome in Holocaust Testimony." Lecture presented at the University of Sheffield, 14 Dec. 2011.

Wendell, Susan. "Oppression and Victimization: Choice and Responsibility." *Hypatia* (1990): 15–46.

Wessells, Michael. *Child Soldiers: From Violence to Protection*. Cambridge, MA: Harvard UP, 2006.

Wilder, Kathleen. "Overtones of Solipsism in Thomas Nagel's 'What Is It Like to Be a Bat?' and *The View from Nowhere*." *Philosophy and Phenomenological Research* 50 (1990): 481–99.

Wilkomirski, Binjamin. *Fragments: Memories of a Wartime Childhood*. Trans. Carol Brown Janeway. New York: Schocken Books, 1997.

Williston, Byron. "The Importance of Self-Forgiveness." *American Philosophical Quarterly* (2012): 67–80.

Zarogoza, Kevin. "Forgiveness and Standing." *Philosophy and Phenomenological Research* 84.3 (2012): 604–21.

INDEX

from the publisher

A name never says it all, but the word "broadview" expresses a good deal of the philosophy behind our company. We are open to a broad range of academic approaches and political viewpoints. We pay attention to the broad impact book publishing and book printing has in the wider world; we began using recycled stock more than a decade ago, and for some years now we have used 100% recycled paper for most titles. As a Canadian-based company we naturally publish a number of titles with a Canadian emphasis, but our publishing program overall is internationally oriented and broad-ranging. Our individual titles often appeal to a broad readership too; many are of interest as much to general readers as to academics and students.

Founded in 1985, Broadview remains a fully independent company owned by its shareholders—not an imprint or subsidiary of a larger multinational.

If you would like to find out more about Broadview and about the books we publish, please visit us at **www.broadviewpress.com**. And if you'd like to place an order through the site, we'd like to show our appreciation by extending a special discount to you: by entering the code below you will receive a 20% discount on purchases made through the Broadview website.

Discount code: **broadview20%**

Thank you for choosing Broadview.

Please note: this offer applies only to sales of bound books within the United States or Canada.

The interior of this book is printed on 100% recycled paper.